START AND RUN A

Business from Home

D1537145

START AND RUN A

Business from Home

How to turn your hobby
or interest into a business

PAUL POWER

howtobooks / **smallbusinessstart-ups**

Published by How To Books Ltd,
Spring Hill House, Spring Hill Road,
Begbroke, Oxford OX5 1RX, United Kingdom
Tel: (01865) 375794 Fax: (01865) 379162
info@howtobooks.co.uk
www.howtobooks.co.uk

How To Books greatly reduce the carbon footprint of their books by sourcing their typesetting and printing in the UK.

First published in 2006
Second edition 2009

British Library Cataloguing in Publication Data.
A catalogue record for this book is available from the British Library.

ISBN 978 1 84528 301 8

Produced for How To Books by Deer Park Productions, Tavistock
Typeset by PDQ Typesetting, Newcastle-under-Lyme, Staffordshire
Printed and bound by Bell & Bain Ltd, Glasgow

NOTE: The material contained in this book is set out in good faith for general guidance and no liability can be accepted for loss or expense incurred as a result of relying in particular circumstances on statements made in the book. The laws and regulations are complex and liable to change, and readers should check the current position with the relevant authorities before making personal arrangements.

For Brian

CONTENTS

PREFACE TO THE SECOND EDITION

Welcome to the second edition of this book.

At the time of writing the first edition, I had started and was running a number of mostly home-based businesses, all of which had been started from my kitchen table. This gave rise to the first edition which was titled *The Kitchen Table Entrepreneur*.

Some years on, I still run my own businesses. Today, none are located in my kitchen, which is probably just as well, given the high number of visitors to one of our most successful enterprises, The Littlehampton Dutch Bike Shop.

But despite the changing locations, my advice is still the same. If you want to start your own business, travel light. Forget the fancy gismos, the expensive high street rents, the accountants, business advice gurus, and so on. Instead think big, but start small. Learn first to survive, then succeed and finally prosper.

For example, it always makes me laugh when I overhear someone discussing with another that they're about to start their own business (or in some cases, already have). The conversation usually is full of well-meaning advice from the person who is not actually starting a business themselves, and ironically, probably never will. But as you will soon discover, if you haven't already, as soon as you start your own business, or announce your intention to do so, you'll be bombarded with all sorts of free advice, usually from people who – without wanting to sound too unkind – probably don't have a clue! Their free advice will usually include such gems as: 'make sure you get yourself a good accountant', or another favourite, 'be careful what tell you tell the tax people or they'll take everything you own.'

The underlying theme of this free advice is that you need to protect all the money you're going to be making from being gobbled up by greedy tax people. If only it was that simple. In my experience, and one that is shared by every successful entrepreneur I've ever spoken to, is that the biggest problem you face is learning how to make any money at all.

Think about this for a moment. Whatever business you're planning will have to make money and enough of it to cover your business costs and make a worthwhile profit. All this comes before you should even think of hiring accountants, tax experts and so on. The golden rule of any business is that you need to make money. Without cash, neither you nor your business can survive. Although this should be obvious to anyone wanting to start a business, I must admit that it took me a couple of years, and a few attempts before I got the message.

Whilst not wishing to put you off entirely, please don't underestimate the challenge ahead. Anyone, and I mean anyone, can start a business. The difficult part is to make it successful. So be prepared for the rough road ahead. However, the good news is that once you have mastered a few of the basic concepts, you're well on the way to success. You don't need a business degree or formal business training to make a success of your venture. Many of the most successful entrepreneurs have had no training and in my opinion this is why they are so successful. For example, have you ever heard of a professor of economics who actually runs their own business? Perhaps such people exist, but if they do, they must prefer to keep it to themselves as we certainly don't hear much about them.

Since writing the first edition, I've had lots of correspondence from would-be entrepreneurs asking for my advice on their 'great idea'. Many of them apologise right from the start that they're unable to tell me too much about their idea as their friends have warned them not to divulge their master plans in case I, or someone like me, might steal their idea and beat them to the fortune that lies in wait for them.

The fact that I haven't solicited their correspondence or wish to hear their ideas is beyond them. That said, it's always nice when I get an email or a letter from a grateful entrepreneur who has found what I have had to say helpful to them. So while I welcome your correspondence, please note that I'm not a business consultant ready and waiting to sell you my services. Neither do I write from the position of business guru or millionaire. I'm neither and I certainly have no ambitions to be the latter.

What I am is someone who tired of working the nine-to-five trap and was sick of paddling someone else's canoe. And if the truth be told, I couldn't stand working for bosses who I wouldn't trust to lead me safely across the road, let alone determine my future.

So I'm not a business guru, and I'm sorry to say I won't be able to give you the brilliant idea of how you can make more money than your neighbours, colleagues, relatives and friends. Making millions doesn't interest me.

My own view of life is that we are all leaseholders. No matter how much wealth you accumulate, you won't be able to take it with you. However, that shouldn't stop you from aiming to become a millionaire if you so wish. Indeed, if that's your ambition, then great. Off you go and good luck to you. But that's not my aim and ambition. Indeed if you really want to be seriously rich, then you'll still find the information in this book useful and helpful to get you started.

Everything I share with you in these pages is information I came across the hard way. Indeed, when I started my first business, I drove ahead blindly with my plans, without really thinking about where I should have been going. It shouldn't have come as a great surprise to me when my first business venture crashed soon after starting. If only I'd known back then what I know now. But I was surprised, hurt even, that I could have possibly failed. After all, we all know someone who is extremely successful, yet we believe them to be less talented and knowledgeable than ourselves. How many times have you looked at someone and thought, if they can do it, so can I?

Well, the good news is you can. But starting your first business is a bit like driving a car without really knowing how. Dangerous stuff. Don't be surprised when you end up driving off the road, writing off everything you own. Obviously it would make sense to learn how to drive first. But learning how to drive is only the start of it. Next you have to master taking directions, then reading the road signs and so on, until at last you're really ready to drive on your own.

If you grasp the above concept, you're off to a good start. No book, however comprehensive, can cover all eventualities. But what I hope to provide in this book is a basic driving guide, together with rules of the road and a short map to get you on the highway to success. The rest is up to you. Whether you choose to ignore my advice, or implement it in your own business, only you can decide. But at least you're getting the chance to decide what's right for you and your circumstances. And you can be assured that the advice you're taking is from someone travelling the same road as yourself.

I hope through sharing my experiences and those of others that by the end of it, you'll have more knowledge than I had when I first started. Even if you only read this Preface, and understand that the cardinal rule in any business is that you must make money, you'll certainly at least have a raincoat to keep the rain off your back in the first few months.

Let me know how you get on and beware of 'free advice' and advice from business gurus whose only business is advising other business people. In my experience, advice from them is by far the worst. For example, if they know so much about how to run a successful business (other than one offering others advice) how come they're not acting on the advice they you want you to pay them for and making their own fortunes?

Good luck!

Paul Power

1

SO YOU WANT TO START YOUR OWN BUSINESS?

My story

I can still remember the day way back in 1998 when I decided that there must be more to life than seemingly endless monthly appraisals, unachievable monthly targets, vacuum-packed sandwiches, foul-tasting coffee, uncooperative lifts, difficult people, and management I truly detested. Like so many others before me, and countless since, I decided to cash in my career with all its perks, including paid holidays, sick leave, generous pension benefits and a relatively decent salary, and go it alone starting my own business. I'd like to open this book by saying that nothing beats the feeling that came when I told my bosses where to stick it and the liberating feeling of swapping days in fluorescent hell for the altogether more preferable experiences of running my own successful business, and enjoying more free time while earning truck loads of cash and being the envy of friends and ex-colleagues.

But it wasn't like that.

The joy of telling an employer where to stick their lousy job is, sadly, short-lived. Indeed any emotional feel-good factor quickly wears off as soon as the next round of bills starts to fall through the front door.

Why am I telling you this? Because starting your own business is going to be, with the exception of coping with a life-threatening illness, one of the most challenging and difficult things you're ever likely to embark on.

And for those who stay the course, it's also going to be one of the most rewarding experiences ever. But I don't want to start you off under the impression that it's all plain sailing. It's not. Neither is starting a business, for those who crave security, and want assurances that everything will work out well in the end. With this business, there are no guarantees of success. So if you're the type of person who avoids risk at all costs, then my advice would be to stay employed, or unemployed, as the case might be.

The route to self-employment is a difficult and often seemingly impossible journey where only a few will actually achieve any real success. Notice how I haven't used the words 'lucky few'. Because in reality your future success will *not* depend on luck. Indeed luck has nothing to do with it. If I've learnt one difficult lesson through the last few years it is that those who start and go on to run their own successful businesses do not rely on luck. If there is such a thing, then I believe that you make your own luck. Certainly if you're sitting somewhere reading this book right now and wishing for a lucky break in your life, stop reading now, find the nearest shop that sells lottery tickets, and buy yourself one. Then you can sit back and wait for Lady Luck to come knocking on your door.

An alternative is for you to decide as I did that life is too short to worry, and regardless of how hard you work for someone else you'll never really be in control of your own life. If you're prepared to go for it, then commit to the hard work ahead, be prepared for the failures, disappointments, let-downs, bureaucracy and fear, and start to enjoy the massive benefits that will come when your start your own business.

Prepare yourself for some difficult times ahead

After leaving paid employment, I was euphoric. Sadly, it wasn't to last. Six months after starting my first business it failed spectacularly, and I was left with no way to pay the mortgage and household bills. Despondent, I was forced to return to the ranks of the employed. At the time, it was a bitter blow to have to find another job which paid a fraction of the salary I had been previously earning and with none of the benefits.

Even vacuum-packed sandwiches, fluorescent lighting and uncooperative lifts all seemed like a dream compared to my new job where my circumstances were far worse than before.

At the time, I made myself a promise – to get back on my feet, overcome my fear of failure and as soon as I could to dive back into the depths of self-employment, but this time more prepared than before. I passed the time working for others as best I could. I worked hard and committed myself to my new job: after all, it wasn't my employer's fault that my business had failed. But then one day I realised that I was once again stuck in that nine-to-five, Monday-to-Friday routine and, despite three promotions and the fact that I was now earning more than I had been in my previous job, I remembered why it was that I had had to return to employment. It was to pay my way until I could leave again.

On the day I left this job, I made a promise to myself that I would never again work for someone else. Regardless of my circumstances, regardless of how low my life could sink, and even if I was to lose my house, furniture, etc., I would never again return to being an employee.

To date, I have kept this promise.

Today, my businesses are successful and I enjoy every minute of my working life. Since leaving employment my health has improved, I am happier, and I get to steer the course of my own life and those of the people I love without being at the mercy of others.

Self-employment is not for everyone. As I said earlier, not everyone is are suited to this life, which is probably just as well as you'll soon discover this when your business grows and you need to employ talented people to move it on to the next level.

Undoubtedly there are those folk who will pick up this book and, once they recognise how tough the road ahead can be, will decide they're better off where they are now. Good for them, I say. Far better they realise, after the relatively small investment of buying and reading this book, that self-employment isn't for them than to discover later when they have lost everything that they weren't really cut out for it after all.

Not everyone has the stomach for self-employment. As I've said, it can be a difficult road, often long and seemingly unending. But for those who persevere and, more importantly, for those who travel light and carry a map, that road can be made all the easier.

Let's start by looking at some of the attributes that make successful entrepreneurs different from those who fail.

The five secrets of being a successful entrepreneur
1. Develop self-reliance.
2. Work with written goals.
3. Develop a 'can-do' attitude.
4. Maintain a sense of humour.
5. Keep your 'own counsel'.

DEVELOP SELF-RELIANCE

Through starting and running my own businesses I've met lots of successful entrepreneurs, who have overcome all sorts of challenges to start their own successful businesses. Without exception, what they all have is an acute sense of self-reliance. They believe entirely that whatever life or business can throw at them, they have the power to overcome, whatever this may be.

They also accept fully that they alone are responsible for their own future. This is crucial to their success – that unshakeable belief that they, and they alone, are in charge of their lives. Yes, their businesses are led by events that are often outside of their control. But by accepting that success isn't dependent on what happens to you, but how you react to these events, you will start to realise that your success ultimately depends on no one else but you.

WORK WITH WRITTEN GOALS

I wish I had discovered this secret earlier. If I had, I would have undoubtedly spared myself much heartache and false starts. For when you set a written goal you commit to achieving whatever it is you want, which could be anything from simply spending a half an hour a day researching your new business to setting a start date for your new business.

Just think for a moment how motivating it is to write down the date you intend to start your first business. Imagine for a moment the forces that begin working on a conscious and unconscious level, moving you towards this goal.

For example, once you set your date you can:

- ☐ Write a list of all the things you're going to have to do before you can get started.

- ☐ Break this list down into smaller achievable goals. For example, set dates to meet with bankers, suppliers and anyone who you're going to need to be involved to be in your business.

- ☐ Create a written timetable for these things. There's no point in saying you'll get them done by such and such a date. You need to work to a timetable so you can achieve your goals.

- ☐ Where necessary, revise your initial date. It may be that you haven't given yourself a realistic timescale to work within. This is a common mistake made by novice entrepreneurs who will underestimate how long it takes to get funding, supplier agreements, and so on, in place.

As you can see, when you set written goals you will go from simply thinking or dreaming about doing something to actually working to a set, written goal. And by doing so, your future chances of success will be greatly improved.

DEVELOP A 'CAN-DO' ATTITUDE

Similar to developing a real sense of reliance, successful entrepreneurs also have a real 'can-do' attitude. You know the type of person I mean. You'll find them heading up local community campaigns, tackling problems head-on, and refusing to take 'no' for an answer from anyone. You'll have met these people when you've been on holidays. They are the ones that when there's a problem get it sorted quickly without fuss or insult.

Unlike others, can-doers live their life with an unshakeable belief in their abilities. They refuse (whatever the circumstance) to be told that whatever it is they're about to do is impossible. Imagine for a moment how it must have been for the Wright brothers, the first people to fly an aeroplane across the Atlantic. Picture if you will all those from the 'it-cannot-be-done' camp, arguing and forecasting impending danger. Lesser men wouldn't have bothered with such a challenge and some would say they were stupid and reckless. But their achievement brought world-wide admiration, and at the time ushered in the reality that soon ordinary people could be travelling from America to Europe by aeroplane.

A 'can-do' attitude is vital to your future success as a self-employed business person. If you can only achieve results where the odds are stacked in your favour and success is guaranteed, you might as well stay doing whatever it is you're doing now. Because at times on the journey ahead, the only thing between you and failure will be your attitude. It's not so much what happens to you in this life, but *how you react to it*.

Start working on becoming a 'can-do' right away. Guard against listening to the floods of people who'll tell you whatever it is you're about to do won't work. Believe in yourself and work towards eliminating personal doubt and fear.

MAINTAIN A SENSE OF HUMOUR

I'd love to tell you that I've laughed at each and every one of my many shortcomings and numerous failures, but I won't lie to you. Most of my life I've taken things far too seriously, and it's only as my businesses have begun to see the faint, flickering light of success in the far-off distance that I can finally begin to understand the importance of being able to laugh at myself. Today I'm getting better at it, but I firmly believe that if I had realised earlier on in my self-employed career that being able to laugh at yourself is as important as paying your rent or mortgage, I believe I would have achieved more and far quicker.

Let me take you through one episode that happened to me.

The boating lake

Some time ago I ran a boating lake in our town. As you can imagine, given our current climate in the UK it was pretty much a seasonal business. We'd open the lake at Easter and it would close again in early September when the children returned to school. Our busiest times were bank holidays, and it was on these days (weather permitting) that we would actually finally see a financial return on all our hard work.

One August bank holiday, I woke up early on Saturday morning to visit the lake and ensure that everything was clean and ready to go for later in the morning. I should tell you here that the lake had been built by the Victorians employing the most remarkable engineering that allowed it to be filled by the sea through a series of underground chambers. As I walked the short distance from the house along the sandy beach to the lake on what was a beautiful morning, I couldn't help but think how lucky I was. After all, how many people could undertake their daily commute to work along a beach with two happy dogs playing at their feet?

However, that morning I was in for a shock.

When I caught a glimpse of the lake in the distance, I knew right away something was wrong. Our boats which were usually tied up in the centre of the lake were not yet visible. I panicked. My first thought was that someone must have stolen them. It certainly wouldn't have been the first time that one of our boats had been stolen. But as I walked towards the lake, the boats came into view. Relieved, I continued towards the lake. But there was still something wrong. Indeed something seriously wrong, but I couldn't yet put my finger on it. Only when I finally stood at the edge of the lake did I realise what the problem was.

All of the water had drained away!

The lake was completely empty save for a few small puddles of water, totally drained. I couldn't believe it. Here we were on the busiest bank holiday of the year. Beautiful sunny weather – and our lake had utterly disappeared.

Ask yourself, what would you do? Well, I got angry. Very angry. And even angrier when some people began to come up to me with all sorts of petty worries. Questions like 'Do you think the crabs will be okay?' or, 'What time will you be opening today?'

Can you imagine going up to the owner of a boating lake, which for some unknown reason has lost all its water, and asking them what time they'll be opening?

Of course, I took it badly. Replying sarcastically that we would obviously be opening in a few minutes. 'A few minutes?' one man said indignantly, 'but the lake's dry.'

'Don't worry, we'll let you have a boat half price', I told him, which as you can imagine didn't help the situation.

Today, some years on, I can look back at this incident and laugh. It was a truly hilarious situation, as was pointed out to me at the time by one of the local business owners who advised me to see the funny side of it. 'What's the point in getting stressed about it?' He said. 'After all, you getting angry isn't going to fill the lake up, is it?'

He was right and I was wrong. Laughing at what the world throws at you is something I've only learnt recently, and I must say it's definitely the best kept secret of successful entrepreneurs. You really do need to be willing to see the funny side in every calamity. I'm not recommending you adopt a 'couldn't care less' attitude. Far from it. There's nothing funny about losing your takings for what was potentially the busiest weekend of the year. But it's far worse, wouldn't you agree, to lose your takings *and* be entirely miserable and angry?

KEEP YOUR OWN COUNSEL

I cannot stress this one enough.

If you're the type of person who has to tell all and sundry your forthcoming business plans, then save yourself from future agonies and decide now not to start your own business. Sharing your plans with everyone else really is disastrous.

Let me give you an example of this via something that happened to me a while ago.

When I decided that I'd had enough of working for someone else for a living, I had already given a lot of thought as to what sort of business I was going to start and run. I'd worked through the figures, carried out lots of research, and had actually found a business that was easy to set up and run, and more importantly, was already making money for someone else. I believed entirely in this business idea. In fact, it was more than a business idea as other people were obviously already doing well with this same business. All I had to do was replicate their idea. Nothing wrong with that. As their business was not even in our area, I wouldn't be competing with them. And so I believed I was on to a winning idea.

Then one night I was out for dinner with some friends and relatives, none of whom were their own boss. At the time all of them had successful careers and were happy working for someone else. During dinner I shared my ideas with the gathering who, it has to be said, were mostly horrified at my plan. Later on, after the meal, when we were sitting in the hotel foyer polishing off a bottle of wine, I then made the further (fatal) mistake of trying to justify my business idea to the group.

I was overrun with 'What ifs' and all sorts of well-meaning advice. Thus in the weeks that followed I changed my business plans to take on board all the well-meaning advice I'd been given.

When I discussed my plans sometime later with an already successful person who'd started a similar business they advised me against my new plan and told me I should stick with my original idea. This caused me a great deal of more confusion and heartbreak.

Eventually I made the decision to go with my revised business idea, thereby turning my back on this successful entrepreneur's advice. Six months later, my new business collapsed (and looking back, I'm actually surprised it lasted as long as it did).

So here's the lesson, dear reader – *keep your own counsel.* As soon as you choose to tell someone that you're thinking about starting your own business, you'll get bombarded with free, well-meaning, and entirely useless advice. So with the best will, keep your ideas to yourself.

The only people you should ever discuss or take advice from when you are starting your own business are those who are already running successful businesses of their own. No one else. If you still have a problem with this concept, let me ask you a question. Have you ever been to a party where you've met a professional such as a doctor, architect, engineer, dentist, or similar who asked *you* for *your* advice on how they should treat their patients, design their buildings, or make their machines?

Of course not. And the same is true for entrepreneurs. No one but you is really qualified to understand what's involved in starting your business, let alone qualified enough to offer advice.

So remember, keep your own counsel!

Before we go any further, have you got what it takes?

So far, I've talked about myself and shared with you what I believe to be the five strongest attributes that all successful business starters have in common.

It would be silly in the extreme if I was to assume that every person who picked up this book, or indeed any other on the subject of starting your own business, was already well-endowed in the 'skills' department. Certainly if my own initial experiences were anything to go by, few of us actually know clearly what it takes to start a business, or once up and running how to keep it going.

But don't despair. What you don't know, you can find out. Simple as that. However, this can only happen if you first recognise exactly what it is you are lacking. So before we go any further, I want you to take a few minutes to undertake a stocktake of your lifestyle. All you need is a paper and pen, or if you haven't got any paper, simply write the answers alongside the questions below.

Lifestyle questionnaire

1. Are you the type of person who constantly craves someone telling you how well you are doing?

2. Are you motivated enough to be able to work alone, at home, solidly, without resorting to phoning friends, watching day-time telly, or spending hours surfing the Internet?

3. When you take on a new task do you always need encouragement from your friends and family?

4. If you're living with a partner, husband, or wife, have you discussed your proposals and the implications of what you're planning and how these will affect both your lifestyles?

5. Are you giving up a career to start your own business? If so, how are you going to cope without your colleagues, salary, pension entitlements, and so on?

6. If your business venture fails (and lots of first ones do), would you be able to cope and get back on track again?

7. Are you really serious about starting your own business, or is it just the romantic notion that attracts you?

8. Can you keep going under the kinds of circumstances where others would pack up and clear out?

By reading through these questions you should be able to start to see the sort of personality that's more suited to being an entrepreneur. For example, if you're someone who loves being part of a team, sharing anecdotes and gossip over the water or coffee machine on a Monday morning, then the loneliness that invariably comes when you work for yourself will not be for you.

Don't work under the false assumption that everything will be alright on the night. This is never the case. In fact, usually what can go wrong will go wrong, as well as a host of other unforeseen problems. However, in my experience, if you plan for things to go wrong they usually don't. Why? I believe that once again when things go wrong it's not down to bad luck. Remember, I don't believe there is any such thing as good or bad luck, only poor planning. Indeed, if such a thing as luck does exist, I am certain you make your own luck.

So – have you got what it takes?

Allow me to be brutally honest here for a moment and ask you a few personal questions. Just between you and me. For example, have you got the get-up-and-go needed to start your own business, and accept responsibility for your own future?

What I'm talking about here is you getting up each and every day, regardless of how well or unwell you feel, and going to work in your own business. Remember, when you work for yourself you're not going to have those others in the office, or factory, or on the shopfloor that you can have a good old chinwag or moan with. Initially, it will most likely be you and you alone who you undertakes every task imaginable, from answering the phone, to meeting with high-powered executives, to negotiating with suppliers and landlords for better rates.

In my experience, none of these people will be really interested in how you feel about things. Your customers generally will only be interested in what your business can do for them. And why not? After all, your job is simply to satisfy their needs. Your suppliers, landlord, bank, local council, and anyone else who'll be taking a slice of your profits isn't really interested in your wellbeing. All they will be concerned about is whether you have any debts with them (be this loans or commitments like rent) and whether you will be able to honour them.

Sorry to be blunt here, but that is how it is.

The sooner you understand that you will be on your own here, the better. That way you won't be in for any unpleasant surprises and you can plan accordingly.

Here's an interesting experience that happened to me when I was doing a radio interview promoting the first edition of this book.

First of all, I must say that I really enjoy doing promotional radio interviews. I get to go all around the country chatting to interesting, would-be entrepreneurs. Usually it's all fairly light-hearted and good fun. However, on one show, I took a call from an extremely irate lady who berated me for suggesting through my book that anyone could turn a hobby into a successful business. She told me that her daughter had lost everything when she decided to pack in her career and open a teashop.

Once she'd calmed down, I asked her what did she believe was the biggest factor in her daughter's business failing. Without hesitation, she blamed greedy bankers and a landlord who charged her 'over the odds for a piddling little shop that no one else, but her daughter would rent'.

Note, the two parties she blamed:

1. Greedy bankers who had charged too much in interest and fees.
2. A landlord who had charged too much in rent.

What's telling about this lady's daughter is that her business hadn't had a hope to begin with. Let's face it, both the costs of her bank/loan charges and shop rent would have been known to her from the outset. I'll take you through what's involved in negotiating for a shop premises later, but suffice it to say it's a bit like renting a flat or house. You will know in advance the monthly rent and will have agreed to that figure when you sign the lease.

Similarly you will know in advance your bank charges, loan repayments, and so on. So there is absolutely no reason why your business should close down owing to foreseen costs, provided of course that you have created a realistic business plan. Later on, I'll take you through the research you'll need to do before signing anything or indeed deciding to start your business. An all too common mistake and one of the main reasons for business failures is that an entrepreneur, similar to this lady's daughter, has failed to consider the costs. Instead they have rushed into a half-baked idea without any real idea of how they were going to make it a success. And then when it fails, they blame others for their own basic mistakes.

So ask yourself now – are you willing to take responsibility for your future? If you are, and I hope you are, great. If not, fine. At least you can walk away now without losing any money, your home, your relationship, and so on.

Starting and running your own business isn't for everyone, but everyone can do it provided they're prepared for what lies ahead. Ultimately, the rewards will change your life for the better. So be prepared for a life-changing journey and all the fun and excitement that goes with it.

To do list

1. Grab a notebook and start working on planning some initial written goals. This could be anything, from setting a deadline by which you will have finished reading this book to choosing a date for starting your business.

2. From now on start working on developing your self-reliance. Work out as many ways as you possibly can of ending your dependence on other people. If you're the type of person who loves to be praised at work, then make a conscious effort to stop seeking others' approval. Remember, one of the greatest attributes of successful people is that they really don't give a damn what others think of them. They live their lives on their own terms.

3. Learn to laugh more and not get worked up about things. Start shrugging off the inevitable problems you encounter every day. Whatever you do, don't take yourself too seriously.

2

GREAT BUSINESS IDEAS START AT HOME

Many of the world's largest businesses began life at home in a back bedroom, garage, or spare room.

American computer magnate, Steve Jobs, the founder of Apple Computers, began this business in his bedroom and initially traded from his garage.

Closer to home, Sir Alan Sugar, legendary Chief Executive of Amstrad (Alan Michael Sugar Trading) began his business life at home, selling electrical parts to retailers from the back of a van.

Karan Bilimoria, the entrepreneur behind the hugely successful Cobra Beer brand, had prior to launching this dipped his toes in a variety of import businesses until he finally found the right opportunity with this now famous drink. His sales method was to visit as many Indian restaurants as he possibly could to persuade them to stock Cobra. He used an elderly, and often unreliable battered green Citroen 2CV to carry around his initial stock. He started off already in debt from his previous ventures and has gone on to literally change entirely the way Indian beer is sold in the UK. All of this was achieved initially from his kitchen table and delivering from the back of an elderly car.

The founders of Innocent Drinks, Richard Reed, Adam Balon and Jon Right, started creating their fruit juice drinks at home. And after an difficult initial trading period that would have seen most fair weather entrepreneurs folding their tents and seeking once again the shelter and convenience of paid employment, the trio proceeded to build one of the country's most innovative and sought after drinks brands.

James Murray-Wells, the student founder of Glasses Direct, began his online spectacles mail order business from home. Glasses Direct is now a household name and trades from offices at Charlton park, Malmesbury.

The late iconic activist and entrepreneur Anita Roddick, founder of the Body Shop, set up her first business in a bed and breakfast in Littlehampton (the town where she grew up and where her mother ran a local café). Although the Body Shop began life as a small shop in Brighton it was initially a home-based idea, started up by Anita as she wanted to sell products that hadn't been tested on animals or otherwise brought about by harming anyone.

Online social networking site Friends Reunited was started at home by Steve Pankhurst and Jason Porter, who later sold the company for a reported £120 million a few years after. Once again, the idea and business began at home with the initial intention of creating a part-time business.

Legend has it that Richard Branson, founder of the Virgin Group, used the telephone box closest to his home as his office to make and receive calls. Whether this is true or not I'm not sure, but what is remarkable is that he founded his business from home, and later on ran his empire from a houseboat moored in London.

Why do so many businesses start from home?

The answer here is because great ideas begin at home.

Also, and let's be brutally honest at this point, the reason most business empires initially trade from home is that their founders simply haven't got the necessary resources to start anywhere else.

Sure, we'd all love bright modern offices, a fleet of freshly liveried vans to deliver our goods, bellboys in sharp uniforms at the doors of our shop and some posh sounding people to answer our phones, but alas starting a business isn't at all like this. A typical home-base entrepreneur will have little or no money, can either be in debt or previously bankrupted by a failed venture, yet will still believe enough in themselves and their ideas to continue with their global dream – which inevitably can only begin from their kitchen table.

The next time you see a successful business that interests you, take the time to find out how and where it all began. I can guarantee you that nearly all the ventures you come across will at one time have been home-based.

Are all the best business ideas already taken?

When you sit down and try to come up with the next million-making idea, it may seem like all the best ideas are already taken. You may sit there thinking, if only I had come up with the idea for an online social networking site like My Space, Bebo, or Friends Reunited. You may also regret not being the first in line with the idea of smoothie drinks, which up until a few short years ago were relatively unheard of. But don't despair. There is no reason why you cannot come up with a great idea of your own and build a successful business from it.

Where to get great ideas

It's vital to explore all of the possibilities that present themselves. Often the greatest ideas won't be immediately apparent, which is why we need to have some sort of strategy for unlocking them.

By far the most difficult way of coming up with ideas is to sit down with a blank piece of paper and try to think of things.

My favourite methods are:

☐ looking for ideas while enjoying my hobby
☐ brainstorming
☐ readers' letters.

LOOKING FOR IDEAS WHILE ENJOYING YOUR HOBBY

By far the easiest, and I believe the most enjoyable way of getting your creative juices flowing is to get out there and throw yourself into your hobby.

But rather than just enjoy yourself I want you to think about what frustrates you most about your hobby. You see, very often the best business opportunities lie in what we don't like about something.

Experience

Every dog lover will know how frustrating dog leads have been. In the past, all you could buy were short leads that meant your dog often pulled one way and you the other.

The problem was finally solved when someone came up with the simple idea of the retractable dog lead, which meant that at last you could let your dog walk in the direction they wanted to while still being on their lead. And if you don't want your dog to walk any further you simply apply a brake using your finger. When your dog walks closer to you the lead retracts back into its housing.

But why did it take us so long to get this simple tool?

I'm convinced the reason is that those who manufacture dog leads never actually walked a dog themselves, because the only person who could have come up with such a product is someone who has long suffered the frustrating limitations of the traditional dog lead.

Experience

Gardening can be really back-breaking work. A much-needed improvement for gardeners came about when one garden tool manufacturer introduced a new range of gardening tools.

These included such things as spades with extra-long handles, clipping shears with cushions to stop your elbows from getting jarred when you used them, and lightweight seats set at specially low heights to allow you to weed while sitting down.

Again, just like the modified dog lead, the reason these tools became overnight successes was they were designed by people who gardened, who believed their favourite pastime could be made more enjoyable and less painful by adding a few thoughtful modifications to the original products.

So ask yourself:

What's the one thing you find most frustrating about your hobby?

The 'thing' needn't even be connected to your hobby. For example let's say you're a keen walker and you find the maps you're using difficult to store comfortably when you're walking, or hard to keep dry in the rain.

For an entrepreneur this type of problem represents opportunities.

☐ You could design a map that suits the particular needs of your hobby, and either publish your own maps or approach map companies with your ideas on how their product can be improved, and offer your services as a consultant.

☐ You could come up with some sort of carrying case that makes it easier to store maps and read them in the rain.

☐ If one is already available elsewhere in the world you could apply to the manufacturers for a distributor's licence to sell the product here in the UK.

☐ If it's already available in the UK, you could investigate buying the product wholesale and maybe offering it as one item in a mail order business.

 TIP   Identify the problem and find an easy way of solving it.

Brainstorming

Brainstorming is another way of coming up with fresh and innovative ideas. In its simplest form it involves you sitting down and writing down every idea that comes into your head on a given subject. It doesn't matter what you write down, as the objective of the exercise is to 'storm' the right-hand side of your brain – the creative side – while ignoring any signals from the left-hand side of your brain – the side that deals with logic and order.

Although an extremely effective way of generating ideas, if you're new to this technique it might take you a little time to get used to it. So don't be despondent if it doesn't work for you. Stick with it and I promise it'll pay dividends.

You may find the following 'rules' and techniques helpful, but do whatever you're comfortable with and fairly soon you'll reap the rewards.

'Rules' for brainstorming

1. Do not judge any of your ideas.

2. Write down everything that comes into your head regardless of how silly or irrelevant it may sound.

3. The exercise is all about quantity, and not quality.

4. Work in five-minute bursts, stop, and then do something else for a few minutes before starting again.

5. Don't do it if you're tired or irritable. This technique works better when you're fresh and in a positive frame of mind.

Techniques for brainstorming

1. On a large, blank piece of paper write down a number of key words associated with your hobby. For example if your hobby is fishing you could write down: fishing rod, fish, hook, bait, fishing boat, beach, pier etc.

2. Allow yourself to go wild with your ideas and remember not to judge/evaluate anything you write down. As soon as you get an idea down on paper move on to the next one.

3. Use pictures to generate ideas. Open any page of your favourite hobby magazine, look at the pictures, and write down whatever comes into your head.

4. Use questions to generate ideas. Six great questions to get going on are: How?, Why?, Where?, When?, Who?, What?.

5. Don't take this too seriously. Try to think of some funny ideas and write them down. For example if you're hobby is water-skiing, imagine the Queen learning to water ski with Prince Phillip being towed behind in a doughnut.

6. Use a stopwatch to time your five-minute session and as soon it ends, STOP.

What can you expect at the end of a session?

Given time to master this technique, you'll find that you start coming up with some exciting potential business ideas. But I stress that just like any other worthwhile technique it takes time and patience before you get the best out of it.

If you find after trying it a number of times that you're still getting nothing – don't despair. Take a break from it and come back to it later when you're fresh and make sure you use all the techniques above. I find pictures a great help. It's amazing what looking at just one picture can do for your imagination.

READERS' LETTERS

The readers' letters section of your hobby magazine and the online forums and message boards for your hobby websites are fantastic places to get new ideas for your business.

Browse through them and you'll start to see common moans, usually directed at manufacturers and suppliers who are perceived as failing to satisfy their customers' needs. It's a great place to find out what others are thinking and what people would really like to buy.

Most large businesses work on economies of scale and will only introduce a product or service if they're sure there'll be a large enough demand to justify full-scale production. Often this reluctance creates an ideal opportunity for a creative entrepreneur to hop in and plug the gap in the market.

In my own gardening business I regularly read online forums and the letters in gardening magazines and have found it to be enormously helpful when planning marketing campaigns and finding out what customers really want.

Experience

When I started studying the letters pages of one of the gardening magazines I subscribe to, I began to notice that certain readers' questions kept coming up in the spring, usually from readers who were new to gardening and wanted to know how to plan their first garden. From this information I launched my first gardening course – How to plan your first garden *which I run in springtime.*

Some hobby magazines also have a readers' tips section, which can be full of useful ideas on creating innovative products.

But beware of sharing your top tips with anyone else. A couple of years ago a reader of a sailing magazine I subscribe to submitted a simple solution for safeguarding an outboard motor against theft. To his surprise, and I believe understandable annoyance, he later saw an exact replica of his device on sale at the Southampton Boat Show. When he enquired further about the origins of the product the salesman told him his company had got the idea for the product from a reader's tip in a sailing magazine.

The company in question is one of the largest in the world and is selling thousands of these gadgets worldwide without paying a penny to the original inventor.

If you are developing a prototype product you should look to have it patented to stop this from happening. To do this you'll need to get specialist advice from a solicitor who deals with this sort of thing.

Keeping a notebook

Ideas are like jokes – you can never remember the good ones. So it's essential to record everything you come up with in a notebook. Personally I prefer to use an A4, hardback, spiral-bound notebook, which I keep safely at home. I use a small pocket-sized notebook when I'm out and later transfer my notes into my master notebook when I get home.

Some tips for keeping a notebook:

- ☐ Find a notebook that you're happy with and then as soon as you fill one book buy the same type of notebook so when you come to filing them on a shelf they'll fit together. This way there's less chance of you losing your information.

- ☐ Use your notebook to record everything about your intended hobby business.

- ☐ Record all your ideas in your notebook, even those you don't like.

- ☐ Always be on the lookout for contacts. For example, names and addresses of businesses that make things you might need for your business etc.

- ☐ When you come across an interesting magazine or newspaper feature, cut it out and paste it into your notebook.

- ☐ Using your PC as a notebook is fine. Just make sure you back it up on either a disk or CD.

Evaluating your ideas

As someone once said, great ideas only work if you do.

While undoubtedly true, this doesn't mean that every idea you come up with, regardless of how you work on it, will bear fruit.

Neither should you get frustrated if some of your ideas seem to be too far-fetched at this stage.

Instead, see your ideas as doorways to your future business. Some you can open today; others may have to wait until you have sufficient resources to put them into action; and a few doors you won't be able to open at all until you do a bit more research.

Regardless of how many potential ideas you come up with for turning your hobby into a business you'll need to have some sort of system for evaluating them.

Generally there are three areas you'll need to consider:

1. your resources
2. your lifestyle
3. feasibility.

Your resources

However brilliant your idea may seem you will only be capable of starting it if you have adequate resources.

Be brutally honest with yourself here. It's no good starting something and then finding that you haven't got what it takes to continue with your venture.

FINANCE

Unfortunately too many new businesses fail simply because their owners hadn't forecasted how much it was all going to cost to get started and survive the first and often difficult months trading that face every new business.

SKILLS

Unless you've got enormous financial backing for your venture you're probably going to have to do everything yourself. This means being able to negotiate with suppliers, sell to customers and be shrewd with the books.

There are lots of places to get help from. You can either buy specialist books written entirely on sales, bookkeeping etc, or you can go on courses.

Regardless of your experience you should contact your local Enterprise Centre where you'll find a wide range of courses specifically run for people starting their own businesses with little or no previous experience.

The courses are subsidised by the government so the fees are affordable.

Your lifestyle

Ignore this one at your peril! Starting your own business is one of the most exciting things you can do. Get it right and you'll never have to work for anyone again. You'll also enjoy the enormous satisfaction that comes with building and securing your own future.

But, and here's the but!

Starting your own business comes with responsibilities that you might find are incompatible with your lifestyle.

If, like many people, you're the type of person who values your free time and never wants to work weekends, and the business you're planning to start will only work at weekends, then obviously you have a problem. One of the top dream businesses that people imagine themselves working at is running their own seaside guesthouse. Just imagine waking up every morning with a fresh breeze blowing through your chocolate box rose-adorned cottage. While you prepare breakfast your guests wait in patient anticipation complimenting your carefully chosen colour scheme. Unfortunately the reality is something different and there will undoubtedly be occasions where running this type of business means you have little time to enjoy where you're living.

Don't do what most people do and adopt the, 'It'll be ok, I'll be able to hire people to cover weekends,' attitude because this won't work. If your business idea will only work at times when you don't want to work at it then find another opportunity.

 TIP To succeed you'll need to be able to devote 100 per cent to your business, at least in the crucial early make or break period.

Feasibility

Before you invest time and money in any business idea you must be sure that what you're proposing is feasible.

Later we'll look at what's involved in working out cash flow and profit and loss forecasts for your business. We'll also look at formulas for calculating how much you need to charge for your products or services.

CONDUCTING A SIMPLE FEASIBILITY STUDY

When you're working through your ideas get into the habit of having a calculator to hand and working out very quick, rounded-off figures. Test your idea on a best scenario basis followed by a worse case scenario.

Let's say you're planning to run walking holidays.

So you work out very roughly what you're hoping to charge your customers, taking into account all the costs you're going to incur. Your basic costs should include provisions for:

- ☐ marketing
- ☐ stationery, brochures etc
- ☐ public liability insurance
- ☐ salary costs, including a provision for hiring in additional staff if you think you'll need them
- ☐ stock if applicable.

I stress you're making rough calculations here. You don't need to work in the cost of every nut and bolt. Just try to be as realistic as you can, being generous with your allowances for expenditure.

 One of the things I've learnt from running my own businesses is that things always seem to cost far more than I initially think they will.

Armed with some rough figures you're ready to work out three useful and very difficult scenarios.

1. Best case scenario.
2. Worst case scenario.
3. Most likely case scenario.

Best case scenario

For your best case scenario work out how many holidays you could actually run, given your resources in terms of time, money etc.

What have you come up with?

For example, if the net amount you're hoping to earn per customer, per holiday, is £80, and given your resources in terms of time available etc, the most holidays you can expect to sell is 100, then that means at the best case you'll earn £8,000.

Are you happy with the amount of the effort you're going to have put in?

If you are, great – obviously you've got an idea worth continuing with. However if your figures are disappointing it doesn't necessarily mean that your idea is unworkable. At this stage all you've worked out is that in its present form it's not going to be sufficient to make a profitable business.

Worst case scenario

Don't forget to calculate a worst case scenario. My favourite way of doing this is to imagine I'll sell nothing.

Obviously this is the sort of scenario we all hope will never happen and provided you undertake sufficient market research before you invest any of your money, it should never arise.

However there will always be factors outside of your control which could destroy even the most carefully-laid business plans. For example, who could have foreseen the impact that the foot and mouth crisis would have had on local tourist business? Many of the walking holiday companies went out of business because most of the countryside in their areas was closed to the public.

Despite investing in advertising and successfully filling their holiday bookings they ended up with no customers and therefore no revenue.

Thankfully this sort of scenario is rare, but it's worth taking a bit of time to ask yourself what would happen if the business you're planning to start had no customers.

How would you survive?

Is the potential financial loss that you would suffer something that you can bear, or would you end up losing everything?

If it's the case that you would end up losing you might like to revise your plans so as to reduce your risk.

Most likely scenario

All being well this is the scenario you most likely expect to achieve. although it's impossible to predict exact expenditure and sales figures, you should be able to work out what you think is possible.

Again if the figures you come up with during this scenario fall below what's needed to make your idea worthwhile then either re-work your idea or start afresh.

Get into the habit of working out feasibilities for everything you come up with. Not only is it a brilliant way of coming up with new ideas, but you're also starting to think like an entrepreneur.

Don't limit your feasibility studies to your own business ideas. It's always interesting to look at what other entrepreneurs are doing. You'll soon start to see businesses that are doomed from the start, and hopefully learn from others' successful business ideas.

Your findings

Regardless of how brilliant, innovative or otherwise your idea might seem to be, it must be:

☐ capable of making enough money to make it a worthwhile investment in terms of your time and money. This needn't be immediate, provided there is some identifiable period in the future when your idea will come into fruition

☐ capable of being started within your current resources in terms of finance, skills and knowledge.

The time spent working out some rough figures and projections at this early stage is time well spent and will highlight the strengths and weaknesses of your idea.

Don't be despondent if your initial ideas don't come up to your expectations. Now is the time to find that out. Better to suffer the disappointment now and get on with building new ideas than end up at some time in the future with a hopelessly loss-making venture.

Hobby business ideas

Most hobbies can find an opportunity somewhere in the following ten business models.

My advice is that you read through the following list with an open mind. Don't dismiss anything immediately. Simply read through them all a number of times and then write them down on a piece of card or in your notebook. Then in the next few days, whenever you get a moment, start working through this list and seeing how many businesses you could start from your hobby.

Remember that most successful home based entrepreneurs have more than one business. They don't risk their futures on one venture, but rather have a number of smaller independent businesses on the go at any one time. So even if you have already decided on the structure of your proposed business, don't be afraid to let your imagination run riot and see what else you can achieve.

SALES BUSINESS

Probably the most common of all business models – this is where you either buy in a product wholesale or make your own product and then retail it.

Examples of this type of business are antiquarian book dealers, craft shops, art dealers, antique dealers etc.

SERVICE BUSINESS

A service business is one where you either sell your own skills, for example a gardener offering a gardening service, or you offer a business where you employ others and market their skills.

Examples of service businesses are: gardening services, dog walking services, interior design services, garden design service.

You could also consider employing others.

Another way is to employ others, and then 'rent out' their skills and experience. For example in our gardening business we employ people to a do a range of things including gardening, teaching and designing. Essentially we 'rent' their skills and sell them to our clients earning a profit on what we pay them and what we charge our clients.

TUITION BUSINESS

Regardless of what hobby you're interested in, there will always be new enthusiasts joining who will want to find out as much as they can about their new hobby.

The business opportunity here is to organise classes and courses so that both newcomers and those with some experience can learn the ropes.

Examples of tuition businesses include organising and running creative writing courses, fishing courses, cookery courses, flower arranging and craft making courses, candle making courses.

You don't have to be an expert yourself to start and run this type of business. Provided you are a skilled organiser and capable of advertising and marketing your courses you can employ teachers or those with specialist knowledge to give your courses.

For example, I run gardening courses and never have any difficulty finding suitably qualified teachers for my classes.

ACTIVITY BUSINESS

Hobbies offer unlimited business opportunities for anyone with organisational skills.

The sort of businesses we're looking at here are organising painting holidays, creative writing holidays, walking holidays, sailing holidays, tours to public gardens, and/or places of interest, deep sea angling trips.

The possibilities are endless here and the great thing about this type of business is that all you really need to get started is your kitchen table. For example, if you're planning to run creative writing holidays you don't need to have your own B&B, hotel or venue to run them from. All you need is to find suitable hotels or venues to run your courses from, negotiate the best deal you can with the proprietors, and organise your holidays.

EXHIBITION BUSINESS

This is a business where you arrange local, national and/or online exhibitions of work.

It is particularly suitable if your hobby involves photography, painting, flower arranging, crafts, candle making etc.

Your revenue comes from charging your exhibitors fees to exhibit at your shows, and/or commission on what they sell.

WHOLESALING

Rather than simply retail products, you could also become a wholesaler. It's worth investigating to see what products you could import and then sell to the UK market.

There are a number of international trade fairs held annually where you can meet and find businesses looking for agents for their products.

The secret with this type of business is to steer away from the main products of your hobby and look for those things that people have difficulty finding. Products that the larger businesses will ignore as they don't believe they can sell them in large enough quantities to justify their expenditure.

COMPETITIONS

You can run all sorts of hobby-based competitions, for example painting competitions, creative writing competitions, poetry competitions, photography competitions.

Revenue comes from charging entrance fees, a portion of which then goes as prize money.

Whilst not a huge business on its own, running competitions can be an excellent way of generating publicity for your business while earning a modest income.

INFORMATION SHARING

Information sharing business is where you sell information regarding your particularly hobby or interest.

Examples of this type of business:

☐ Setting up a website where you list all the events that would be of interest to those participating in your hobby and charging a membership or subscription fee.

☐ Publishing your own guide books or annual directories listing all the information about your particular hobby.

☐ Publishing your own regular magazine or newsletter.

HIRE BUSINESS

Whatever your hobby, the chances are there will be something you can rent out to other hobby enthusiasts.

Examples of this type of business include cycle hire business, fishing rod hire, boat hire, photography equipment hire, holiday home hire, tents and camping equipment hire, garden furniture hire, pot plant hire for offices, hotels, residential homes, stage and movie props.

A hire service can be an excellent way of generating additional revenue for a traditional sales business. Let's say you've opened a cycle shop – why not offer cycle hire as well?

Whatever you're planning to sell – what can you hire to boost your sales?

If you're a classic car collector, could you hire your vehicles out to film companies?

Or if you're an outdoor caterer could you also include a glass hire service in your business?

Don't limit your ideas to your hobbies or what interests you

Don't be afraid to broaden your search for your future business idea.

Although lots of successful business ideas come from hobbies, don't limit your thinking to only those areas you're knowledgeable in. When Sir Alan Sugar founded

Amstrad, he wasn't a computer or software guru but an entrepreneur who saw a niche in the market.

Similarly, when Karan Bilimoria began his Cobra Beer company he wasn't a brewer or had any previous knowledge of the drinks industry or Indian restaurant market. He simply saw a gap in the market and worked out a way of plugging that gap.

Neither had Richard Branson any previous experience of running an airline when he began Virgin Airlines, providing flights across the Atlantic.

And the late Anita Roddick, founder of the Body Shop, wasn't previously a cosmetic retailer prior to starting up. Her previous business experience included running her own guesthouse and upmarket café, neither of which, as she said herself, were really successful.

What all successful entrepreneurs have in common is a seemingly uncanny ability to spot the 'next good thing'. At least that what non-entrepreneurs will usually tell you. I've often heard people remark, 'they (successful entrepreneurs) have a gift or inside knowledge for spotting the next best opportunity'. The actual reality is somewhat more mundane. There's no magic or specialist knowledge involved at all. It's more a case that the successful entrepreneur will continue to slog away, enduring failure after failure, setback after setback, until such times as they hit on the right idea at the right time.

And that, dear reader, is the key to success in your venture.

Be prepared for setbacks. Be ready for the crushing blow when you think you've come up with what you believe is the mother of all ideas only to find either someone else has beaten you to the post or some other unmovable obstacle is standing in the way of you getting going.

When you consider that according to the banks only one in every four new businesses survives the first year of trading, and from then only one in every four will actually survive beyond their third year trading, you don't need me to tell you that the odds of you being successful are fairly much stacked against you. But that should neither worry you, nor deter you.

My belief is that many business failures could have been avoided had the entrepreneur given enough thought to their initial idea. For example, I met two entrepreneurs this week who had just opened their first restaurant. The menu displayed in the window is handwritten, prices are cheaper than cheap, and the lady serving behind the counter looks like death has taken a break. In all honesty, why would anyone want to eat there?

When in passing I spoke to the couple behind the new venture, they told me of their plans to open a whole chain of these restaurants. They seemed to believe they were going to be the next McDonalds. Somehow I don't think they'll make it, but I do hope that before it's too late they'll realise that they are actually offering nothing. Yes, they're offering cheap food. But the problem is that so are half the restaurants in the road they've just opened up on. And those that are offering cheap fare already enjoy a loyal following built up over many years, which means there's no incentive for anyone to visit our cheap and cheerful friends except perhaps the bailiffs.

A great idea should be at the core of your business

If you're simply offering something that's already available then you might as well not bother. A successful business is one that doesn't follow the crowds, but instead carves out a nice little niche for itself before the big boys try to move in on that market.

Prepare to work through lots of ideas. Some ideas you will have might look good initially, but make sure you work your way through all of these *before* starting your business.

I started the Dutch Bike shop from my kitchen table. I'd be embarrassed to tell you (but I will anyway because it makes for a better read) that when we first started our business we only had one model of a Dutch bike available and that could only be supplied in one colour. Today we have considerably more models, and a variety of colours and specifications, but the important thing here was the key idea.

When people ask me how I came upon the idea to import Dutch bikes into the UK, I tell them that when I wanted to buy one for myself I couldn't find a single outlet selling them. So I decided to fill the gap in the market.

Try to remember for a moment all the times you've tried to buy something you simply couldn't get hold of, but still dearly wanted. Think big. Don't think small items that cost a few pence. If your idea involves selling something that costs pennies to buy, you'll only make a fraction of that in return for selling one, so whatever it is you're thinking of selling it will have to be sold in huge quantities. The area of mass retail isn't suitable for us kitchen table entrepreneurs. That's really the domain of the multi-retail giants. Think instead of the things these multi-retailers aren't providing, or won't currently sell, as it's too specialist, too niche for them.

Start looking in such areas and I promise you will find some great ideas.

Summary

1. Getting ideas is simply a process of looking at things differently and working through lots of different ideas until you find the gems hidden in the sand.

2. Try to see if your idea fits into the hobby business ideas as these business models represent enormous potential.

3. Be prepared to start from where you are right now. If your dream is to run a florists' shop, but you can't afford to buy one or take on a shop lease, then be prepared to start with a bucket, selling door-to-door.

3

WHAT'S INVOLVED IN STARTING YOUR BUSINESS

As soon as you've got your ideas together you will need to get a framework from which to start your business.

These are the main areas that you need to consider when starting your business:

- ☐ Naming your business.
- ☐ Deciding where to base your business.
- ☐ Complying with the law.
- ☐ Deciding on a trading identity for your business.
- ☐ Deciding whether or not to register for VAT.

Later we look at what's involved in deciding which trading identity would be suitable for your business and also look at what's involved in VAT. My advice is for you to read Chapter 10 when you feel ready for it. For now though, let's look at some things you'll need to consider when christening your new business and where your new venture is going to live.

Deciding on a name for your business

Choosing the right name for your business is important and is something you need to really think about because whatever name you give to your business will need to create the right image for potential customers.

Let's say you're planning to organise painting holidays in Cornwall. You could call your business simply 'Painting Holidays in Cornwall', but the obvious problem here is that it doesn't give any more information than the obvious.

Before you go any further you need to ask yourself more questions about your proposed business:

- ☐ Are your holidays aimed at the budget-conscious artist looking for cheap hostel-type accommodation with arranged visits to local beauty sites. Or at would-be artists looking for a luxury break, which includes painting tuition and pampering?

- ☐ Where in Cornwall are your holidays based?

☐ What's your own painting expertise?

☐ Are painting holidays the only holidays you're intending to run or will you include other holidays at some future date, such as creative writing courses?

Obviously you are never going to be able to answer all of these questions with the name of your business, but you can improve on the initial name by making it less restrictive and more imaginative.

One of the problems with the original name is that it concentrates on two words – 'painting' and 'holiday'.

The difficulty here is that anyone interested in learning how to paint might get the impression that this business runs holidays for seasoned painters and not beginners, while experienced painters might find the word 'holiday' a turn off.

But by far the greatest difficulty is that it limits your business from offering anything other than painting holidays.

So what's the alternative? You could go for something like 'Creative Breaks Cornwall'.

The advantage with this name is that it conjures up a number of intriguing possibilities without taking away from the core business – painting holidays.

You could also include a strap line on your business advertisements, websites etc:

Creative Breaks Cornwall
Discovering the artist within

If and when you decide to offer other types of holidays your business name is not going to hold you back.

YOUR BUSINESS NAME DOESN'T HAVE TO DESCRIBE YOUR BUSINESS

Your business name doesn't have to describe or even suggest what your business offers.

Take Amazon as an example. Here we have the world's largest retailer of books with no mention of books anywhere in the company name. Yet everyone knows they retail books. Although originally marketed as an online book retailer, Amazon now sells a whole range of non-book products including software and games.

The advantage of choosing a name like Amazon is that not only is it easy to remember and intriguing, but the name doesn't restrict the future growth or diversity of the business. Richard Branson's Virgin Group is similar.

Be imaginative and make sure whatever name you choose doesn't restrict your future business by pigeon-holing you into something that's too narrow.

BEWARE OF CHOOSING CLICHÉ NAMES

It's also a good idea to avoid choosing a cliché business name. By this I mean something like Green Fingers Gardening Company or Joe's Bloomers, or Harriet's Heavenly Pastries etc.

While names like these might seem like a good idea at the time just wait until you discover there's already more than one of them in the country and suddenly your business isn't unique after all.

BARGAIN HUNTING

The exception to the rule is when you're absolutely certain that what you're offering is going to be cheaper than offered by most other retailers, you should include this information somewhere in your title.

Let's say you're planning to open an online fishing tackle shop where offering rock bottom prices is the basis of your marketing strategy.

The Fisherman's Warehouse
Cheapest tackle online

Choosing to use a word like 'warehouse' as opposed to 'shop' suggests large quantities at low prices.

PERSONALISING THE NAME

You could also personalise your business name and call it something like Joe's Fisherman's Warehouse.

Some businesses are ideal for this sort of personalisation, particularly if they involve looking after something that your customer treasures, like children, pets, gardens etc.

While John Browne's Dog Walking Service might seem boring and unimaginative, it does suggest to potential customers that John Browne and not someone unknown to them will be looking after their dog. Including your own name in your business name can under the right circumstances create a feeling of trust, which brings credibility. So don't be afraid to include your own name particularly if the business you're planning to run involves looking after other people's treasures.

OTHER FACTORS

Is the business name you want actually available?

There is no absolute right to a business name unless of course that name is the name of a company or another business trading in the same area as you're intending to.

So if there's already a Flo's Dog Walking Service or Martin's Organic Vegetables in your area then obviously were you to start up a similar business using the same name they would have a legal argument to say that you are trading using their name.

Of course it would also be silly to knowingly use another business name as not only are you bound for legal conflict, you are also denying your business any opportunity of being unique.

 One of the easiest ways to check whether anyone is already using your name is to surf the Internet, which is a good idea anyway because when it comes to creating a website for your business you want to be sure that the domain name you want is available.

Search through as many search engines as you can, including, Yahoo!, Google, Ask Jeeves and any web directories relating to your chosen field.

Don't get too despondent if you find your name is already being used by another business. Better to find this out now than when you've ordered all your stationery, brochures and the like.

When you've decided on your name, ask yourself:

- ☐ Will it fit comfortably on your stationery. For example if you're planning to have labels printed for your products, will the name fit on a small label?

- ☐ Will it create the right image for your business?

- ☐ Will it build trust and credibility?

- ☐ Can you get a website domain name to fit in with your business name?

- ☐ If your business expands, diversifies or changes completely, can you keep this name or will another be needed?

- ☐ If you abbreviate your name, what do you get. For example, my gardening business is called Paul Power Landscapes, which abbreviates to PPL. Can your name be abbreviated, and if so are you comfortable with the abbreviation?

Opening a business bank account

There is no legal requirement that I am aware of that says you must have a business bank account. However, there are banking terms and conditions, which if you ever have the time and patience to read will tell you that you cannot use your personal account for business banking.

OPERATING WITHOUT A BUSINESS BANK ACCOUNT – CASH ONLY

If you're planning to run a small hobby business where all of your customers can pay you in cash then you don't necessarily have to open a bank account.

You could manage your money by simply paying it into a cash till, which you then record as business income. You keep a float in your till to pay your business bills etc, and then finally you pay yourself using cash.

Because this money has now effectively gone from being business cash to personal drawings, I can't see why any bank can object when you lodge this money as it is after all your wages. Not business income!

Obviously there'll only be a limited amount of businesses that will want to operate on this sort of basis and with credit card usage becoming more and more popular it looks like cash will become a thing of the past.

WHAT TO LOOK FOR IN A BUSINESS BANK

At the time of writing there are four main high street banks and I believe all of them offer more or less the same thing. Certainly their charges are similar and once you get past any initial period of free banking, there's not much difference.

Experience

The bank our businesses are with gives us free banking provided we operate our account within certain restrictions, which include a limit to how many lodgements we can make.

I've found the 'limits' to be more than generous and if you do exceed your limit you then only pay to lodge those items over the pre-agreed quota.

But there's a drawback: cash. Our free banking account is basically a postal bank where the only way to lodge monies is either via the post using their prepaid envelopes or in an envelope using one of their branch's cash dispensers, which means lodging cash is pretty impossible.

However this suits our business as most of our payments are either made by cheque or credit card and the small amount of cash we do get we can use as petty cash.

These arrangements suit us but might not suit your business. Shop around and get the best package for your business.

Ask yourself:

1. Are you looking for a bank account to simply lodge and withdraw money, or are you looking for a bank where you will need to apply for overdrafts, loans etc?
2. Are you planning to take credit cards?
3. Will you be taking large amounts of cash?
4. Will you buying your products from abroad?
5. Will you be hiring staff?

If you answer yes to most or all of the above questions then you're going to need a business bank as opposed to simply a business bank account.

Anyone who is considering future borrowings for their business, employing staff and taking large amounts of cash will need a bank where they can actually speak to a business bank advisor who will be sympathetic to the sort of problems you face.

Experience

The owner of a small cleaning business lodged a number of cheques into her business bank account. Unfortunately she failed to make sure the cheques had actually cleared before writing cheques for her employees' wages. She believed she'd left plenty time before writing her salary cheques.

The results were disastrous. The cheques bounced, which meant her employees hadn't been paid. This started a panic with staff telling her customers that they thought her business had gone bankrupt. It might as well have done because staff were now unwilling to work and customers' offices not cleaned.

It was difficult for her to rebuild her business but she did. The bank, as you would expect, dismissed her complaint telling her that it was her responsibility to ensure she had sufficient funds in her account prior to writing her cheques. Her argument was that her cheques had taken an extraordinarily long time to clear.

Situations like this can arise when you run your own business so it's important that you choose a bank that you are comfortable with, and most importantly that you have a named contact in that bank who you can speak to and is familiar with your business.

Ask your bank manager some questions

Someone once described a bank manager as being: 'someone who loans you an umbrella when it's sunny, then asks for it back when it rains.' This bears out my own personal experiences!

Before committing yourself to opening your business account you should ask prospective banks as many questions as you can. The list below is by no means exhaustive:

1. Will you have your own personal contact within their bank who you can call on for help and advice?

2. What is their criteria for granting business overdrafts? Some banks will insist you have an established track record with them for a period before they will consider your application.

3. Ask them to explain their bank charges, particularly in relation to free banking offers. Most banks only offer free banking on the basis that you manage your account within certain parameters. If you exceed those limits will you have to pay charges on all your transactions or just those that exceed their limits?

4. Ask them how they can help your business. This is where you'll find out if you're talking to a member of staff in a call centre reading from a crib sheet or someone who is actually interested in working with your business.

Finally, remember that banks exist to make profit for their shareholders.

 When it comes to bank accounts – keep your personal and business accounts at separate banks.

While it might seem like a good idea to keep your personal bank account and business bank account with the same bank, I'd advise against it.

The reason I recommend you keep your accounts at separate banks or building societies is that in the event that you have a problem with one account, the bank may, at its discretion, enforce its power and put a freeze on your other accounts thus rendering you completely impotent.

Let's say, for example, that you find yourself in the same situation as the proprietor of the cleaning company I told you about earlier. Were you to find yourself in this unfortunate situation it's quite probable that the bank would freeze your personal account as well as your business bank account, which as you can imagine would even be more disastrous.

Believe me, in business things can always get worse!

Despite your best efforts there may be times when either your customers let you down or an unforeseen bill presents itself and suddenly you find yourself overdrawn beyond your limits. Before you know it everything is frozen.

 Contingency plan your banking by having a number of bank accounts with different banks or building societies.

Creating a business identity

TELEPHONE LINES

Do you need another line? Yes, I believe you do. Nothing will put potential customers off more than a badly answered telephone. In the past I've phoned businesses where children have answered the phone and I've given up trying to get them to put mum or dad on so I can order something. Instead I've done what most people would do – moved on.

A separate business line will not only give your business credibility, but also make life easier for you. When the phone rings you know it's business.

The disadvantage to having a separate business line is, of course, cost. Telephone providers charge more for a business line than they do a domestic, but I believe that this cost is a relatively small price to pay to give your business an enhanced professional image. By using a domestic line as opposed to a business line you miss out on free listings in the business section of the phone book and of course when anyone searches directory enquiries you will only be listed if you have a business line. Also, were your line to go down for any reason repairs to business lines get priority over domestic ones.

Freephone numbers

When deciding on a business number you could also consider introducing a freephone number or a number where your customers only pay the cost of local call to contact you. Incentives like these can be useful if you're operating in a competitive environment where potential customers are faced with lots of different companies to choose from.

The fact that your number will cost either nothing to call or the cost of a local call will give them an added incentive to call your business first.

STATIONERY

Now that you have decided on your trading identity and chosen a suitable name you are ready to create your business identity, which will include things like deciding on a logo for your business and ordering company stationery.

When it comes to publishing stationery you have a number of choices:

- ☐ Put together your own simple letterhead without a logo and print your own stationery using your PC.

- ☐ Design your own logos and letterheads either freehand or using a software programme then either print your own stationery or give it to a printer.

- ☐ Employ a graphic designer to create your logos and letterhead and then either print it yourself or have a printer do it for you.

Your choice of methods will obviously depend on how much money you have available to spend on this. By far the simplest and cheapest way is to do everything yourself. Not every business will need a logo or fancy letterhead and many hobby businesses can get by having their business name, address and telephone number printed somewhere on the page as the example below.

Creative Holidays Cornwall
Primrose Cottage
Seafront
Cornwall
Tel: 12345678
www.chhcs.co.uk
email: info@chhcs.co.uk

Dear Mr Visitor

We have pleasure in enclosing our latest brochure on our painting holidays for this season.

Should you have any questions, or to book your holiday, please call us on the above number or book online using our website.

Thank you for your interest in Creative Holidays Cornwall and we look forward to welcoming you in the not too distant future.

Kind regards

Bill Holiday
Proprietor

Nothing fancy is needed

The important thing when deciding on how to approach your stationery is to remember that nothing fancy is needed. A clean, crisp letterhead is far easier to read than a multi-coloured splurge of print complete with clip art.

Clip art is the image/cartoon graphics you receive free with most software publishing programmes. It should be avoided. If you use it when creating your identity, the chances are that other similar businesses will too.

If you really believe that artwork is crucial to your business success then commission a graphic designer to come up with something brilliant and unique. While clip art is fine for party invitations and birthday announcements, the image of your business will undoubtedly suffer if you use it.

BROCHURES

For many businesses, brochures are an important marketing tool. Although it's relatively expensive to employ a specialist company to design your brochure, letterhead and so on, it can pay enormous dividends especially if what you're going to be selling is high value and the buyer needs to be assured of your credability.

 When a professional designs your brochure you are benefiting not only from their design, but also from their marketing experience.

Before employing a designer to work on your behalf make sure you:

- □ **See examples of their work.** Not just online; ask them to send you samples so you can determine the quality of the print, paper and get an overall impression of what they're offering.

- □ **Ask for a written quotation.** Designer's bills are a bit like solicitor's – if left unchecked they can run wildly over your initial budget. Before you enter into any commitment make sure you know exactly what you are getting for your money.

- □ **Insist on copy-ready proofs.** Hopefully this won't be necessary as professional design companies will always send what is known as 'copy-ready proofs' to you for approval. A CRP is basically a mock-up of how your finished brochure, letterhead or compliment slip will look. It's vital you check these thoroughly for mistakes as once you have given your approval the proofs will be printed and you will have to pay for any amendments or alterations.

☐ **Ask for a credit account.** Some businesses will insist you pay upfront. I don't agree with this as I like to be sure that I'm getting what I pay for. In the event that you're not happy with the quality or you don't get what was originally agreed you will have far more influence if you haven't already settled the bill. The problem you might find is that if you are a new business, designers may be reluctant to undertake the work unless they are convinced they stand a good chance of getting paid for it. If this is the case, offer to pay a deposit on order with the balance falling due when you collect your work. It's also worth asking for an account facility, particularly if you intend using the company for all your future printing requirements.

Before printing anything make sure you check the proofs for errors and omissions. Pay particular attention to things like telephone and fax numbers, website addresses, postcodes and email addresses.

Remember, if you are operating as a sole trader and trading under a different name then by law you must include something like 'Paul Power trading as Walking Holidays Cornwall' on your letterhead. You can do this discreetly by adding it somewhere in the lower header in small print. (See Chapter 10 for more information.)

SMALL BUSINESS START-UP KITS

Many printers now offer an all-in stationery package for new businesses, which usually includes: 250 letterheads, envelopes, business cards and compliments slips.

Provided the quality of print and paper is of an acceptable standard these packages can offer great value for money and in my experience printers are generally happy to include some free artwork and layout.

Prior to confirming your order make sure you ask your printer to show you samples of the type of paper you will be getting and samples of the printing.

Envelopes

When it comes to posting out your letters, brochures, direct sales materials etc, you're going to need to think about envelopes. My advice is that you go with window envelopes. These are the ones where all you have to do is fold your letter in the correct place and the address is automatically displayed through the window. They are particularly useful when you're sending out a mail-shot etc.

Ask your printer to give you a quote to have your business name printed on your envelopes. Your customers will be more likely to open your letter as they'll recognise your name on the envelope. Otherwise it might get mistaken for junk mail and binned without being opened.

You could also consider hand-writing your envelopes, although depending on your handwriting this can give an amateurish back-bedroom sort of feel to it.

Whatever you decide on make sure everything is consistent.

Which means that you should make sure that:

☐ the colour of the paper matches the colour of the envelope;

☐ the quality of the paper matches the quality of the envelope;

☐ the colour scheme and logos are similar throughout your business – letterheads, website, company vehicles, staff uniforms, business cards etc.

If you're unsure don't commit yourself.

Getting it wrong can be expensive. I've known of small businesses who've rushed their stationery order through only to find something as simple as the telephone number was incorrect. Remember that once you approve the proofs and give your go ahead you have no recourse. The fact that you haven't checked your telephone number, business name or postcode is not the fault of the printers and therefore not only will you end up with the most expensive scrap paper money can buy, but also have to have everything redone.

Always work to a budget.

Starting a business is a bit like organising a wedding. It's so easy for costs to spiral out of control. An extra colour here and little embellishment there, and let's just go for that satin finished paper and suddenly your costs have quadrupled.

 The best way to prevent costs getting out of hand is to work out a budget and stick to it.

During your first meeting with your printer let him know what your budget is and make it clear that you will not be spending more than this figure. Provided you've picked a professional printer this won't be a problem. Our printer has been extremely helpful in coming up with novel ways of getting the printing we want done to our budget.

Choosing a printer

It's important to choose a printer that you are comfortable with and someone that you can build up a relationship with. Because I run a number of small businesses, my natural instinct is to choose a similar business to mine to undertake our printing requirements. Once I went to one of those high street printing franchises, and I knew as soon as I walked in the door that the young, disinterested shop assistant who couldn't understand that my surname was Power and not Powers was not going to work out.

Personally I prefer the smaller independent who understands and appreciate the problems that come with running a small business.

Your insurance company

The fact that most entrepreneurs will have at sometime worked from home will have an impact on their home insurance policies. It's important therefore to check with your insurance company that you are covered in the event that someone burgles your home office and steals your computer, printer etc that your cover includes you running your business from home.

Obviously if you're going to be holding stock at home you will also need to ensure that your stock is covered in the event of theft, fire or damage.

Unfortunately the relatively high cost of insurance cover means it's usually one of those things to ignore when starting your own business from home, but you do need to ensure that by running your business from home you don't invalidate your ordinary home contents and buildings insurances.

Local authority

Planning regulations generally do not allow private residences to be used for business. So if you're planning to turn your garage into a workshop, you should check with your local planning office to see whether or not you will need planning permission.

However if running your business from home involves little more than working from your kitchen table or spare room then the chances are that nobody will object. But be aware that if you are running a limited company from home the law requires you to display somewhere outside your office the name of your business. You doing this may bring you into conflict with neighbours who may then complain to the local planning officer.

Where to base your business

It may seem odd that a book promoting the home based entrepreneur advises you to consider working from somewhere other than your home, but there will be times when this will make sense.

Take for example our businesses, which include a general gardening business and cycle hire business.

Our gardening business includes trailers, machinery, vans and all that goes with that. I don't believe that it would be fair on our neighbours to base this sort of thing either outside our home or in our garden. The other problem we'd face is that there is now so much of it we wouldn't be able to fit it all in.

Similarly our cycle business includes bikes and accessories with a need for a small workshop area from where we can service and maintain the bikes. We then have a large showroom area where customers can browse a large selection of Dutch bikes, we offer free parking and customer toilets.

But our office is still home based.

The reason for this is that I prefer working from home, and the additional cost of hiring an office on top of workshop/storage space was astronomical. In addition to the costs of hiring office space you also have to pay for water rates, lighting, heating, building insurance, contents insurance, burglar alarms, business rates – which in my mind makes it more sense to be home based.

Of course this arrangement may not suit every business, particularly those employing office-based staff.

If you are planning to rent office space, make sure that you shop around for the best deal and avoid if you can having to agree to a lengthy lease period. Although you may find you get a better rent figure if you agree to a longer let, you might find that after a year the property is no longer suitable for your business and the costs terminating the lease may be so great as to make it impossible.

 Consider having a home office and a workshop/storage unit elsewhere.

Just like I've done with my businesses you may find that you're better off sourcing some form of cheap storage/workshop area where you can keep stock, machinery etc, and then base your office at home.

Again make sure you work to a budget. Estate agents are paid commission on rent and in my experience will always be pushing towards that 'ideal property', which costs just little bit more than the one you're looking at. Before you know it you've taken on a monthly rent commitment the size of the national debt.

SHARING A UNIT

It's also worth considering sharing a unit with another business. Obviously you've got be careful who you decide to share with and make sure they're able, and willing, to pay their share of the rent, but doing this can substantially reduce the costs of renting premises.

If you are going to do this make sure you:

□ get the permission of your landlord. Do this before you agree to rent the property as it's unlikely they'll agree to your sub-letting it once you've moved in;

□ draw up an agreement detailing who is responsible for what and what happens if one you wants to terminate the agreement;

□ set up separate standing orders to pay your rent (if your landlord agrees) so that in the event your sharer doesn't pay, your landlord will pursue him and not you.

Although useful for reducing the costs of renting somewhere, you really do need to be sure about whoever you share with.

SMALL STORAGE UNITS

Gone are the days when renting a storage unit meant you had to take on something the size of a small house. There are now companies who specialise in renting a variety of sizes and who offer easy in-and-out terms, which usually mean that you can rent these units on a weekly or monthly basis. Useful when you're starting out and not sure about how much space you actually need.

 The golden rule when it comes to renting anything is not to be tempted to rush into it.

Even if it seems the most idyllic property for your business you should always:

□ stop and think about it before rushing in and signing on the dotted line;

□ ask for a copy of the lease agreement, which you then take away with you and read thoroughly before committing. The best place to read lease agreements is away from wherever it is you're planning to rent;

☐ get a solicitor to read the lease for you if the property is anything other than a self-storage type unit.

Complying with the law

Unfortunately, small businesses are facing an ever-increasing barrage of legislation and it would be impossible within the scope of this book to cover all possible legalities that you will need to consider. Not every business will be subject to the same laws. For example a business involving food will be subject to different legislation than a business organising water sports.

 It's up to you to check what legislation your business will have to adhere to. Ignorance of the law is no defence.

Important legislation you should be aware of if you're planning to open business involving food:

☐ The Food Safety Act 1990
☐ Food Safety (General Food Hygiene) Regulations 1995
☐ Food Safety (Temperature Control) Regulations 1995

You can find full details of the requirements of these acts at The Foods Standards Agency Website: http://cleanup.food.gov.uk.

You should also be aware of the legislation covering the following areas:

☐ employing staff
☐ health and safety legislation
☐ Data Protection Act.

EMPLOYING STAFF

The most important thing to know is that all your employees are entitled by law to be given a **Written Statement of Employment** setting out the main particulars of their employment.

You are also required to undertake a number of checks on anyone you intend employing. These will include things such as:

☐ **The prospective employee's age.** Their age will affect the types of work they are allowed to do; the hours they are allowed to work; rates you must pay them.

☐ **Whether or not they are allowed to work in the UK.** You must be sure that their status in the UK allows them to work. If you employ someone who is not allowed to work in UK, you commit an offence and risk being penalised.

☐ **Their skills and aptitude for the job.** You will have to take up references, background checks etc.

Visit the government's Business Link website http://www.businesslink.gov.uk.

You can use their free software tool to create a Written Statement of Employment for all your employees and use their interactive tool to check your legal responsibilities when taking on staff. There is a whole wealth of information on this site concerning all aspects of employment legislation.

Health and safety

As a business owner you have a legal responsibility for the health and safety of your employees and anyone that may be affected by your business and its activities. You also have a legal responsibility for the impact your business has on the environment.

It's essential you have in place a properly written health and safety policy for your business.

You can get all the answers to your questions by phoning the Health and Safety Information Line on 0870 1545 500, or visiting the website http://www.hse.gov.uk.

Data Protection Act

The provisions of the Data Protection Act 1988 will affect most business owners. It works in two ways:

1. By governing the way personal information is used and stored. Personal information would include your customer's addresses, dates of births, telephone numbers etc.

   The Act requires you to follows the eight data protection principles, which state that all data must be:
   – fairly and lawfully processed
   – processed for limited purposes
   – adequate, relevant and not excessive
   – accurate
   – not kept for longer than is necessary
   – processed in line with the data subject's rights
   – secure
   – not transferred to countries outside the EU without adequate
     protection.

2. By giving all individuals certain rights.

These rights, which are known as 'right of subject access', give everyone the right to see the information that is being held about them on a computer, and some paper records. This means that if in the course of your business you record details about your customers, they can request that you provide them with all the information you hold about them.

 TIP Make sure that, whatever it is you're recording about your customers, you'd be happy for them to see it.

The information must also be accurate and up to date. For example if you run a walking holidays business where you regularly send information to customers on your mailing list, periodically you would have to make sure that the details you have are correct and up to date. So it's good practice to include a slip with your mailings asking customers to tell you whether or not they still want to receive your information and inform you of any change in their details.

(There are some exceptions to this, for example when the information stored is being used in the detection and prevention of crime.)

NOTIFICATION

The commissioner maintains a public register of data controllers. Notification is the way in which a data controller's processing details are added to this register.

The data controller could be you, as business owner, or an employee of your business.

Unless you are exempt from Notification, you must notify the commissioner and pay a fee, currently £35, to be added to the register. This is an annual fee. Failure to notify when you are not exempt is a criminal offence.

To find out whether your business will have to Notify telephone the DPR on 01625 545740 or visit their website at http://www.dpr.gov.uk.

THE RIGHTS OF SUBJECT ACCESS

Because individuals have a right to see the information that is being held about them – the right of subject access – you need to know what to do if an individual makes a request to your business.

If you receive a request you must:

☐ send them the information you hold on them;

- ☐ tell them why this information is processed and anyone it may be passed to or seen by;

- ☐ explain the logic in any automated decisions;

- ☐ deal with their request within 40 days from the date you receive it.

You may charge an administration fee of no more than £10.

COMPENSATION

Be aware that individuals may seek compensation through the courts if they have suffered damage, or damage and distress, because of any contravention of the Act.

As I said earlier, there is a whole raft of legislation that can affect your business and you must be familiar with it all. I really recommend a visit to the Business Link site, which is an invaluable tool for small business owners and entrepreneurs.

Summary

1. Give plenty of thought to the name you're going to give your business. Your business name creates the first impression of your business, therefore it's important to get it right.

2. Choose a base for your business that suits you in terms of affordability and adaptability. There's nothing wrong with the kitchen table.

3. A successful business is impossible without creating credibility. Therefore it's important that you get it right from day one.

4. Get a dedicated business line for your business and make sure it's answered in a business-like way.

5. Research all legislation that might affect your business and be sure to register where appropriate.

4

RESEARCH: THE DOORWAY TO SUCCESS

The two huge mistakes you can make when starting your business are to:

1. First decide on a product or service to sell and then go out and try to find customers to buy what you're offering.

2. Start without a fully-researched business plan.

Deciding on a product first and then looking for customers to buy your goods is a common problem, and the reason many businesses fail. What happens is this. The novice entrepreneur comes up with a great idea for a business, stocks up his shelves, opens his doors and then nothing happens. In our town I've seen so many examples of this, where would-be entrepreneurs arrive full of optimism that our town wants their gift shop, book shop, candle shop solely on the basis that we haven't got one already.

Why haven't we got one of these shops? Is it maybe that no one either wants or needs whatever it is you're trying to sell them? Or if they do, perhaps there aren't enough potential customers to make the business viable. It's an easy mistake to make and I believe if you were to take a quick nationwide survey of everyone's garages, lock-ups, spare rooms and garden sheds, I bet you'd find thousands, probably millions, of products that were all part of that initial great idea, which ended in failure.

To succeed you must first identify your target market and understand their needs before you get your products and services together.

 Only when you have researched thoroughly, and decided that an actual market really does exist for whatever it is you're selling, should you actually go ahead with your business.

Not having a winning business plan is the other most common mistake made by would-be entrepreneurs.

If you go on an unfamiliar journey do you plan your route first, or wait until you're hopelessly lost before asking for directions?

I know a lot of you would say you wouldn't plan a route, and wait until either you got lost, got lucky or gave up.

But the point is you reach your destination faster and far less stressed if you invest a small amount of time preparing and familiarising yourself with the best route.

Why businesses fail

There are many reasons why new businesses fail.

☐ Overestimating how much the business will sell or underestimating how long it will take to achieve initial essential sales targets.

☐ Underestimating costs.

☐ Failing to identify your market correctly because of inadequate market research, or no research.

☐ Failing to control costs.

☐ Carrying too much stock.

☐ Being personally and financially unprepared for running your own business.

Or in other words **failing to have a winning business plan**.

Experience

When one of the shops in our small seaside town was up for let, I was intrigued to know who would rent it. In fact, I had thought about renting it myself and turning it into a cycle shop. However when I found out what rent the landlord wanted and the local council's business rates, I decided that it wasn't viable.

Personally I thought the rent was too high for our town. When I mentioned this to the letting agent they scoffed and dismissed my surmising as rubbish. Not only had they already had one offer, but were now turning down others.

The new tenant duly arrived and I watched with interest as what was once a tired sweet shop was transformed into a state-of-the-art Internet café.

I was shocked. Who in their right mind would consider opening an Internet café when the local council had just extended the library to include free Internet access for all library members? And those who weren't library members could pay a nominal fee of 50p to surf the web for 30 minutes. Needless to say the new Internet café proprietor didn't appear to have any trade at all. Within weeks they closed only to reopen a few days later as a second-hand bookshop. Again surprising as there was already a large second-hand bookshop in what is a very small town.

Soon after the doors closed for good and the property went on the market again.

I don't take any pleasure telling you this story, but the reason it's important is that any one of us could end up in the same unfortunate position as that entrepreneur if all we do is follow our heart and go with the business idea that suits us most.

Unfortunately business doesn't work this way. Before you can even think about success, you need to be able to survive. There are two important words that I want to stress in the above list of reasons for business failures. They are:

- □ overestimating
- □ underestimating.

I speak from experience when I tell you that it's so easy to overestimate how much you will sell and underestimate how long it's going to take to get your business fully up and running.

I believe it can take at least three years to establish any worthwhile business. So prepare yourself for a long ride.

Researching your idea

There are various areas of your idea that will have to be researched and looked at. The primary area that you need to concentrate on is to thoroughly research your product or service. Look at these from every possible angle.

PRODUCT OR SERVICE

You need to be as sure as you can that either the product or service you are about to launch will actually appeal to your target market. Here's something to think about – why was the teabag a roaring success and the coffee bag a huge flop? I don't think anyone has actually managed to answer this one, but it does go to show that sometimes even though something similar has been an enormous success it doesn't mean that your new idea will work too. You can stack the odds in your favour by undertaking thorough research.

Question everything about your product or service and ask yourself:

- □ **What makes your product/service unique?**
- □ **Why would customers choose you in favour of anyone else?**
- □ **How easily can you source your products?**

In the initial burst of enthusiasm for your new business venture it's easy to overlook the question of sourcing. You need to be sure that not only you can obtain your products (or raw materials if making your own) but also that the price you're paying isn't subject to frequent and excessive price fluctuations.

Experience

Our local fishmonger relied entirely on supplying his business from local fishing boats until recently. Although his unique selling point is to be able to sell fish so fresh it's often hopping and flipping all over his counter, the downside of this is that when the weather was too bad for the fishermen to fish, his business ran out of stock, which meant his customers began to buy elsewhere. To overcome this he now buys a percentage of his stock from fish wholesalers where he still manages to get fresh supplies for his business as well as offering locally caught fish when it's available.

The result has been an overall increase in his business as he has gained not only a reputation for always having fresh fish available, but also a greater variety than previously.

CURRENCY FLUCTUATIONS AND TRANSPORTATION COSTS

If you're sourcing either products or raw materials from abroad you'll need to make sure that you allow provision somewhere in your costings for those inevitable currency fluctuations and other costs that can adversely affect the price you pay for your goods. Remember that the price that suppliers quote you when you're working out your initial costings may not be the price you actually have to pay when you open for business.

Another factor you'll need to consider is transportation costs, which can rise significantly in the event of an oil price increase, civil unrest or natural disaster.

I know an entrepreneur who sells sailing boats that he imports from France and Poland. He goes there himself and transports them back to the UK on a road trailer towed by his four-wheel drive. He believes this is the only way that he can ensure he gets his goods on time without paying excessive transportation costs and waiting weeks or even months for his boats to arrive.

MINIMUM QUANTITY ORDERS

Beware of the effect that having to order minimum quantities can have on your business.

We buy our Dutch bikes direct from Holland, which means we have to pay shipping costs. To keep costs to an absolute minimum our suppliers send our bike deliveries as fillers for other business trailers, so our bikes travel with all sorts of other goods such as fruit, flowers, vegetables and even cakes. The benefit to us is that we pay low transportation costs, as our order is nothing more than a way of the haulage company ensuring they fill all the space in their trucks.

Another often unseen problem with minimum orders is you may not be able to order further stock as you haven't got the cash as all your money is already tied up in your stock.

This is why it's essential to work out a cash flow forecast.

MAKING YOUR OWN PRODUCTS

You're intending to start a business where your unique selling point is that you make all your own products. How quickly can you make them? You'll need to be sure that you can keep making them while still running your business.

Whatever it is you're selling, make sure you can produce it as quickly as will be needed to make your business profitable. If you're marketing home-made produce, your customers will expect that's what they're getting. Offer anything else, and you may well destroy your uniqueness.

Experience

A friend of mine makes the most beautiful dolls houses, together with a range of accessories.

Her attention to detail has gained her an enviable reputation both in the UK and abroad, with many of her products being purchased for the lucrative American market.

She was doing so well that she decided to move her business from exhibiting at craft fairs to taking on her own shop. However, soon after opening her shop she had to close it. Not because she couldn't find enough customers to support her expanding business, but because she couldn't make her products fast enough to keep up with demand.

Whereas before she spent her days working at her kitchen table crafting her products, she now had a shop to run, which meant she had little or no time left to make her products. Of course she could have hired someone to run the shop for her, but her business couldn't support employing staff as well as paying the hefty rent, business rates and all the other costs that come with a high street premises.

She's now back at her kitchen table doing what she loves most and her business is booming.

PACKAGING AND PROMOTION

Packaging and promotion of your goods often go hand in and. A product that is imaginatively and attractively packaged will obviously have greater a chance of being sold over one that is not. Toy manufacturers spend millions of pounds annually on making sure their products grab the attention of their intended audience, children.

Mail order

If you're intending to offer your products by mail order, you'll need to be sure:

☐ that your products are suitable for dispatch by either postage or by courier;

☐ they don't get damaged while in transit. You should also considering offering your customers insurance to protect their goods once they leave your business.

Selling at craft fairs and exhibitions

☐ Try to make all your customers walking advertisements by giving them something eye-catching to put their purchases in.

☐ Where possible choose packaging that has either been made from recycled materials or is capable of being recycled.

☐ Consider encouraging your clients to return their packaging to you for use again. You'll be surprised how many will do this and how many will buy from you because you offer this as a service.

Wholesaling your products

If you are selling your products wholesale you need to be sure that whatever you're selling remains in the same pristine condition once it reaches your customers' shelves as it did when it left you. Even though your clients are retailers and not the public, if your goods turned up damaged and unappealing few retailers will want to restock your orders.

PRICE

Unless you are proposing to sell a truly unique, sought-after product to a small niche market, consider very carefully the price at which you sell your goods and services before you throw open your doors.

If your prices are too low you may get the business, but not earn any money; too high and you won't sell anything.

The ethos that runs through all of the businesses that I am involved in is that we offer a value-for-money service where customer service is our number one priority. We're not bargain-basement clearance merchants. We offer a quality products at prices customers find attractive and leave enough profit to make it all worthwhile.

Market research

COMPARING LIKE FOR LIKE

When researching the competition, make sure that you are actually comparing like with like.

I recently came across an Internet business offering what appeared to be bicycles similar to the ones we sell. Naturally I was concerned that this business appeared to be offering considerably lower prices. However when I compared their cycles to ours it was apparent that they were not the same product in terms of specification and build quality.

MAKE A CHECKLIST

The best way to approach your research is to make a checklist of all the things you need to know about your competition before you start researching.

To be successful, research needs to be carried out over a period of time as opposed to on one occasion, as every business has seasonal peaks and troughs. Prices will vary depending on what time of the year it is. For example, most retailers suffer in the early part of the year when business is slow after Christmas. On the other hand this can be a boom period for gym owners and travel agents.

So make sure your research gives an accurate picture of the market in general and not one that is either enjoying a seasonal boom or a temporary famine!

HOW TO FIND POTENTIAL COMPETITORS

Obviously before you can start researching your competitors you must first identify who they are. The important point to remember is that it's not always the readily identifiable ones that you need to worry about.

Remember the poor guy who opened up an Internet café in my local town only to find that the local library were offering Internet access? These sorts of events aren't as uncommon as they might sound. Around about the same time as the Internet café

55

disaster our local council opened a new restaurant, which they offered as a concession to a private company. The location of this restaurant is superb in that it gets the best views of the harbour. Naturally it's doing very well, but what about the private restaurant owners who are having to work doubly hard on the almost impossible job of winning customers back to their restaurants which have no sea views?

It's always a good idea to keep an eye on what your local council is up to. If nothing else you may well spot a business opportunity – a worthwhile concession up for tender.

The main ways to find your competitors is to check:

- □ advertisements in your hobbies' magazines, club websites and your local paper;
- □ the Internet – using the main search engines (Google, Yahoo!, etc);
- □ trade directories;
- □ *Yellow Pages*;
- □ *Thompson* directory.

CHECKING OUT THE COMPETITION

When checking out the competition make sure you find out:

- □ Exactly what it is they are offering. How do their products or services compare to yours in terms of quality as well as price?

- □ The total price of their product once you've included all the extras. For example is VAT included or added on at the point of sale?

- □ The sort of guarantees your competitors are offering. Can you match or better what they are offering?

- □ How quickly they can deliver their goods. How does this compare to what you are offering?

- □ Customer testimonials. Have they included any customer testimonials in their sales material/website? If they have been established for any length of time they should have testimonials from satisfied clients. If they haven't, why not?

- □ How close they are to where you will be based. If they are on your doorstep is there really enough room for the two of you?

- □ How busy they are. If they have a retail business you should camp yourself discreetly outside at various different times to see how many people not just go into their shop, but also come out having made a purchase. If they are mail order or website based, monitor their site to see how often it is updated. Also send them some query emails to see how quickly they reply. It'll soon become apparent whether or not a business is doing well or dying on its feet.

CUSTOMER SURVEYS

Sometimes the only reliable way to be sure that whatever it is you're about to sell is going to appeal to your potential market is to carry out customer surveys.

You can do this in a number of ways:

- ☐ If your hobby has a magazine with a readers' letters page, write to the editor with your idea asking for the readers' help with your research. Make sure you include your email address.

- ☐ Post messages on website discussion forum boards. Again, invite comments and suggestions regarding your proposal. This is a great way of getting some useful marketing feedback and if you encourage people to email their thoughts to you, you will then have a ready-made sales list for introducing your products or services.

- ☐ Send out questionnaires to clubs, groups and organisations relating to your hobby. Encourage participation by offering an incentive for everyone who completes them. For example, everyone who returns their questionnaire before such and such date will automatically be entered in our free prize draw to win a whatever it is you're offering.

- ☐ Network and mingle. Wherever your hobby enthusiasts gather, get out there and network with them. Most hobbies will have regular group get togethers, which can be great places to test drive any ideas you might have. For example, if you're introducing a new product or service you could go along and offer free test runs/trials for whatever it is you're offering. I use this technique a lot in my businesses when I'm planning to introduce something new. Not only have I found this a brilliant way of getting new ideas, but also for finding new customers.

UNDERSTANDING THE MARKET PLACE

Obviously it's unlikely that you will be the only business operating in your chosen field, but if you do find that the competition is thin on the ground this doesn't necessarily mean good news for your business. It may be that businesses like the one you are proposing have come and gone. So it's worth further research if there isn't any sign of real competitors.

Investigate as much as you can about your potential market. The following are good sources of market information.

☐ Internet search engines.
☐ Local libraries.
☐ Council records.
☐ Speaking to other shop owners who are operating in the geographical area you are considering.
☐ Newspaper archives.
☐ Posting 'information wanted' notices on web forums.
☐ Speaking to potential customers.

Prior to starting our cycle business, my partner and I spoke to as many of the local shop owners as we could, trying to find out whether or not they thought there was any future in our idea. Without exception everyone we spoke to was extremely helpful and offered us the benefit of their experience and came up with some useful suggestions.

So if you're planning to open a shop or business in a particular locality don't be afraid to ask existing businesses for their thoughts. That way you've got a good chance of finding out what's gone on in your area, and whether or not a business similar to what you're proposing has come and gone.

 I worry more about lack of competition than competition itself.

HOW MUCH CAN I CHARGE?

There's no easy answer to this one, and how much you sell will depend on a combination of factors including:

☐ how big your market is
☐ how well you promote your products and services
☐ your unique selling points
☐ your competitiveness.

The first thing you must get right is to actually ensure that there is a demand for whatever it is you are offering. Once you've established this you then need to be sure that there will be sufficient demand to make it profitable.

The cost of starting a business

To succeed you will have to have a fairly accurate idea of how much it is going to cost to start your business.

A common mistake is to decide on the type of business you want to start and work backwards finding out, often too late, that you can't afford to keep going what you've already started.

 Make sure that you work out as accurately as you can how much it's going to cost you to start up.

When calculating your initial costs, you should consider:

- ☐ How much you will have to pay for your initial stock.
- ☐ Any specialist equipment or machinery that may be required.
- ☐ Vehicle costs.
- ☐ Registration or professional fees – for example you may need to employ a solicitor to read and report on a lease agreement, patent a product or pay local authority registration fees.
- ☐ Insurance costs.
- ☐ Costs of hiring additional storage space.
- ☐ Website costs.
- ☐ Stationery costs.
- ☐ Working capital.

WORKING CAPITAL

Working capital is the amount of money you have available to run your business on a day-to-day basis, and without it, you will be unable to trade successfully.

This is as opposed to fixed capital, which is the capital you use to buy your fixed assets, for example what you spend on items such as buildings, vehicles, machinery etc.

A common problem when it comes to working capital, and one that I've made in the past, is to underestimate how much working capital you actually need to keep your business up and running. For example, if your business involves selling a range of products you will always have money tied up in unsold stock. Not only that but when you sell your stock you will then need to buy additional stock to replace what you've sold. Thus even though your business will be receiving sales revenue (income from sales), you will have to reinvest some, or even all, of this revenue in purchasing replacement stock.

You'll also to have pay your ongoing business costs, which might include rent, business rates, heating, lighting, advertising and so on as well as paying yourself and any staff you may have.

You need either to have money available in the form of working capital, or access to a bank overdraft to cover your regular business expenses until such time as your business is fully able to support itself.

 TIP Always include a generous provision for working capital in your business plan.

Initially you might find that although you're busy, you are not earning very much, if indeed anything, because you're having to reinvest your revenue in your business.

It's a common problem and one you need to address at your business planning stage.

Who is going to finance your new venture?

There are a number of options available to you:

- □ use your own funds;
- □ bank loans;
- □ business angels;
- □ small firms loan guarantee.

OWN FUNDS

Wherever possible you should use your own funds. That way you won't be burdening your new business with loan repayments. Obviously this won't always be possible.

BANK LOANS

My experience of banks and their lending policies has been dismal to say the least – so much so that I don't think I will approach them again. Your ideas may be more successful than mine, but if you do get turned down for a loan don't take this to mean your ideas don't have any potential.

BUSINESS ANGELS

This is my favourite funding option. Business angels are other successful entrepreneurs who, in return for a share in your business, will loan you money to start or expand your business. Obviously, you'll need to be satisfied that you can get on with your business angel and that you're happy to have someone else have a role in your business. The advantage of course is not only funding for your business but also the expertise these entrepreneurs can bring to your business.

You can find business angels by using the Internet and searching under key words: 'business angels', 'funding for business', 'venture capital' etc.

SMALL FIRMS LOANS GUARANTEE

The SFLG guarantees loans from banks and other financial institutions for small firms that have viable business proposals but have failed to get a conventional loan because of lack of security.

You can apply for a loan for sums of between £5,000 and £100,000, or if your business has been trading for more than two years you can apply for up to £250,000.

To be eligible you must be a UK company with an annual turnover of no more than £3m, or £5m if you are a manufacturer.

The SFLG guarantees 75 per cent of the loan. In return the borrower has to pay the Department of Trade and Industry a premium of 2 per cent on the outstanding amount of the loan.

You can get a loan for most business activities although there are some restrictions. Further information can be found on the DTI website at http://www.dti.gov.uk.

Dealing with slow and non-payers

Hopefully you will have few instances where customers either refuse to pay you, or are slow in settling invoices.

When this happens you have a number of options, culminating in taking them to court. In my experience most customers will pay their bills before ever getting to the stage of having to threaten legal action. So it's important when dealing with an overdue account not to rush in wielding a sledge hammer when one isn't needed.

These are some things we do to encourage prompt payment in our business:

- ☐ Confirm our prices and what is included in a written estimate so customers know exactly how much they are going to have to pay. By doing this you reduce the likelihood of having a payment dispute at some later date.

- ☐ Do not routinely offer credit terms. We include in all our written estimates that our terms of business are that payment is made immediately upon completion of the job. When it comes to our retail cycle business, we only release the cycle when the bill has been paid, and not before.

We adopt the following procedures for dealing with late payers:

- ☐ Where a customer does not settle their bill immediately, we allow a period of no more than seven days for their cheque to arrive, after which time we send a polite reminder letter.

- ☐ If after a further seven days we still hear nothing, we phone our client and ask what the problem is. It's vital to keep dialogue friendly and non-threatening. There can be a number of genuine reasons why customers are late in paying.

- ☐ If after a further seven days we still haven't been paid, and there isn't a genuine reason why the bill hasn't been settled, we then write a final letter, sent by recorded delivery. It asks that payment in full is made by return, or if this is not possible, we are contacted immediately to advise when payment will be made. We also include in our letter that if we don't receive payment within seven days, we will reluctantly have to take out County Court Summons.

THE COUNTY COURT

Taking non-payers to the County Court should always be a last resort. Although the system is easy to use, it is far better to have your debt settled without the costs and time involved in preparing your case for court. You can if you wish employ a solicitor, however you will have to pay their costs upfront. If your application is successful in the courts you can reclaim your fees from the other side.

But be warned that even if the court makes a judgement in your favour, your delinquent customer might still not pay their account. Then you have to make a further application to the court to allow you recover the debt from them.

It can be a lengthy, tiring process, and you really must be sure the debt is great enough to be pursued.

You can get the all the information, forms etc you need to make a County Court Claim by visiting your County Court or their website at http://www.courtservice.gov.uk. Or you can phone the Business Debtline on 08001 976 026.

Writing a winning business plan

Most small business gurus (you know the types – the ones who've recently been made redundant having spent most of their corporate lives killing careers with PowerPoint presentations and now want to sell their perceived skills to small business entrepreneurs) will have us believe that the most important reason for having a business plan is so that we can borrow money for our businesses.

And their angle on this? To write one for us, for which of course we will have to pay them a fee.

Let's get one important thing clear about business plans – you don't need to have someone write one for you. I don't care if they've been Richard Branson's personal business planner for the past 20 years, the only person that can really write a truly winning business plan for your business is you.

Because these experts will never tell you that your idea is absolutely farcical and you'd be wasting your money. An expert's expertise is in writing business plans. So if the business you're planning to start is in anything other than business plans, the truth is that they probably know absolutely nothing about your business. But you do because it has something to do with your hobby. You know your idea better than any paid expert whose real motivation for helping you will be his extortionate fees.

THE TEN ELEMENTS OF A WINNING BUSINESS PLAN

1. **A well-researched business idea** which includes information on what products and services you intend to offer, who your target customers are, details of your competitors and a general assessment of the market you are proposing to work in.

2. A clear idea of **how much it's going to cost** you to start your business.

3. A clear idea of **how long it is going to take your business** to become fully operational.

4. **A personal survival plan** detailing how you will survive during the initial period when your business is not actually earning you money, but costing you.

5. **A contingency plan** for what to do in the event that something unforeseen happens to either your business or you.

6. Details of **how you intend to fund your business** and, if you intend to borrow money, the plan should include details of those who you are hoping to borrow this money from together with anticipated repayment periods.

7. **Profit and loss forecast** where you work out how much your business is going to cost to run versus how much you're going to achieve through sales.

8. **Cash flow forecast**. Essential for every business because you work out how quickly and often you will receive cash into your business versus how much you will have to spend to continue trading.

9. **Operational details for your business**, which will include:
   - details of where your business will be based, including any additional business premises that you may need to rent (for example additional storage space for stock etc);
   - information on how many staff (if any) you will need to hire, where you intend to get these staff from and how much you're intending to pay them.

(You should never rely on the goodwill of friends and relatives who offer to work for you for nothing. This is wholly unrealistic and if your business relies on others supplying their labour free of charge then you should be asking yourself if your business is really viable.)

10. **SWOT analysis** – what are the strengths, weaknesses, opportunities and threats facing your business?

BUSINESS PLAN FORMAT

If you're considering approaching a bank to help finance your business, your business plan will need to be presented in a certain format. In addition to the above information they'll want to know more about your career history including details of why you're suited to start and run this type of business. If you are in partnership with someone, or you are hiring specialist help, they'll want to know more about these key people before they are willing to lend you any money.

 Most banks now offer a very useful business planning software programme, which you can get free from your business banker. The business plan is laid out in template form and all you have to do is fill in the blanks.

Even if you're not planning to borrow any money, I'd recommend you take advantage of their free software as I've found the spreadsheets for calculating profit and loss to be invaluable. Having a system where you can change one item and then immediately see the effect on profit and loss figures saves enormous time working things out.

PRESENTING YOUR BUSINESS PLAN

The golden rule when presenting your business plan to prospective lenders is that you must be completely confident with the facts, figures and projections.

Your presentation should be:

- ☐ Clear and to the point: free of superfluous and distracting things such as jokes, anecdotes and over-familiarity.

- ☐ So well-rehearsed that it doesn't actually sound rehearsed.

- ☐ Convincing. Remember you're asking someone to invest money in your business, which means they are sharing in your risk. They need to be convinced you know what you're doing and that above all else you are confident that you can achieve what you are saying.

What to wear

Dress to impress, but make sure that whatever it is you choose to wear you feel comfortable and confident. Nothing is more soul-destroying than making a presentation to someone when you feel at a disadvantage because of the way you are dressed. Certainly if the business bankers that I've met in the past are anything to go by, traditional smart dress is essential as many are still trapped in some sort of unique time warp.

Summary

1. The two most common and potentially disastrous mistakes made by novice entrepreneurs are to decide on a product or service and then try and find customers to buy from them and to start a business without a written business plan.

2. The advantage of working out a winning business plan is that you can identify and address potential problems before it's too late.

3. When researching your market make sure that you are comparing like for like when considering the competition. Even though two businesses may on the surface appear to be servicing the same market, they can be world's apart.

4. Try to get an accurate picture of your set-up costs before you start your business.

5. Don't forget working capital. Insufficient working capital is often a cause of many otherwise potentially good business ventures going under. Remember that in the early stages you will need to reinvest much of your initial earnings to build and develop your business.

5

SALES: THE BEATING HEART OF YOUR BUSINESS

Selling — there really is nothing to fear

Whatever business you're planning to start – be it to sell a product or offer a service, you're going to have to be able to sell, because if you are to survive and succeed your business will have to compete with other businesses. The only way to truly beat the competition isn't to undercut them or outdo them, it's to outsell them.

You don't have to be a sales expert to sell

An expert is often described as 'someone from out of town carrying a briefcase'.

Nowhere is this truer when it comes to the perceived mystery and magic surrounding successful salespeople. All sorts of misconceptions abound with many people believing that if you haven't got the 'gift of the gab', or a 'killer instinct' then you won't possibly be able to sell anything.

The next time you have nightmares about having to do your own selling I want you to know that often selling is nothing more than you being able to ask potential customers one simple question. I'll tell you what that is in a minute, but first I want to explain what selling *isn't*.

Selling isn't about:

- □ talking your customers into buying something they don't want;
- □ selling them something at a grossly over-inflated price;
- □ developing a 'killer instinct', whatever that might be.

OK. That's what selling *isn't*. So what *is* selling?

> Selling is helping your customer buy what they want and then making sure that what they decide to buy, they buy from you.

Imagine you've just decided that you want to take up canoeing as a hobby. You're going to need a number of things to get you started, which might include finding a suitable training course, buying a new canoe, lifejacket, suitable clothing, books, videos, roof-rack etc.

You visit your local outdoor shop and once inside you're approached by a friendly and obviously knowledgeable salesperson who encourages you to have a good look around the shop without feeling under any obligation.

While you're busy browsing you overhear the sales staff answer others' questions and you're impressed with their knowledge. You also like the range of canoes in the shop but are a bit unsure about which ones might be suitable for you. So you approach the salesperson for some advice.

Now put yourself in the salesperson's shoes. Here you are with a shop full of canoeing goodies. You stock everything from books, videos and clothing to a wide range of canoes to suit a range of uses and budgets. And anything you haven't got in stock you can generally get in within 48 hours, or sooner depending on the item required.

You've just finished serving a regular customer when this person you have never seen in your shop before nervously approaches you asking for advice, which you freely give. Now you've got to make a choice – you can either smile at them as they walk out of the door on their way to search the Internet looking for a cheaper deal than you can offer, or you can be professional and sell them what they want.

Now if I was that salesperson, I'd want to sell them a canoe and all the bits and pieces they need. After all, I've given them the benefit of my advice, I know my products are quality and offer excellent value for money. Makes sense, doesn't it?

So why do so many otherwise competent salespeople allow their customers to walk out of the door of their shop without asking them one simple question?

WHAT IS THE MOST POWERFUL SALES TECHNIQUE IN THE WORLD?

Some salespeople will never grasp this, because it's so simple. The most powerful selling technique in the world is to *ask for the order*.

That's it. No expertise or killer instinct required. The most successful and simplest sales strategy that you can employ in your business is to say to someone, 'Would you like to buy it?'

Of course there are lots of different ways you can ask potential customers to buy whatever it is you're selling, but the question remains the same.

Selling has nothing to do with foot-in-the-door techniques or pushiness. We all know that these so called sales techniques are used by all sorts of individuals and corporations on a daily basis. But the reason for this is because they can only sell whatever it is because either nobody wants it, or it is grossly over-priced.

You won't have to employ any of these unscrupulous tactics because as a home business you're going to be offering quality, value-for-money goods or services to people who really need them.

So you have nothing to fear!

Remember that people like to buy things. The only thing that is worse than a morose, unhelpful salesperson is one that leaves you to 'think' about things.

The three golden rules for selling anything to anyone

1. Remember that people buy *benefits* not features.

2. You must give your customers a reason for buying from you – otherwise they'll buy from someone else.

3. If you're doubtful about selling whatever it is you're selling, people will be afraid to buy it.

RULE 1. PEOPLE BUY BENEFITS NOT FEATURES

Believed to be the first rule in marketing, the 'people buy benefits not features' mantra is at the heart of every advertisement you're ever likely to come across.

To sell anything to anyone you must understand this concept and appreciate that if you're adhering to this rule in your face-to-face sales presentation, brochures or website information, the chances of your sales being anything less than average are greatly reduced.

Why is this concept so important? To answer this we need to look at the reasons we buy anything. Factors that influence what we buy include things like:

- price;
- what we need the whatever we're buying for;
- attractiveness – is it 'us'?

Price

Of course there can be an infinite amount of reasons why we might buy anything, but unless we've unlimited resources price will certainly be a deciding factor.

Marketing companies are aware of this, and many competing products highlight price as being a benefit.

Next time you hear a radio commercial, watch a TV advertisement or pick up a magazine, start looking for the benefit messages. What's in it for you? What will you get if you buy a certain product? Will you feel better? Slimmer? Fitter? Wealthier? Sexier? Younger?

Selling is all about benefits

The reality is that we don't buy things because of features, we buy because of the benefits that come with owning a certain product or service.

One of my businesses is running a gardening maintenance company. Many of my clients lead busy professional lives, which means that they are 'time poor'.

All of them want to enjoy a nice relaxing garden to unwind in, without having to spend all of their free time cutting lawns, weeding borders, trimming hedges and so on.

So the features of the service my business offers are that we undertake all aspects of garden maintenance, including lawn cutting, hedge cutting, pruning etc.

But the benefits to our clients are that they enjoy more free time in their wonderful garden because they no longer have to spend hours maintaining it.

When we market our service we list our features (what we offer), but we sell our benefits. Therefore in our business our advertisements are always built around powerful *benefit* messages.

Tired of spending all your free time mowing the lawn, cutting hedges and travelling to and from your local dump?

Here at Paul Power Landscapes we're experts at doing the things you hate.

Isn't it time you enjoyed your free time and your garden?

The features are:

- ☐ lawn cutting
- ☐ hedge cutting
- ☐ dumping of garden waste.

The benefits are:

- ☐ enjoyment
- ☐ free time.

PUTTING YOUR SALES MESSAGE TOGETHER

The way to construct your sales message is to highlight the features first, followed by all the benefits.

Start looking at as many advertisements as you can. The glossy magazines that come with weekend newspapers are very useful as they usually contain lot of imaginative ads often with the 'benefit message' innovatively hidden somewhere within the message.

We can learn lots from looking at how other businesses market their products.

Get into the habit of either cutting out advertisements and keeping them in a file, or writing down the advertising message and keeping it in your notebook. Then when the time comes to write your own ads you can browse through your file for inspiration.

Don't forget that the feature/benefit rule also applies to face-to-face selling. Next time you're out shopping listen to what salespeople are telling potential customers.

Ignore the completely inept ones, usually hired by larger DIY stores and electronic warehouse retailers, but wait until you find real salespeople. You will hear the same message: 'But the great thing about this is that it ...' – and you'll hear the *benefit* loud and clear. The more skilled the salesperson the more suited the benefit will be.

But not everyone buys the same benefit!

We all have different reasons for buying anything. Take, for example, someone buying a flight ticket. Unless it's a holiday charter airline the people buying a seat on a flight will have different needs.

Some will be travelling on business, others holidaying and others wanting to travel as cheaply as possibly.

To overcome the problem of differing needs, airlines target their marketing campaigns at different sectors. Comfort and getting you there on time will be key benefits for business travellers, while value for money might be the message for holidaymakers.

In your business it may not always be possible, owing to budget restrictions, to target different market sectors, so make sure the benefits you're selling appeal to the widest audience possible.

TIP If you're face-to-face selling then all you have to do is to correctly identify the buyer's needs and sell them a benefit that they want.

If they need whatever it is you're selling right now, and you have it in stock, then the obvious benefit is that they can have it now. Wait and think about it and it may be gone.

If they're working to a budget and whatever it is they want comes within it, the benefit is that not only can they have it, but they can save themselves money by not spending all their budget.

LOOK AT WHAT YOU'RE PROPOSING TO SELL

Whatever it is you're planning to sell, start by listing all its features and then work on the benefits.

Be imaginative here. Many of the benefits may not be immediately apparent to you even though it's your product or service.

Start by trying to see whatever it is you are selling from different perspectives:

- ☐ Is it only suitable for everyone who shares your hobby, or could it be of use to a wider market?

- ☐ How does it compare with other like goods or services in terms of price and quality?

- ☐ How quickly can you deliver?

- ☐ Can you give five reasons why anyone should buy your product/service instead of your competitors'?

- ☐ If your product/service has no competitors, why? Some of your reasons should make excellent benefits.

Once you've come up with your list of benefits you're almost ready to sell anything to anyone, but you must learn and follow the remaining two golden rules of selling.

RULE 2: YOU MUST GIVE YOUR CUSTOMERS A REASON TO BUY FROM YOU

Ideally you should give your customers as many reasons as you possibly can for buying from you, although often this isn't possible. But the bottom line still remains – if you don't give a good enough reason, people will buy elsewhere.

I want you to think about something you need to buy. This could be anything – an essential item, luxury treat or something you buy everyday like a newspaper or carton of milk.

Now on a blank piece of paper write down the item you've just thought of and draw a big circle around it.

Immediately underneath your circled item write down where you intend to buy this item and draw a circle around it. Don't give this too much thought; just write down where you'd first go to buy it.

Done?

Now draw a line from the item and then draw another big circle. In this circle write down all the places you could actually buy this item. Write down as many places as you can think of, stopping only when there is no more space left in your circle. (If you can't think of any alternative places to buy from then choose another item and start the exercise again.)

Finally, draw a line and another big circle from the circle where you've written where you're planning to buy this item. Then write in it as many reasons as you can think of why you've decided to buy from this source.

Your findings

This exercise is to show you that although you made an initial choice where to buy your item, there are other places you could buy it.

In business, these other outlets are called competitors, and to survive and compete with our competitors we must be able to offer would-be customers a reason to buy from us.

Why did you make that initial choice? Cost? Location? Or something else? Marketers often refer to these reasons as a business's **Unique Selling Points** (USPs).

What are your business's Unique Selling Points?

To do this, break down your product/service into set categories:

- ☐ price
- ☐ quality
- ☐ availability
- ☐ uniqueness.

Price

Unless you intend building an out-of-town pile-'em-high sell-'em-cheap style warehouse, it's unlikely that you will want to sell on price alone. However, price will still be a deciding factor for potential customers. For example if you're planning on running your business as a mail order shop, your goods will need to be keenly priced to get customers buying from you. The USP for mail order businesses is often that they offer goods cheaper than anyone else.

On the other hand, if your business will involve lots of personal attention and fussing over your clients' every wish, your prices will be higher than your competitor offering a bargain basement, no-frills service.

In this case your USP could be that you are expensive, but well worth it because you are offering personal service.

Quality

What makes your goods and services better than anyone else's?

It's not enough to simply say the word 'quality'. Your USP needs to paint a picture. Bed manufacturers are a good example of this. We all know that the difference between a good and bad night's sleep can be the quality of the bed, so a cheap bed may mean a bad night's sleep. Buyers will therefore spend more on a bed that promises restful sleep.

Again it's not enough simply to promise a restful night's sleep, as most of the beds in the shop will be claiming the same thing. The unique selling point will often be to highlight how many springs or layers this bed has over its competitors.

Availability

Ignore this one at your peril.

We're living in a world where the words 'next week' often lose a sale. Even next-day delivery can be too late for some people, so if your product is available to be bought and taken home today, it is a Unique Selling Point.

For example I've now given up furniture shopping in chain stores for the simple reason that no matter how small the item, even a chair, it has to be ordered by the sales staff. Even though you have paid for the item you have no idea of when it's likely to arrive. Finally, after what seems like an extraordinarily long wait you get a phone call to say the furniture will arrive 'sometime on Friday'. When you explain you'll be at work on Friday and need a specific time so you can arrange for someone to be there, you're told this isn't possible.

I'm not alone in switching my allegiance back to the small independent retailer who either has the item already in stock or will personally get it in for you and deliver it to you at a mutually convenient time. Availability is always a powerful unique selling point.

Uniqueness

Many businesses based around a hobby are successful because what they are offering is unique.

Large retailers, travel companies and the like steer clear of what is often referred to as niche markets. The last thing they want is a large amount of their store shelf space clogged up by products that relatively few customers will be interested in.

Therefore your unique selling point could be that you're offering hard-to-find items such as books, memorabilia or even specialist holidays.

Highlight whatever makes your business unique as a selling point. It can even be something as simple as your personal knowledge of what you sell.

Experience

A few years ago the rudder on my sailing boat broke in half while we were in heavy seas. Although the boat was fibreglass, the rudder was wooden. I searched everywhere to find a replacement rudder with no avail. Even desperate surfing on the Internet brought no results.

Finally, on the advice of a friend, I spent a morning walking around what I'd previously thought were disused warehouses. Here amongst the carcasses of forgotten old boats, I found John's workshop. As soon as I met him I knew he was skilled and competent. Not because of anything he said. It was everything about him. The way he lovingly handled his measuring tape, the way he examined my broken rudder – everything about him told me he loved what he was doing. He had the entrepreneur passion.

My instincts were right and a couple of weeks later my new rudder was ready, but when I went to collect it he had bad news. He told me he was sorry that he was going to have to charge me so much, but he'd put a lot of work into it and it was made from mahogany.

The rudder was a work of art. He handed it to me lovingly wiping it down with a cloth to remove his hand prints from it.

'How much?' I asked expecting to pay at least £150. He apologised again. '£20,' he said.

I was shocked. So much so that it was obvious on my face. Unfortunately he took it to mean I was shocked at the price and began to justify his costs again.

After convincing him that not only was I very pleased with the new rudder but also believed he was grossly under-pricing his work, he told me that no one wanted wood any more. 'Everyone wants fibreglass now,' he said, 'wood is just too high maintenance.'

When I next passed John's workshop the doors were shut and soon after the whole area was redeveloped for luxury housing.

Clearly John's USP was that he was a skilled craftsman and experienced boat builder. Since meeting John I have spoken to many people who would give almost anything for his skill and experience. While the new boat market is dominated by no-maintenance fibreglass crafts, there are still a large number of sailors who prefer wooden boats, and some would say there has been a high revival in wooden boats in recent years.

It's difficult to say why John failed to see that his USP was his uniqueness, but I do think that probably one of the reasons why he decided to close his business was that he wasn't earning enough. Certainly if his prices were anything to go by he was seriously undercharging, and these super-low prices could only be sustained for so long.

Was John trying to compete on price with the plastic boat builders? I don't know, but what I can say is that it does look like he failed to correctly identify his USP.

Having something unique to offer is a great selling point. Our lives are dominated by mass-produced, over-priced garbage. We'd give almost anything to be able to get our hands on something different.

What makes your future business different from others is that you are going to be working at something you really enjoy doing. The enthusiasm and passion you bring to your products and services is what makes your business as unique and special as you are.

 Never undersell yourself.

RULE 3. DON'T BE DOUBTFUL ABOUT WHAT IT IS YOU'RE SELLING

One of the reasons that many otherwise professional salespeople fail to reach sales targets is that they don't really believe in what they're selling. It is often the problem when you work for someone else where the sales department has little control over the quality of the products or service they're selling.

This is the problem with the large furniture stores I mentioned previously. My experiences have been that you walk in and are pounced on by an over-zealous salesperson who follows you around the store like a puppy saying how wonderful and nice everything that you look at is.

As soon as you say something negative about a piece of furniture they agree with you and do their best to move you on to the next equally unimaginatively piece in the hope that you will say yes. And all throughout you're subjected to the information that there's 50 per cent off this weekend, and that the now mandatory interest-free credit is available on that particular item.

Text-book sales stuff. The salesperson sells you the benefits (as they see them) – interest free credit, etc. And of course somewhere along the line they will get in their unique selling point, which could be something like, 'Of course this suite is part of our super-duper executive range and is exclusive to us,' and just in case your comprehension of the English language is as bad as they assume your financial position to be, they'll add 'which means you can't get it anywhere else.'

However, where it all falls apart is when you test the confidence they have in their product.

Some good questions to ask are:

- ☐ Who makes the furniture?

- ☐ Where is it made?

- ☐ When can you deliver it? Get specific here – 'when' as in morning? Afternoon? Mid-afternoon?

- ☐ Has anyone ever cancelled an order with your store?

- ☐ What happens if my furniture is late – will you phone me, or someone from your call centre?

If the store prides itself on its reputation for customer service, and consequently has little or no problems, then this will quickly become apparent from the salesperson's response.

However if they don't have such good customer service, the cracks will soon start to appear. Don't be surprised when the salesperson decides to leave you alone to 'think about it' while they go and badger someone else.

The problem is that they're not confident in their product. They've been at the store too long now to know that many of their orders won't be delivered on time, and that there can be a whole range of other problems, such as the wrong product being delivered or an incorrect colour suite.

 Unless you're a seasoned conman, you won't be able to sell unless you believe in what you're selling.

Before starting your business make sure you have confidence and faith in what you're about to start. There's often a temptation to cut corners and decide that whatever you're selling will be 'all right on the night' sort of thing.

Trust me – it won't. Home businesses succeed because their owners believe completely in what they're offering. Their enthusiasm and passion sells and builds their businesses.

Special offers, interest-free credit and free delivery are the domain of the stack-them-high sell-them-cheap brigade. Our businesses are different. You are different. Go out and create something unique and wonderful and you won't need any costly, frilly incentives to get customers queuing at your doors.

Overcoming objections

The most notable difference between giving something away and selling it, is objections.

If you've already set up your business and you find you're not at least on occasions getting objections from potential customers then it probably means you're giving it away! Because customer objections are a natural part of the *buying* process, not the *selling* process.

Unfortunately many sellers misinterpret an objection as being a reason someone doesn't want to buy, when in fact it is a clear buying signal.

As soon as the 'but's, and 'what if's start flowing, the inexperienced salesperson incorrectly assumes that what they thought was a potential buyer isn't one after all. Consequently the seller's shutters go down, the wrong message is given out to the would-be buyer, and in an instant any chance of a sale is lost.

An objection is a clear buying signal.

If you're to successfully overcome customer objections you must understand that they're actually not objections at all. They are buying questions, or buying signals.

Imagine for a moment someone is planning a holiday to some far-flung exotic destination. Somewhere they have never been before. They know roughly the area where they want to go to because friends went there some time ago and said they really enjoyed it.

So they go off to the local high street travel agent. They could search the Internet, but they really want to talk to someone about this holiday because although their friends told them it was lovely, and they saw the breath-taking holiday pictures, others have since said that the area is dangerous and holidaymakers can be at risk from local criminal gangs.

You are the travel agent. You are very helpful and pull out all the brochures on the areas. When you run through some of the prices they're a little taken aback because their friends didn't pay this much. So they tell you that it sounds a bit expensive, and isn't really what they were hoping to pay.

Expensive, is the first objection.

Now you have two options:

1. Decide to stop wasting their time and politely invite them to browse through the brochures when they get home while you get on with the next customer.

2. Overcome the objection, or, if this is not possible, interest them in an alternative holiday that fits their budget.

If you are a more inexperienced salesperson you are more likely to opt for number one. On the other hand if you are more experienced you will know from experience and hopefully training that saying it's too expensive means that the customer is interested in buying the holiday.

Why?

Well let's look at the obvious first. You're sitting in your high street shop and they walk in asking about a holiday to a specific destination. In anyone's mind that should be seen as a fairly strong buying signal.

When you start telling them how much it's likely to cost they indicate that sounds a bit expensive and is more than they were hoping to pay. Again this is a positive buying signal. They haven't said, 'I don't want to go there,' all they've said is that it's more than they were hoping to pay.

So what you need to do now is to overcome their objection. The easiest way of doing this is with some gentle questions, beginning with, 'I'm sorry to hear that because obviously you're very keen on going there. Well let's not give up yet and see what we can do for you.'

You've told your customer two important things. First that you're sorry it sounds expensive, and second that you are going to help them get the holiday they want.

Before going any further you need to know:

- ☐ Is it too expensive because the customer can't afford it?
- ☐ Have they found a cheaper deal elsewhere?
- ☐ It is just more than they thought it would cost?

You can ask anyone anything you want without them getting offended, provided you're polite about it. So you ask them: 'When you say it's more than you expected to pay is that because you're seen a cheaper deal elsewhere?'

Notice I used the word 'cheaper'. I could have said 'better', but that would have been commercial suicide because what I've told my potential customer is that somewhere out there, there is a better deal to be had.

 TIP | Always use 'cheaper' and not 'better' when dealing with a price comparison.

Cheaper doesn't mean better, it usually means inferior, so when you're in this sort of situation choose your words carefully.

Your customer now tells you the full story. 'Well the reason it's more than I expected is because my friends went there and they paid a lot less.'

Because you know your business you will know why there is a price difference. There may be a number of reasons why it's more expensive now and you might even find their friends' holiday company isn't around any more having gone bankrupt.

Now you're ready to overcome the objection.

Because you've probed a bit more into the reason your customer believes it may be too expensive you're in a better position to overcome their objection. But before you do that you need to know whether or not the holiday is within your customer's budget. You do this by asking, 'How much are you planning to spend on your holiday?'

Some salespeople will disagree with me when I tell them this saying that you're going to insult your customer. However, in all the years I've been running my own businesses no one has been insulted by this question. In fact quite the opposite has happened and they've been pleased to be able to give me something that I can work on to come up with a package to suit their needs.

Provided the holiday is within your customer's budget then there is no reason why they shouldn't want to book their holiday with you. Unless of course there are more objections!

Which in this case we know there will be, because our customer has heard some negative things about others who have gone to this area.

But of course in your position as salesperson you don't know this and just as you thought you'd got the order, your efforts are under attack again when you're told, 'I don't know how true it is but I've heard that a number of tourists have been robbed when they go to this area...'

Fear of being robbed is now your second objection.

Provided the area isn't marred by frequent robberies you'll be able to allay your customer's fears. Obviously honesty is the best policy and you do have a legal duty of care to your customers, which includes not misleading them.

HOW TO TURN OBJECTIONS INTO IMMEDIATE SALES

As we've seen, objections are really buying signals because the buyer is really asking questions that, if answered favourably, will mean they can buy whatever is being sold.

Certain types of objections, if handled the right way, can be turned into immediate sales. In a few moments we'll look at different ways of closing a sale. Often objections offer the easiest way of closing a sale so that everyone is happy; what's often referred to as win-win situation.

 A win-win situation is where the buyer gets what he wants at a price the seller is happy to sell at.

The price objection

One of the most common objections you're likely to encounter is the customer who tells you you're too expensive. Often buyers use this objection hoping to get a better deal. You can use this strategy to your advantage by leaving a degree of negotiation in your pricing structure.

I say 'degree' as the last thing you want to do is get a reputation for having prices that are always negotiable. That said, I don't think there's any harm in having a small negotiating margin where your overall profits won't suffer if you agree somewhere below your original asking price.

This is how it works. You give absolutely nothing away unless you get the sale there and then. No more buts, ifs, I'll think about its. Simply, 'If I agree will you buy it right now?'

If your buyer says no, he won't or can't, then there's no deal and it remains fixed at its original price. However if he does agree to buy now he gets the item at a reduced price.

THE POWER OF SILENCE

Silence is a much underestimated selling technique. Too often salespeople rush in and spoil a sale because they just can't stay silent for long enough. Unfortunately many of us are programmed to find silence unbearable, but silence is a natural part of the buying process.

Think of the last time that you either made a significant purchase or bought something you wouldn't usually buy. Chances are that you didn't simply waltz into the shops, see the item, holiday, house, service and immediately buy it. Like most of us you'll have needed some time, even if only a few seconds, to think it through.

During this thinking time you say nothing. Your mind is on what you're about to do and any sort of conversation can at best be an extremely annoying interruption and at worst make up your mind that you don't want whatever it is after all.

 Silence is a powerful selling technique.

It's also something that takes a bit of getting used to because most of us find silences uncomfortable. Therefore rather than wait until you're at that crucial moment where everything depends on your staying quiet long enough to win the sale, start practising now.

A good way to do this is to start using the silent technique next time you're buying something. You'll be amazed at how quickly prices come down when you simply say nothing.

The most effective places to try this technique are at large retail chain stores where the salesperson's income rely heavily on them closing sales. Although many of these outfits have perpetual sales and give-away offers this doesn't mean there isn't room for further negotiation.

The technique works as follows:

1. Make yourself known to someone from the sales staff.

2. Discuss your requirements.

3. Even if the price is displayed, ask how much it costs.

4. When the salesperson tells you the price, say absolutely nothing. Instead keep staring at the item.

5. Wait.

6. Do not say anything. Savour the silence while the salesperson starts to shift uncomfortably. If they're working on a commission the chances are the first thing they tell you is that the price could be reduced...

Trust me, this technique works, which is why when you're selling something you must out-silence your buyers.

Although silences can last an agonising amount of time, it will actually only be a matter of seconds. A minute at the most and during that time your buyer will be thinking about what they're about to do, not trying to outwit you.

Being mentally prepared is important. Remember, as soon as you give your price, *shut up*. Say nothing until your buyer speaks.

And when they say 'I'll take it,' you know it's all down to the power of silence.

Closing techniques

The technique of turning a buyer's interest into a sale is known as closing a sale.

Depending on which book you read you will find a bewildering choice of techniques to choose from. However, I believe you only need to concentrate on three. We've already covered the most important one.

ASK FOR THE ORDER

In my experience this is often the most appropriate and easiest method of getting the sale.

It's amazing how often sales staff don't do this. Instead they talk on and on and round and round, desperate to do anything but actually ask for the order. Then wonder why the customer buys somewhere else.

So always ask for the order. Even if the customer doesn't appear too interested in what you're selling – still ask for the order. And if they say no, ask them why. After all, you've invested your time in showing them whatever it is you're selling, so it makes sense to know why they now don't want it.

THE ASSUMPTIVE CLOSE

My second favourite method is to simply assume your customer is going to buy from you. The secret to using this method is to start planting the seeds of success right from the beginning.

When I meet a prospective client for my landscape gardening business, I always include lines like this somewhere during the meeting:

'When we come and do your garden would it be all right if we parked on your driveway?'

'Do you have an outside tap that we could use?'

'Generally we like to get onsite everyday at about 8am. That wouldn't be too early, would it?'

'Would you like me to arrange for you to see examples of some of our work?'

Not only am I assuming that I will be getting the order, but I'm also asking questions. I always ask the last question as this shows my prospective client that I'm confident enough to be able to show them examples of our company's work. I don't wait for them to ask me.

Questions like these help build up a rapport with your client and also establish you as a professional. Few cowboys will give a stuff about what time they get to their customers' gardens, and most will never want anyone to see examples of their work.

You can use the assumptive closing technique for any business. All you have to do is work out some appropriate questions and introduce them into your discussions at appropriate intervals.

Try and avoid using sentences like: 'If we're lucky enough to get your order,' or, 'If we can agree a price,' and so on. Sentences like these create doubt. They are based on 'if's and also give the impression that your price is in some way negotiable.

Be positive in your assumptions.

Generous use of the word *when* will pay dividends. *When* we come, *when* you book with us, *when* your order arrives, *when* you decide which colour, *when* you stay with us, etc.

Remember that very often people 'buy' people. This is especially true of many businesses based on hobbies.

For example, if someone is planning to go on a painting holiday they're going to have to be certain they like who'll be teaching the course. These are people businesses where those attending want more than just a painting course. They want to enjoy the whole experience.

The assumptive close has always worked for me and I think it takes a lot of the fear out of selling. One of the advantages is that there's no big build up to a grand finale where suddenly you must close the sale.

Relax and assume they'll be your customers and most likely they will.

THE ALTERNATIVE CLOSE

Another powerful closing technique is to use is what's often referred to as the 'alternative closing method'.

The idea here is that rather than offer your customer the choice between buying and not buying, you include an alternative. So the decision is now *what* to buy, as opposed to *will* I buy?

It's an effective technique that's easy to introduce. In its basic form all you need to do is offer a choice. So if someone is browsing your hand-crafted, keep-out-all-draughts knitted sweaters, then all you need to do is introduce a choice, which could be a different colour or size. Then ask your customer which one would they prefer. 'Would you like the black one or the grey one?' 'Small or large?'

You're using two closing techniques here. Assumptive and alternative. So you're assuming your customer will buy one – but which one. You're not being pushy here, just helpful. After all how many of us have walked out of shops because they didn't have the size or the colour we wanted and were either too shy, too busy or whatever to bother asking.

But imagine you've offered an alternative colour and your customer says no to both. What then? Ask them what they're looking for. The important thing here is to keep the dialogue going. Keep them interested and stop them from going elsewhere.

Remember that lots of people browsing your goodies may not be buying for themselves. They could be looking for gifts for someone else. By asking them what they're looking for and who it's for you'll get a better understanding of their needs and be better placed to help them and close your sale.

So the alternative close can go on until they either buy something, or you run out of alternatives. Provided you don't come across as pushy or stalk them! Remember you're there to help them find the thing they most want to buy.

Price alternatives are good, too.

Let's say that your business involves you selling home-made soaps. Because your product is unique and all of your scented, bubbly delights are lovingly created, they're considerably more expensive than traditional off-the-shelf soaps.

Limiting yourself to one price range can lead to problems and you could find, as many gift shops do, that your shop is full of 'Sunday browsers' oohing and cooing over everything, but buying nothing. The problem here is often that the prices are just out of reach of the average impulse purchaser.

The way to address this is to offer two price ranges. One that appeals to those who appreciate the quality and uniqueness of your soap and will buy it whatever the cost, and one for those who would love to buy your soap if it was more affordable.

If you're creating your own products then you could offer a certain product range at a reduced price to the second group. Or have a special offer bucket where you include all your soaps that haven't come up to the same exacting standards as the others.

Whatever you do, try to offer alternative prices. If someone looks interested but then disappointed when they see the price of your soap and makes for the door, get in there. Tell them you do a special range of soaps which are excellent value and bring out your irresistible soaps with a more appealing price tag.

We all like choice. Whether it's choice within a product range or choice of prices, we're more likely to buy when we don't feel as if we're simply buying the first thing we've seen.

Mastering the three Ps of selling

Undoubtedly, closing techniques are important. Nothing is worse than seeing a potential customer buy from the competition when they've already been discussing their requirements with you.

That said, there's much more to selling than just closing techniques. What happens along the road to agreeing the sale is often where any chance of a sale is lost. If you pay enough attention to the three Ps then many of your sales will close by themselves.

The three Ps are:

1. Prospecting
2. Presentation
3. Price.

PROSPECTING

Selling is one thing that you can't leave to luck. Few, if any, businesses have ever succeeded, let alone survived, because they got lucky. Successful entrepreneurs make their own luck by getting out there and preparing the ground for future success. Great sales figures don't just happen. It's a combination of making sure the product is right for the market we're selling in.

Experience

A few years ago I wandered around Brighton market hoping to find some old vinyl records on behalf of a friend. After a short time browsing the stalls I found what I was looking for, a stand specialising in records, posters and memorabilia.

You could say I got lucky. How many markets, boot fairs and the like would have someone selling records? But there was nothing lucky about it. I must confess I'm not a fan of boot fairs and the thoughts of having to spend a Saturday or Sunday morning wandering round a wet field with the waft of sausages and onions doesn't do it for me.

Careful not to either waste my time, or make myself miserable in the process, I asked everyone I knew where would be the best place to pick up vinyl records and they all pointed me in the direction of this particular market. So my success was really down to spending a little time preparing and planning.

While I was there I took the opportunity of browsing the stalls. To my amazement many were full of all sorts of interesting things and ideas and these businesses were doing a brisk trade.

However other businesses weren't. It wasn't difficult to see why. The people who were browsing in the market were either looking for something unique and interesting, or something regular but at a much cheaper price than they would expect to pay in a high street shop.

Therefore the businesses that were doing well had matched their products to the people who visited the market, and the traders that weren't doing well clearly hadn't thought about the type of market they were selling to.

A bit like selling football strips at a chess conference.

PRESENTATION

One of the most powerful selling techniques I know is simply to present both yourself and your product with the utmost respect, which means dressing appropriately and packaging your product correctly.

Dressing well

When I meet a prospective client for the first time I dress appropriately. Although most people say they wouldn't mind their landscape gardener turning up covered in mud, sweat and cement, often they do. And even if they wouldn't be put off, I still wouldn't turn up looking like this – because it would put me off.

Dressing to impress is important. If your appearance is dirty and sloppy people will expect whatever you're selling to be the same. Similarly if you handle your product as if it is a piece of rubbish you immediately devalue it.

Whenever I give anyone my business card I hand it to them as if I were giving them a precious gem. I do this because I know that our business delivers a quality, value-for-money service, something all too rare these days.

If you're going to slap a dog-eared, ink-splurged home-produced card in a prospective client's hand you may as well be giving them your competitor's phone number.

Displaying your product

Next time you're out for a Sunday afternoon stroll, take a closer look at why you want to spend time looking in some windows and not in others. It's all to do with presentation. Most antique shops have retail display down to a fine art, as do successful florists. It's all about display. Even the most mundane product can be made to look appealing in the right window.

Whether you sell at craft fairs, exhibitions, boot fairs, church halls or with an online shop, presentation is the key to success. Get that right and you will at least have customers coming through your doors or stopping at your stand. Get it wrong and everyone loses out.

Creating atmosphere

Often the difficulty with a small shop is creating the right atmosphere. A small, silent shop can be as intimidating as a large austere public building. Make it easier for potential clients to browse your wares. Invite them in with the sound of relaxing music and heavenly scents.

Inviting people in

Display a notice on your door. Something like, 'Please do come in and browse – you're under no obligation whatsoever to buy anything.'

And then once they are inside, make your visitors feel at home. Be warm and friendly but not in an overpowering way. Have some music playing in the background as this helps take away that church-like silence you often get in smaller shops.

Remember to offer them alternatives. 'Too big.' 'We've got smaller ones as well.' 'Too expensive.' 'We do have some on special offer.'

'Not really me.' 'What is you?'

'Can't make up my mind?' 'Why not have them both?'

Listen to what your visitors are saying without intruding on their viewings and then at the right moment offer them the alternatives.

And at all times avoid that awful, insincere greeting: 'How can I help you?' To which I'm always tempted to reply, 'You could pay this month's mortgage...'

 People like buying things, especially something that they'll be using for their favourite hobby. So make it easy for them to buy.

PRICE

Whatever you're selling it must be priced to appeal to your target market.

Too expensive and you won't sell any, too cheap and you won't earn enough profit to stay in business long enough to repay your initial financial investment.

From now on start becoming price aware. Whenever you see products or services that you're thinking of offering in your business, stop and really look at what price they are being sold at.

Ask yourself: Can you sell them any cheaper?

If your products will retail for more, ask yourself why should anyone choose what you're offering over a cheaper alternative?

Many products, even so called hand-crafted products, are mass produced in sweatshops in developing countries. You face an impossible task competing with these businesses who can retail goods and earn a profit for far less than it would probably cost you to buy these goods wholesale. While no business should compete on price alone, your prices still have to be attractive in order to sell your goods.

Record your price findings in a notebook along with details of potential suppliers, wholesalers, packaging companies etc. All useful information when it comes to finalising your plans.

Five ways to turbo-boost your sales

My top five recommendations for turbo-boosting your sales:

1. Accept credit and debit cards.
2. Include a mail order facility.
3. Offer customer referral incentives.
4. Publish your own newsletter.
5. Send a card.

ACCEPT CREDIT AND DEBIT CARDS

Even if you don't have a shop you should still consider taking credit and debit cards, especially if you sell at craft fairs, exhibitions and so on, and what you sell is of relatively high value.

Let's say you're selling bespoke bird boxes with every imaginable treat for bird and buyer, and the price starts at £30. Not a huge amount by any means but how many of us have £30 in our wallets?

People like buying things, especially something that they'll be using for their favourite hobby. So make it easy for them to buy.

Experience

A local photographer did some brochure work for me recently and told me that if it weren't for him accepting cards his business would have closed years ago. The chances of anyone having as much as £20 in their wallets these days was about as likely as snow in August.

Even though expensive, it's worth it. Obviously you'll have to shop around to see which bank offers the best deal and work the costs into your business and pricing, but like my photographer friend it could make the difference between having customers or no business.

Just look at the restaurant business. How many of us would still go into a restaurant if they didn't accept our debit or credit cards?

INCLUDE A MAIL ORDER FACILITY

I believe every business that sells a product should have way customers buy their goods via mail order.

Let's go back to the homemade soap business example again.

Here you are selling a unique, desirable product to customers who visit your shop, stand, stall or car boot. Chances are that many of these customers do not live in your immediate area and probably won't be able to return to buy some more. The product itself can be posted almost anywhere relatively inexpensively, which makes it ideal for mail order. Yet an amazing number of businesses ignore the potential additional sales that mail order can bring.

 If you are retailing your product and it is capable of being posted, then why not offer it mail order?

Nothing fancy is needed

All that's needed is to include a small advertisement somewhere, either on the outer packaging or on a small note inside, telling your customer that if they're delighted with their purchase, which you trust they will be, then they can order more either via your website or phoning you direct.

You can also use this as an opportunity to promote all the other products you do that your customer may not yet have bought. And in the unlikely event that your customer is not satisfied with their purchase you can ask them to email you with their comments.

By adding mail order to your business you really can increase sales without paying out for further advertising because previous customers will now be able to buy again from you, and will almost certainly start recommending you to their friends, colleagues, and family and this in turn builds further sales.

Customer loyalty schemes are now commonplace amongst the country's largest retailers. There's nothing to stop you introducing similar schemes in your business. And if you have a website where customers can sign up for your regular free newsletter you can include all sorts of things like details of your latest products, competitions and so on.

OFFER CUSTOMER REFERRAL INCENTIVES

The insurance business relies heavily on successfully targeting their existing satisfied customers to introduce them to new customers, often in areas where previously they have been unsuccessful.

Referrals work on the basis that if your customers are happy with your products and services, they should be encouraged to recommend your business to everyone they think might benefit from what you're offering.

Usually a tempting incentive is offered, which could be anything from a pen to a gift voucher or even a holiday. As soon as the nominated friend buys something, whoever referred them gets their gift as a thank you.

 Encouraging referrals by offering incentives is a great way of building up your customer base at a fraction of what it would cost using traditional advertising methods.

Sales leads generated from this type of campaign are far easier to turn into actual sales because the people you will be selling to will be more open to buying your products as you've come via personal introduction.

It's easy to introduce referral schemes

All you have to do is ask your existing customers to recommend someone they know to receive a copy of your latest brochure, sample product, newsletter etc, and as soon as this nominated person starts shopping they will receive their free gift.

To really make this system work you need to create a sense of urgency. Otherwise your campaign runs the risk of suffering from 'I'll do it tomorrow' syndrome. The most effective way of getting your existing customers to recommend someone today is to set a deadline when the offer runs out. Of course there's nothing to stop you then re-running the offer at a later date when hopefully you will get another batch of potential clients.

Ways to make your referral scheme work

1. Offer a desirable gift, but something that is not going to cost your business a fortune. For example you could offer a gift voucher that can be redeemed against future orders. The advantage here is that not only are you getting new customers referred to your business, but you are also encouraging existing customers to buy again so they can use the gift voucher.

2. Set a deadline for when the offer expires. Remember that to make this scheme work you need to create a sense of urgency. Your aim is to get your customers referring their friends to you within a certain period of time if they are to qualify for their incentive.

3. As soon as you get your new customers shopping with you offer them a similar incentive to refer their friends and so on.

4. Keep interest alive by varying your incentives. Gift vouchers are fine for one occasion but try and offer something different next time.

5. Consider introducing a rewards points system where points are awarded for every new customer introduced who spends a minimum predetermined amount. Points are also awarded on future purchases and once a certain number of points have been accumulated a larger incentive gift can be claimed.

Whatever type of business you are planning to start, make sure you introduce some sort of referral scheme, even if it's just to ask your customers if they know of anyone else who would benefit from what you're offering.

PUBLISH YOUR OWN NEWSLETTER

Newsletters are a great way of promoting your own products, keeping your customers loyal and generating additional income for your business by either selling advertising space or earning commission on selling others' goods.

Already got your website?

If you have a website, publishing your own electronic newsletter, or e-zine, is relatively straightforward. (See Chapter 8 for more information.)

The advantages of having an online newsletter is that you'll get potential customers as well as existing customers signing up. For example, I run a *Top Tips For Gardeners* newsletter via one of my websites, and I get as many would-be customers as customers signing up. The challenge is then to convert the would-bes into customers while encouraging my existing customers to recommend my products and services to everyone they know.

If you haven't got a website

You don't need to have a website to publish your own newsletter. What you do need, however, is a customer address list to send it to. This isn't a problem in my gardening business where I automatically get potential customers' names and addresses when they phone up asking me to go and give them a quote.

Building your mailing list

But if you're selling your goods at craft fairs, exhibitions and other retail outlets the chances are you won't be able to get names and addresses. Don't despair – there's a simple way around this. All you have to do is include a copy of your current newsletter with everyone's purchase. Make sure also that you give a copy to anyone who browses your stand. The trick here is to get as many copies of your newsletter out as possible.

The easiest and most effective way of getting people to send you their details and subscribe to your newsletter is to offer an incentive. Again there are a number of things you can offer here, for example, gift voucher with 10 per cent off first purchase, free goody bag, pen, holdall etc, but I believe the most irresistible incentive is to run a competition.

Your competition

It is vital here that you have a worthwhile enough prize for people to want to enter so give it some thought and be prepared to splash out a little. Here's how it works. Give your readers a question to answer. Make sure you include a cut-out coupon for them to complete.

Make sure your cut-out coupon collects the following information.

1. full name;
2. date of birth (*important so you can get a feel of the age group who buy, or are interested in, your products and services. Also useful if you are to send them a card on their birthday*);
3. address including postcode;
4. email address;
5. telephone number.

Remember, the objective of running the competition is to get people to sign up for your newsletter, so don't forget to ask them to subscribe. Something along the lines of:

Please tick here ☐ if you would *not* like to receive our newsletter completely free of charge delivered regularly to your letterbox.

I recommend you ask them to tick the box if they don't want to receive your newsletter because market research indicates that this is the most effective way of getting people to agree to something.

You could of course simply ask them to tick the box if they would like to receive your regular newsletter free of charge. It's up to you.

If you're thinking about offering a relatively high-value prize then don't feel that the draw must take place prior to your next newsletter coming out. This needn't be the case. You can run the competition over any period you want, provided you indicate when the competition closes.

For example, you could start your competition in spring and say, 'Lucky winner to be announced in the winter edition of this newsletter,' which shouldn't have any adverse effect on entries.

Designing and publishing your newsletter

You don't have to go to enormous expense to run a successful newsletter. For my gardening business I publish a seasonal newsletter using a software program on my PC. You don't even have to go to that extent if you don't want to. Provided your document is well laid out, easy to read and attractive then that's fine.

You can get it photocopied or if you have a large mailing list, it's probably cheaper and more efficient to have it done by your local printer.

What makes a good newsletter?

There are two angles you must consider here.

1. Your needs: to make this publication sell more of your products and services and expand your customer client base.

2. Your customer's needs: they've got to get something from reading your newsletter. If they don't they won't read it, and everyone loses out.

It's vital the **content** of your newsletter is informative and interesting in a chatty sort of way. Few, if any, will want to read a newsletter which sounds like an advertisement, or talks down to them.

So you need to work on your content. Make sure your newsletter includes interesting, and if possible previously unknown, facts about your products or services.

For example, my *Top Tips For Gardeners* newsletter always includes something about the flowers and plants that are in bloom at the time. My last spring issue contained the following information about daffodils:

Did you know that daffodil bulbs were used by the Roman surgeons to treat a gladiator's open wounds and gashes?

And Roman soldiers always carried daffodil bulbs in their knapsacks when going to war?

When eaten daffodil bulbs suppress the nervous system, so it's thought that the soldiers used the bulbs not only to treat their wounds, but give them courage!

How are your daffodils looking this year?

I then go on to give five top tips for caring for daffodils and what to do after they've flowered.

I finish this piece by inviting my readers to contact me to arrange for our company to come around and prepare their garden ready for the spring. Because January is usually a quiet month for us, as it is for many businesses, I offer an incentive.

Winter Warmer – Book your spring tidy up before 31 January and we'll give you 10% off our normal rates. Book today on (telephone number) to take advantage of this special offer.

Note that I've created a sense of urgency by asking customers to book before 31 January. This creates a sense of urgency and also means I don't have to discount any work which comes in February, the month our business traditionally picks up.

Some things you could include in your newsletter:

☐ **Any interesting history** behind your products: how did your products get their name? Where were they first sold? Anyone famous using these products? What's the most expensive one to ever have been sold?

☐ **Other customers' tips and advice**. Invite your readers to write and share their tips and advice with others. This works well with hobby businesses where there is a natural sense of allegiance because everyone is interested in the same thing.

☐ **Your business diary**. If you're planning to exhibit at a certain venue, let your customers know in advance by way of your newsletter. Again you could offer an incentive – bring along your copy of this month's newsletter and get your free gift etc.

☐ **Staff profiles**. If you're hiring staff you could include a different staff profile in each issue. Especially if you're offering a mail order service you could introduce your clients to the person or people responsible for taking their orders.

☐ **Product advice**. Tell your readers how to get the most out of what they've bought. Depending on your business you can include all sorts of helpful information here.

☐ **How to guides**. Write your own short 'how to' guides for your hobby. Even though the object of my gardening newsletter is to sell more of our products and services, I like to include short garden guides. The feedback is always positive and if nothing else it provides you with an opportunity to demonstrate your skills and knowledge.

☐ **Now is the time to...** Somewhere in your newsletter you should always include a '...now is the time to' feature, especially if things have some sort of natural deadline. For example if you're running walking holidays in Cornwall and you know that fairly soon your next month's diary will be full – then tell your customers: 'Anyone considering booking their walking holiday in July should do so now as there are only a few places left.' Or, 'You really only have two weeks left to plant your onion sets if you want to have them in time for summer salad days.'

 My advice is to keep it short. You're not printing a magazine or newspaper, so keep it as short as possible. Aim to leave your readers wanting more rather than having them put it down halfway through.

What about pictures?

If you're publishing an online newsletter then you can include picture links in your newsletter. But be careful: depending on your connection it's not always easy to download pictures and they can distract from the main content.

If you want to include pictures in your online newsletter then the best way is either to write in some hyperlinks, which are links either to other websites or web pages, at end of the newsletter, or tell your readers there are now new pictures on your website.

For paper newsletters, I'd recommend you steer away from pictures. I think it's too expensive and doesn't really fit in with what's normally expected of a newsletter.

If you can't write your own

If you really can't write your own newsletter then try to get a friend, relative, partner or even a member of your staff involved with it. Discuss with them what you're looking for and what you hope to achieve by having a newsletter. Get yourself online and sign up to a few newsletters so you can get a feel for what they're about.

But do try to include them in your business. A well-written, regular newsletter is a great way of turbo-boosting your sales, and at a fraction of the cost of traditional advertising.

Making it 'sticky'

Good newsletters are sticky ones. By sticky I mean that not only do your customers read them every month but they find they can't do without them.

There are a number of ways you can make your newsletter sticky:

- **Competitions**. Run regular competitions where you announce the winner in a future issue. You print the lucky winner's name and they have to contact you within so many days to claim their prize.

- **Reader's notice board**. Invite your readers to advertise their items for sale in your newsletter. My advice is not to charge them for this service as you'll benefit from having a more interesting and stickier publication.

- **Ongoing feature**. Choose an interesting area of your hobby and write an ongoing feature as opposed to simply writing it all in one go. Divide it up into, say, four parts. Remember to finish each piece with a taster of what's to come in the next issue.

Naming your publication

Just like when choosing the name for your business, spend a bit of time working on a title for your newsletter.

Originally I called my gardening newsletter *From the Potting Shed*, but when I asked readers what they most liked about it, they said the tips. So I simply call it *Top Tips*

For Gardeners. It may sound a bit uninspiring and unoriginal, but it does what it says on the tin because every issue is packed full of useful tips, advice and information for gardeners.

Finally!

Remember the objective of publishing your newsletter is twofold:

1. By reading your newsletter your customer should get some interesting information and details of special offers, new products etc.

2. You in turn should get increased business and customer loyalty.

SEND A CARD

Another great way to ensure customer loyalty and boost sales is to send your clients cards, which can include:

- ☐ Christmas cards
- ☐ Birthday cards
- ☐ Postcards
- ☐ Get well soon cards

Sending Christmas cards to all your customers can increase your sales by up to 20 per cent.

Christmas cards

In our businesses we send cards to all our customers and also to those who have expressed previous interest in our business. The results are often amazing and I believe that not only do we continue to keep our customers by sending them cards but we win lots of new business, too.

Birthday cards

Earlier we looked at the sort of information you should ask for when getting customers to sign up for your newsletter. This included asking for date of birth so you've no excuse for not sending your clients a birthday card. You could also consider sending them a small gift in appreciation of their business.

Postcards

It might seem an unusual thing to send your customers, but postcards make great inexpensive marketing tool for announcing special offers, end of line reductions etc. You could have your own postcards printed using a picture of your products or something else that depicts your business, or just use off-the shelf postcards with images relevant to your business.

Other cards

Where you're running a business where you get to know your customers and meet them on a regular basis, such as a gardening business, you can send all sorts of other cards including get well soon cards and congratulations cards. When I hear that one of my gardening customers is unwell I always send them a get well soon card. These are the small, inexpensive touches that sets your business apart from the rest.

 Cards are a powerful and relatively inexpensive sales tool. Saying thank you is one way of making sure your customers stay loyal to you and your business.

Summary

1. You don't have to be an expert to be a successful salesperson.

2. The most successful sales strategy in the world is simply to ask for the order.

3. People buy benefits, not features.

4. Objections are buying signals.

5. A professional salesperson will recognise buying signals and work on them to achieve a sale.

6. Turbo-boost your business sales by taking credit and debit cards; offering mail order; client referral schemes; publishing your own newsletter; and sending customers, both existing and potential, cards.

7. Selling – there really is nothing to fear.

6

THE ESSENTIALS OF SHOESTRING MARKETING

One of the most difficult things to get right when starting a new business is knowing how to market your new venture.

Unfortunately it's an area often overlooked. Efforts can vary from large and expensive magazine advertisements to doing absolutely nothing at all. Often both approaches bring the same result. Nothing happens.

Why is marketing so important?

Having a successful marketing strategy for your business is like having a powerful train driving customers through your doors. Once these customers are through your doors, you can then work on selling them your goods and services. All too often businesses concentrate their efforts on the sales function without really bothering about marketing, which results in poor sales because customers aren't coming to buy.

I am going to assume that you don't have thousands of pounds to spend on marketing. Even if you have a large budget available, be forewarned that the amount you spend on marketing your business does not necessarily equal the size of your sales.

Learning from larger businesses

Before we look at marketing techniques, I want to tell you about an excellent, free way of getting up-to-the-minute telesales training. Every year big businesses invest millions of pounds training their telesales staff in the latest techniques for telemarketing. As soon as you open your business, you will get bombarded with all sorts of people trying to sell you something. Personally, I never buy anything over the phone; even if it's something that I'm interested in I will only decide if and when I see written information including terms and conditions.

But rather than get annoyed at this constant stream of telesales people, see them as offering you a free telesales course. After all, they will be sharing with you all the expensive training they have been given. Of course the standard of call will vary from awful to brilliant, but either way you can learn from these people.

WHAT YOU'LL LEARN FROM TELESALES EXECUTIVES

How to approach a cold sales telephone call

You'll learn a lot from how they work the call so as to get through to the decision maker. Obviously the last thing they want to do is waste their time selling advertising space to someone who is not a decision maker.

So listen to how they make their initial approach. What distinguishes professional telesales executives from the others you'll get calling you is that the pro will have their homework done. They'll have the name of who they want to speak to. The amateurs or no-hopers will simply say something like, 'Hello, can I speak to the business owner, please?' or another favourite, 'Can I speak to the person who handles the utility bills...?'

How to overcome common objections

The reason I urge you to tell them you're not interested is because then you'll learn how to handle initial objections. The most important thing when handling any objection is to keep dialogue going and build up a relationship because people find it more difficult to say no to someone they like.

The more objections you raise the better the lesson becomes. I've used many of their techniques with great effect in my own business.

Coping with rejection

Whatever business you're planning to start you're going to have to learn to handle rejection as you're going to get it. Often in truck loads. When a professional telesales executive calls you and you make it clear you don't want whatever it is they're selling you, they won't take it personally. 'Well thank you very much for your time this morning, Mr Power, I appreciate how busy you are, but if you ever do change your mind...'

Professionals will be unfailingly polite, respectful of your time and also will try to leave the door open by saying something like, 'Would you mind if I give you a call, let's say in a couple of months, to see if your situation has changed?'

If they sound nice and reasonable the chances are you'll probably say yes. From their point of view they've succeed in one goal at least – keeping the door open.

Why advertising doesn't always work

Small businesses waste thousands of pounds annually on expensive advertising that will never bring them a single customer. Unfortunately many labour under the misconception that all they have to do to bring business through their doors is go with the biggest ad they can afford. Advertising doesn't work this way.

For an advertisement to work it must have a clear, quantifiable objective, nothing as vague as 'to bring in more business' or 'to increase sales'.

The advertisement's objective must be:

☐ **Specific**. How many new customers do you want to generate? How many products do you want to sell?

☐ **Measurable**. How are you going to work out how successful your ad is? One way is to ask to customers replying to your ad to quote a specific reference number or mention the ad itself to take advantage of a special offer.

☐ **Targeted**. You must make sure your ad is going to reach your potential market. If you're a hairdresser offering a mobile hairdressing service, you need to target those people who for whatever reasons find themselves mostly housebound.

The key to success is to make sure the objective is achievable.

Too many advertisements are dead simply because they can't achieve what's expected of them. For example, a common, and easily made, mistake is to use a small advertisement to try to sell your products. A single advertisement can't do this.

So the objective for the advertisements we run for our Dutch bikes is to get people motivated to get further information on our products. They can do this by either visiting our website or phoning us for a brochure.

Rather than see your advertisement as simply a tool for selling your goods, instead use it as a vehicle for bringing potential customers to either your telephone line or website to find out more about your products and services. This way at least your advertisement stands some chance of achieving its objective.

A WORD ABOUT ADVERTISING SALES EXECUTIVES

Beware, be very aware, that when someone phones you to sell you advertising space their primary concern is to make a sale for their business not necessarily to generate increased business for your company.

Imagine for a moment someone rings you completely out of the blue to tell you all about something great that they say will do your business the power of good. It's expensive, but you agree to go ahead convinced that the investment is worth is because your sales will rocket. You pay your money (unless you've a trading history, most ads have to be paid for upfront) and you wait in eager anticipation until the day of publication.

Absolutely nothing happens – you fail to get even a single inquiry via your expensive advertisement. This scenario isn't as uncommon as you think. It's one that's happened to me in my business and from speaking to other entrepreneurs it's happened to them, too.

Experience

Recently we approached a large glossy gardening magazine to run a specific series of advertisements promoting one of our business's new products. I spent considerable time on the phone with the sales executive discussing our advertisement's objective. The salesperson agreed that not only would our ad do well in their publication but that they would also be willing to do a feature on our product.

Our first ad came and went with a dismal response. Having already sent a sample of our product to the magazine's editor, I was surprised that I had heard nothing. So I phoned and was told they never received it (although they had received the covering letter, which was odd). Undeterred, I sent another sample of our product hoping for the promised review.

The next issue of the magazine arrived and our product had still not been reviewed. Much to my annoyance our competitors' product had, and they hadn't even advertised in the magazine.

When I phoned the magazine for an explanation I was told that the editor did not think that our product was suitable for their readership. But their advertising department had assured me our product was ideal for their publication.

I pulled our advertisement immediately despite warnings from the sales manager that we would be liable to pay for further ads as we had entered into a contract.

Naturally I pointed out that under such circumstances they'd have a struggle to convince a court that we owed them money.

I cannot stress enough that the only thing an advertising executive is interested in is their commission and their publication's future. Your business is simply a means to an end. Don't rely on anything they tell you and make sure that your products and services are right for their magazine. While the offer of a cheap advertisement might seem attractive, it becomes very expensive when you don't get any business from it.

My favourite method for promoting our businesses is using our websites. This is covered fully in Chapter 8.

Here are my preferred shoestring offline marketing techniques.

Ten ways to market your business with a small budget

1. Classified advertisements.
2. Press releases.
3. Sponsorship.
4. Media stunts.
5. Make more use of your business cards.
6. Join a local networking group.
7. Use self-employed sales agents.
8. Leaflet drops.
9. Give talks to other businesses.
10. Write for your favourite hobby magazines or create your own newsletter.

CLASSIFIED ADVERTISEMENTS

You may wonder why after berating advertisements I'm now including them in my list. My reasons are simply that some businesses will have to employ traditional advertising methods to get started and bring potential customers through their doors.

Small, and relatively inexpensive classified ads, can be an excellent, cheap way of achieving sales targets.

However, before rushing off to place your advertisements there are two very important things you must get right.

1. The publication must be suitable for your advertisement.
2. The advertisement must be as powerful as a train in pulling customers through your doors.

Is the publication's readership suitable for your advertisement?

Remember the editor who rejected our product as being unsuitable for her readership. She was right. It was unsuitable, which was why our advertisement achieved nothing. Obviously had I given it more thought and really identified who the magazine's targeted readership was, I would have come to the same conclusions as she did and not wasted our money.

If your ad is going to achieve anything for your business it must reach your target market.

When considering a publication always get a copy of the magazine or newspaper before placing your advertisement. Remember, if your advertisement is to have even the slightest hope of succeeding, your products or services must appeal to the bulk of the magazine's readers. If it doesn't your message will fail to reach your target audience.

- ☐ You don't have to buy the magazine or newspaper. Phone the classified sales department and ask them to send you a back issue and a media pack.

- ☐ The media pack will contain information on how many copies are distributed and an analysis of the typical readership.

- ☐ When you receive your copy go through all the advertisements and ask yourself if what you're offering is the same as what is being advertised.

- ☐ If the answer is no, or you've got your doubts, then it isn't for you. Ignore what the sales staff say. Their job is to sell advertising space, not your products.

How much should you spend?

Rates are based upon a number of factors, which include how many copies are sold monthly, quarterly or yearly, whether the magazine is a glossy colour affair or in more of a newspaper format etc. My advice is that you should initially ignore how much your advertisement is going to cost you until you've first assessed the publication's suitability.

My own experience has been that it's far too tempting to place adverts in publications which offer the best rates, while ignoring the key factor, which is do your customers read this publication? If you're sure that they do – having first worked through the existing advertisements, then you need to work out an advertising budget. The reason this is important is that you need to make sure that you don't overspend unnecessarily.

Don't be surprised when you phone the advertising department of the publication to be told that the attractive introductory offer in the publication isn't the price you'll end up paying. For instance, most will charge you extra for a colour ad and will inevitably try to sell you a larger ad than the one you had planned.

Advertorial

Whenever you do decide to go with a particular publication make sure to ask them to run a small feature about you and your business. Many will, but only if you ask them. An advertorial is a great way of getting additional publicity for your business because it's your ad dressed up as a news story.

Working out a budget

Generally speaking, any advertisement will take some time before it starts to work. Some marketing experts reckon that it can take customers as much as five exposures to your message before they will consider buying what you're offering.

If you doubt this, next time you watch television make a note of how often the same advertisement will come on during your favourite programme or a night's viewing. Anywhere between three and five seems to be the magic number. So if you're planning to run just one ad in one publication then you may as well as forget it and save your money.

I have found that it usually takes about three months of advertising in a monthly magazine before I see any return on my investment. Of course it may take longer, but I make a point of reviewing our advertisements every three months and those that aren't performing well are either axed completely or revised.

When working out your budget try to come up with a six-month or annual marketing budget. Then make sure you to stick to it. It's so easy to get carried away with bigger and better ads in the vain hope that this strategy will reap rewards. It won't and it doesn't.

 TIP   Work out a budget that you can comfortably afford – and stick to it.

WRITING A KILLER CLASSIFIED ADVERTISEMENT

Only after you have carefully assessed the publication's suitability for your business should you think about writing a classified ad that will hook your customers.

Five steps to writing a powerful classified advertisement:

1. Don't try to sell them anything.
2. Create a killer headline.
3. Offer something irresistible.
4. Call them to action.
5. Create a sense of urgency.

Don't try to sell them anything

Strange, but true. Rather than see your classified ad as a way to sell your products and services to potential customers, try instead to view it as a powerful train bringing carriage loads of soon-to-be customers to your business.

The primary objective of your advertisement should be to bring in enquiries and not sales. Succeed with this objective and then you can successfully sell to them when they visit your shop, website or request a copy of your mail order catalogue.

Create a killer headline

Without it your advertisement is going nowhere.

Some years ago when the Internet was still a mystery to most, I was commissioned by our local paper to write a piece on Christmas shopping on the Internet.

My feature was duly published and those I spoke to afterwards said they hadn't seen it. Even when I told them what page it had appeared on they still had difficulty finding it.

The reason? The headline. It was written assuming that readers had already some knowledge of the World Wide Web with the heading: 'Christmas Shopping on the Web', which meant nothing to most people and so they either consciously, or subconsciously, didn't read it.

 Your headline must grab the reader and make them want to read more.

Target your customers by making the heading as specific as you possibly can. If your product will only appeal to those interested in sailing then make it shout at sailors:

ATTENTION FRUSTRATED SAILORS

Or if you're selling to gardeners with bad backs:

IS YOUR GARDEN BREAKING YOUR BACK?

And so on. Be as specific as you can. Grab their attention and make them want to read your ad.

Offer something irresistible

In the chapter on selling I've told you the key to all selling is that people buy benefits and not features. This is also true when it comes to your advertising.

The only way that people will be motivated to bother looking at your website, visit your shop or phone for a brochure, is if your advertisement answers their overriding motivation, which is: What's in it for me?

Following your attention-grabbing headline you must give them a powerful, irresistible benefit.

The way to do this is to write down all the benefits that someone would get if they bought what you're offering. We're not just looking for unique selling points here, we're looking for benefits, which could include:

☐ cheapest in the market;
☐ sole supplier of such a product;
☐ only a few products left – after that you won't be able to repeat these prices;
☐ only so many vacancies left – after that you are full for the rest of the year.

The next step is to prioritise your benefits and decide which one of all them is the most appealing. Highlight this one and then check through the other ads in the publication you are considering and make sure you're not duplicating someone else's advertisement.

When you've got your powerful benefit it can follow your headline:

IS YOUR GARDEN BREAKING YOUR BACK?
Our catalogue is full of products specially designed
to take the hard work out of gardening.

Now you've got your powerful heading and created an irresistible benefit, most gardeners will be tempted to request a copy of your catalogue.

But they'll put the magazine down intending to phone you later and then something else will grab their attention, and fairly soon your ad will be part of pile of papers bound for the recycling centre.

Call them to action

To avoid this happening you must call them to action.

Next time you watch television, listen to commercial radio or pick up a magazine, listen out for the advertiser calling you to action. Car insurance companies are probably the least subtle of all. Many command you to pick up your phone right now and find out how much money they can save you on your insurance renewal. These advertisements shout at you to do something. The reason you do, is because they have already told you the all-important what's in it for you – cheaper car insurance, a cheap holiday in the sun etc.

Don't be afraid to be bold and blunt (without of course being offensive). Something like:

> *Our catalogue is full of products specially designed to take the hard work out of gardening. Copies are limited so order now to avoid disappointment.*

Create a sense of urgency

The response to your call to action can be greatly improved if you create a sense of urgency as well. There are a number of ways you can do this, for example:

- ☐ offer a free gift with every catalogue requested before a certain date;
- ☐ offer a discount on all lines for orders placed before a certain date;
- ☐ make 'only while stocks last' announcements;
- ☐ offer give-away prices for a specific period only.

Remember that the primary objective of your advertisement is to bring customers through your doors so create as much urgency as you can by offering a powerful time-sensitive incentive. You don't have to offer discounts on all your products or services. One will do so long as it's powerful enough to pull them through the doors.

The worst-case scenario for your ad is to have either no one see it to begin with – more common that you think – or for potential customers to read it and not be motivated to find out more.

Spend as much time as you can working on your classified advertisement. Look at it from the perspective of your potential customers and not your own. Keep the 'What's in it for me?' motivating factor at the forefront of everything you do.

 Get it right and a small, relatively inexpensive, classified advertisement can see your sales rocket and guarantee your business's future success.

Don't worry if you don't get it right first time. Review and revise your advertisement as necessary and remember it can take months before you see any great return on your ad.

Press releases

A press release is a marketing tool that is often overlooked by small business owners and is still my favourite.

Nothing will generate sales quicker than a favourable mention in your hobby magazine, local newspaper, radio or television channel, and it's not as difficult as you might imagine. Although obviously the greater your understanding and knowledge of how to write your press releases the greater your chances of success.

Read as much as you can about this subject, but don't be intimidated by the word 'press' or be afraid to contact the media with your ideas.

A SIMPLE, EFFECTIVE PRESS RELEASE

Every day newspaper editors, magazine editors and television producers are deluged with press releases from businesses, politicians, entertainers and more, all trying to get publicity for their interests.

The reason they want to be featured on the news is that people are more receptive to their sales message via the news as opposed to advertisements.

However, editors aren't in the business of running free ads for anyone and they know that if their publication, television or radio programme has even the slightest hint of promoting products and services people will turn off in their droves. So the golden rule when it comes to approaching any media publication is to remember that editors buy news and their publications sell advertisement space.

So to succeed in getting your business featured in their publications, your press release must contain something that is newsworthy and not simply seen as promoting your business. Once you know where to look you'll soon find lots of potential angles for a news story.

Although most local newspapers are pleased to run a small piece on a new business opening in the area, you won't find the glossy monthly magazines quite as accommodating.

Even so, prior to launching your business you should always contact the editor of your local newspaper and also the editor of any magazine that covers your hobby or interest. But when contacting them you must be able to offer them a powerful benefit for featuring your business. After all, what you're doing here is selling them a news item or something interesting and unique that will appeal to their readers or viewers.

WHAT'S NEWSWORTHY ABOUT YOUR BUSINESS?

1. **Human interest.** All news revolves around human interest. Although you might think that an innovative new product is a newsworthy item, it's worthless unless it has a human-interest angle.

Imagine for a moment that you've just found a new product that overcomes sea sickness. Simply writing a press release announcing this fact isn't going to grab anyone's attention or imagination unless you can work it into a human interest story. So rather than saying 'Hey, we've just found the perfect solution to curing seasickness,' you would announce that either you or someone you know who has suffered from seasickness has finally found relief from this awful condition.

The product is the solution, but the story an editor would be interested in is the impact it's had on a previous sufferer.

2. **Previous career or occupation.** Your previous career may well be a news story on its own. For example, a former city banker trading his suit and tie for the kitchen and happily running his own organic catering business is a great story for the contrast in careers. People love to read about how others have changed their lives, especially those who've swapped a high-flying career for something completely different.

3. **Employment and local prosperity.** There isn't an editor in the country who would turn down a story where a new business was going to further enhance an area's reputation, or create new jobs. Stories like these are sought after. So if you're going to be improving an area and offering more employment and greater prosperity – there's your angle.

4. **Gaps in the market.** With every hobby there is something that is either difficult to get, or prohibitively expensive to do. For example, as anyone who owns a boat knows, mooring fees have reached an all-time high. Incredible as it may sound many boat owners are now moving their boats abroad, away from UK marinas, as berthing rates are far more affordable.

A marina near where I lived introduced an innovative solution by offering low cost 'dry berth moorings', something which is popular in the US. Rather than have a berth for your boat, it is dry stored at the marina when you're not using it. As soon as you want to go boating you phone and the marina arranges to have your boat ready in the water for you. Once you've finished it is then lifted and dry stored again. The advantage to everyone is that the cost of dry berth is extremely favourable compared with a traditional water berth.

Because the marina was offering an innovative way of reducing the cost of berthing, the story was taken up in all the press including the local television news.

There are literally thousands of ways your business could be newsworthy; all you have to do is work out the best ones. Remember the key to success is looking for the human-interest angle.

No one will be interested in a product or service alone. It's the 'What's in it for me?' angle you're looking for.

ISSUING A PRESS RELEASE

Once you've found your news item you'll need to communicate it to the editors of the various media you intend to contact.

Many books will recommend you use a set format for your press release, I recommend you don't. Instead, try something that doesn't smack of attempting to get free publicity – rather offer the editor an irresistible story to win favour with their readers.

A simple but effective press release is to write a letter to the editor. The big advantage of doing this is that if the editor doesn't include a piece on your business, hopefully your letter will still appear in the readers' letters section. This is not to be scoffed at, as this is usually the most read section in any publication.

My experience has been that I make my letter as compelling as I possibly can. I include a 'call to action' for the editor at the end of the letter asking them to contact me for more information or to come and visit us for a coffee and a tour of what we're about.

The results are usually positive and I've found that either the editor or a staff journalist has phoned me to find out more information, and then done a nice interesting feature on our business.

WHAT TO INCLUDE

1. That all-important headline.
2. What's special about your business.
3. Briefly how it started.
4. A bit about you.
5. Call to action.

The headline

Just like a classified ad, you will need to make it attention grabbing, but without looking tacky and cheap.

What's special about your business

This is where you describe why you are newsworthy – what makes what you're doing unique and of interest to the publication's readers.

Briefly how it started

It's important to cover this, as often this is where the editor's interest lies. A former estate agent swapping selling houses for opening a herb farm is more interesting than the herbs themselves. The life-changing angle will appeal to more people than the fact that the area is to gct a new herb farm.

A bit about you

What's your vision for the future? Would you like to see everyone eating delicious healthy herbs and getting wonderful benefits? Be bold here. This might be the paragraph that gives the editor the news story he wants.

Call to action

End your letter with a powerful call to action. Something like 'Pick up your phone now and I'll tell you all about it,' probably won't work. So try something like inviting the paper to come and visit your new business to try out your new product or service – it is an ideal way of calling an editor to action.

CONTACTING OTHER MEDIA

Television and radio stations are always on the lookout for local and national news stories.

Our local ITV news runs regular features on small local businesses, which have included boat builders, dolls house makers, book enthusiasts, people who run walking holidays and even a man who makes pub models from things he finds in the local tip.

 TIP Don't be afraid to contact your local TV or radio station. You'll often find they ask anyone with a story to contact them.

Approach TV and radio in same way you would a newspaper or magazine. Again, try to avoid a formal press release style format and go for a more personal approach. You're far more likely to get a positive response if you come across as friendly and enthusiastic as opposed to trying to act like a large corporation.

Sponsorship

There are all sorts of good causes out there that would be delighted to receive sponsorship from a local business. You could sponsor anything from a local football team to building and maintaining a flower border or garden for a hospice or children's home.

Not only are you doing something worthwhile, but also getting some excellent publicity for your business.

You needn't just sponsor charities. There is a now a growing trend amongst budget-conscious local authorities to invite businesses to sponsor the upkeep and maintenance of everything from roundabouts to local parks and gardens.

Having a nice big sign on one of the roundabouts leading into your town or city is a great way of promoting your business.

Whatever your hobby, there will be some group glad of the financial and inspirational help of a business involved in the same field.

 Sponsorship is a win-win situation.

Every year our business sponsors a worthwhile cause. Not only are we making a difference and getting a great feel-good factor for doing so, we are also raising the profile of our business locally.

Media stunts

Richard Branson is arguably the current king of the media stunt machine and we can all learn from his successful strategies.

Contrary to the image of journalists portrayed in films where they're constantly running around searching out that all-important story, most journalists haven't the time or resources necessary to do this. Instead, they look for ready-made stories via their contacts at hospitals, police stations, council offices, undertakers and the like. When they find something they believe would be of interest to their publication's readers they then work on the story.

Although this method is usually successful, the problem arises in that their rival publication makes the same phone calls every day. Editors are aware of this and are obviously keen to either have a different slant on local news stories, or to look for something completely different.

 Doing something unique and inviting the local media to come and witness your stunt is a great way of generating instant publicity.

Let's imagine for a moment that you're planning to run walking holidays but are finding that many of the rights of ways in your area have been blocked by local landowners. Obviously their actions will have a negative impact on your business as your walkers will be unable to follow what are often the more interesting routes. You could arrange for a local protest where you and a bunch of walking enthusiasts set out to challenge the actions of the local landowners.

Doing this will accomplish two objectives. The first thing you might achieve is to open up public walks which should already be accessible to the public. Provided you contact as many of the local press as you can you will also be assured of getting great publicity.

There are all sorts of stunts you can arrange for your business to generate publicity. Think big!

Making more use of your business cards

I have a simple philosophy when it comes to business cards – you can never give out enough of them. You'd be amazed at how quickly you can increase your sales if you start using your business cards as a marketing tool as opposed to simply a piece of information.

Before we look at the all the ways you can distribute your card, you first need to look at your existing card, or if you haven't got one, start planning what you'll need to include in it.

DESIGNING YOUR BUSINESS CARD

The three deadly sins of the business card design are having:

- ☐ blank spaces;
- ☐ no sales message;
- ☐ no call to action.

Blank spaces

If you already have a business card I'd like you to take it out now and turn it over so that you can't see the print. OK? So what can you see? A blank piece of paper? Or a powerful sales message?

I'm not a betting man, but I'd lay odds that the majority of people will be staring at a blank piece of paper. Leaving one side of the business card blank is the first deadly sin of business card design.

If you were running commercial vehicles as part of your business you wouldn't leave one side of the vehicle without a sign, so why leave half your business card blank?

Most people will have had their cards printed like this because this is the way the printer does them. However for a bit more money you can have the back of your card printed with an all-important powerful call to action.

No sales message

Just like your classified advertisement, your business card should have a powerful sales message. Otherwise why would anyone want to call you?

The fact that you sell fishing gear won't be enough to get people to call you. Remember that they need to be told what's in it for them.

So rather than just telling them where your fishing tackle shop is based, tell them why they should visit your business as opposed to your competitors'. And what better place to do this than that great big blank space of the back of your business card?

Even something as simple as what I've written below is better than a blank space.

> Don't forget to visit us online and see for yourself our amazing range of products at prices you won't get from anywhere else.

Call to action

Now you've told them why they should visit your business you must call them to act, otherwise your card will go into the bottom of their wallet, bin or coat pocket never to be seen again.

Call us today to take advantage of our special offers.

Phone us now for a friendly chat to see how we can help you.

Quote reference BiZcard1 and claim 10% off your first order.

The sooner you get your business cards selling for you, as opposed to simply providing information, the better. If you already have 250 business cards with a blank space, no sales message and no call to action then you should consider having some reprinted.

DISTRIBUTING YOUR CARD

You should never miss an opportunity to hand out your card. For example:

- Enclose your business card with every bill you pay or correspondence you reply to.

- Get your business card on every notice board, window or wall where people gather and wait. For example, barber shops, dentists' surgeries, restaurants, bars, staff rooms, shop notice boards – anywhere you're allowed to put your card up.

- Whenever you meet a prospective customer don't simply give them your card, personalise it. If they ask the price of something, write it down on your card as opposed to simply telling them, or worse still writing in on a scrap piece of paper.

- Even if everyone knows about your business, it's still worth giving friends and relatives a quantity of your business cards so they can give them to their colleagues and friends and put them up in their local barbers and so on.

Local networking groups

This may not suit every business, but networking groups are a useful way of building up local business contacts.

Groups generally work on the basis that you attend regular meetings, which can vary from breakfast get togethers to evening meetings where you meet other business owners and entrepreneurs just like you.

Even if you don't think that joining one of these groups will introduce you to new customers, they can still be a useful way of making excellent local contacts. For example if you're looking for funding your new business venture you could well find someone at these events.

If nothing else, it's a good way of getting away from your kitchen table and getting a fresh perspective on your business.

ONLINE NETWORKING GROUPS

You can also network online by joining any of the online forums relating to your hobby or entrepreneurial matters. Just browsing through previous discussion threads can be an excellent way of getting new ideas and solutions to your problems.

Remember if you're having problems with a certain aspect of your business, the chances are others have experienced the same difficulties. The answer to your problems may already have been solved by someone else which will save you time, money and stress.

Online networking is an excellent way of both promoting your business and getting that all-important support.

Self-employed sales agents

It is worth considering whether or not your product or services can be sold either in the UK or worldwide. You can employ a network of self-employed sales agents.

Rather than rely on your own marketing efforts you can benefit from the experiences and contacts of already-established sales agents.

Lots of products and service are marketed in this way, from boats to holidays to books.

How it works

You recruit a number of motivated sales agents who will sell your products or services for which they earn a commission.

Experience

Let's imagine for a moment that your business is making dolls houses and that each house retails at £100. The cost of selling your product on your own can be greatly reduced if you contact existing businesses that already attract your target customers and get them to sell your dolls houses.

The advantage to the sales agents is that they don't have to buy your stock. Instead you provide them with free point-of-sale material, which includes an example of your product. When their customers enquire about these houses, the sales agent will be able to answer all their questions because you will have briefed/trained them in advance. The sales agent then takes the order and the money, contacts you with the customer's details and pays you the amount they have received from their customer less the agreed commission.

Make sure that your commission structure is generous enough to be appealing while still leaving you with a worthwhile profit margin.

Where to find them

You could either approach retailers direct by telephoning, emailing or writing to them with your proposal, or you could run a classified advertisement in the business opportunity section of newspapers and magazines. Another way is to advertise that you are looking for sales agents on your website and point-of-sale material.

Does it really work?

Yes it does. In our businesses we hold a number of agents for a variety of products and we also recruit our own sales agents to sell our courses.

The reason I like using self-employed sales agents is because they are motivated by commission. If they don't sell your products, you don't pay them anything. After a short time it soon becomes apparent which agents you want to keep and invest further in and those you have to let go.

Provided you listen to what your agents are telling you, you can also get some very useful and regular feedback from customers about how your products and services can be improved.

Leaflet drops

If your target customer is locally based, door-to-door leafleting is a very cost-effective way of promoting your products and services.

There are a number of options:

- ☐ do it yourself;
- ☐ employ someone to do it on your behalf;
- ☐ have your leaflet included in an existing paper, for example your local property paper or weekly advertiser.

We've used door-to-door leaflet drops with great effect in our gardening business. Personally I prefer to arrange and do it all ourselves rather than employ a company to do it. All you have to do is recruit some casual help and blitz an area.

DESIGNING YOUR LEAFLET

Your leaflet is crucial to your success. Just like all your other marketing material it must include:

- ☐ **The big offer.** Why should anyone want to use your product or service?

- ☐ **A powerful benefit to potential customers** for choosing you over your competitors.

- ☐ **Credibility.** It is vital that you establish your credibility. So if you have any qualifications or have won any awards in your particular field don't forget to mention them. If you haven't any qualifications then don't worry. You can still establish credibility by including: 'references available', 'fully insured' (if appropriate).

☐ **Create a sense of urgency.** For example offer a discount for anyone booking you prior to the end of the month or a special offer for new customers. Whatever you offer, make sure it has a time limit.

☐ **Call to action.** Never forget this crucial bit. You must tell them to do something, whether it's to call you or visit your website.

☐ **Your full contact details.** Unfortunately we're living in a society that seems to be dominated by rogue businesses and so we're all subject to suspicion and scrutiny. Even if you only include your name and a land-based telephone number you are greatly increasing the odds that people will call you as you're providing them with information that the rogues will never give. If you can go one step further and include your website address and office address you really are taking positive action to establish yourself as a professional. If the only contact detail you can provide is a mobile telephone number, then this type of marketing isn't for you. People are right to be suspicious of anyone providing only a mobile telephone number.

Try to make your leaflet as eye-catching and interesting as possible and always get it printed by a professional. A cheap, home-made appearance is not going to encourage anyone to call you. Shop around for a good printer and ask them if they offer a design facility. If they do, as many will, ask to see examples of their work. As soon as you see anything that resembles those awful clip-art animations then look elsewhere. You want a design that reflects your unique business and not something that looks about as inspirational as a bus ticket.

DISTRIBUTING YOUR LEAFLETS

The benefit of leafleting is that you can target specific areas and even specific houses.

Experience

A few years ago, I owned an Italian car, which developed an intermittent fault. Our local garage was unable to rectify it as were the other two garages I took it to. Then one weekend while the car was parked outside my house a young man put a card on the windscreen, which read: 'We specialise in repairing common faults experienced with (the manufacturer's name of my car). We also undertake servicing.'

I called the number and asked whether or not they had heard of the type of problem my car was suffering from. They told me not only had they heard of the problem but repaired these faults on a regular basis. I took the car around to them and they fixed the problem.

This is an excellent example of targeted leaflet/card marketing, which got their phones ringing every time. If you are planning to start this type of marketing, and I recommend you do if your products or services are suitable, then try to be as specific as possible both in terms of the wording on your leaflet and the area you choose to market in.

Remember the golden marketing rule – people buy benefits and not features. Make sure your leaflet or card includes a powerful and specific benefit.

WHAT RESULTS WILL YOU GET?

We regularly undertake direct leafleting in our businesses and typically we get around a 1 per cent reply rate. On occasions this can be higher, but I'd say 1 per cent is a good average. We always aim to distribute 5,000 leaflets in one marketing hit and this generates approximately 50 sales calls, which we usually receive within around three weeks of our campaign.

The times we haven't achieved these results have been those when we employed another business to do our leafleting for us. So as I said earlier, we now organise, motivate and manage our own direct marketing team.

Giving talks to groups and other businesses

Whether your hobby is popular or unusual there will be always be local groups who'd love to hear you tell them more about what you're doing.

I've given talks to all sorts of local groups about gardening and garden design and have always found them an excellent way of generating new customers. When you give a talk on anything you become an expert and your credibility is immediately established. Even if those who attend your talk aren't personally in the market for your services they will tell their friends and relatives who may be, so it's worth giving everyone who attends your business card and a brochure or leaflet telling them more about what you do.

 Many hobby enthusiasts will travel surprising distances to listen to a seasoned expert share their knowledge, experience and anecdotes.

If you're nervous about having to speak in public, don't be. There are lots of books, audio cassettes, videos and even part-time courses that you can take to turn you from nervous amateur to skilled professional. Whatever you do, don't lose out on the potential of this sort of marketing can do for your business simply because you are nervous. Any worries I've had about speaking engagements have always turned out to be groundless. My experience has been that people are wonderfully supportive, hospitable and grateful for the time I've given to them and their organisations.

WHERE DO I FIND GROUPS?

You can usually find regular updates on groups operating in your area in your local paper. Your library will also have a very useful folder containing the details of all local groups that meet in the area. Spend a bit of time going through this binder making notes of the contact names and details of any of the groups you think might be interested in a talk from you. Either write, email or phone the contact and discuss your idea with them.

Getting paid

I've never asked for a fee for speaking to groups. I believe it's a win-win situation. The group's members get to hear what I hope is an interesting and informative talk on a subject they're interested in and I get to meet potential customers for my business. I also find that I also learn new things from them. So my advice is that unless you're selling someone a course on something, you should never ask for speaking fees. But it's up to you.

Writing for magazines and newspapers

This is similar to the idea of press releases. If in your business you're doing something different or unusual, then you should consider offering to write features for your favourite hobby magazines.

Look through any monthly gardening magazine and you will always find a business owner writing about some aspect of gardening. Whether it's a landscape gardener giving an account of how to lay the perfect lawn or a nursery owner discussing how they rid plants of common pests – it's all there.

 Writing a feature not only gives you valuable, free publicity, but also instant credibility.

Although most magazines and newspapers pay their freelance writers and contributors, I think that if you're writing about your own business then you should not charge. After all, the costs of your taking out a 1,000 or 2,000 word advertisement would be astronomical, and beyond most of our budgets. So don't look at it that you're giving away your services free. You're not. The resulting publicity will be more than just reward.

If under any circumstances you could not consider writing a feature for a magazine, then you should still contact the magazine's editor and tell them about your business, inviting them to come along to see the insider story on how your products are made.

I love boats and nothing grabs my interest more quickly than when my favourite boating magazine visits a boat builder's and we get to see first hand how a beautiful craft is created from an idea on a piece of paper to a finished boat.

Summary

Effective marketing needn't be expensive. A good website supported by a relatively inexpensive, but carefully constructed, classified ad can be far more effective than a large and expensive glossy ad. The most important thing to get right with your marketing is to begin with a budget.

Work out a figure that covers you for a series of small classified advertisements, website promotion, leaflets, business cards and any other point-of-sale material your business will require and then stick rigidly to your budget.

The most important thing to remember about advertising is that the amount of money you spend on your marketing will not guarantee you a pro-rata amount of business.

 Lots of successful businesses are marketing on a shoestring. I know because ours is one of them.

So don't be afraid to go out and look for free publicity, hand out leaflets, put posters up, give talks to groups, and build your own website. Above all, take responsibility for the future of your own business and not do as many do – allow it to fall or succeed on the amount of advertising they have paid for.

1. Spending money on an advertisement will not automatically generate more business.

2. For an advertisement to work it must have a clear objective, which isn't necessarily to sell your goods.

3. A marketing campaign is one half of your sales function and is equally as important as your sales function.

4. Classified advertisements can be a great way of marketing your business.

5. Advertisements take time to work. A single ad is unlikely to give any worthwhile return.

6. Work out a marketing budget and stick to it.

7. Never buy advertisements from cold-calling telesales executives.

8. Make sure your advertisement is somewhere your target customer is visiting.

7

DECIDING WHERE TO SELL FROM

Regardless of how innovative or unique your products and services are you must have some sort of a shop window from which to sell. I use the words shop window loosely here as your 'shop' could be anything from a website to an ad in the small classifieds of your favourite hobby magazine to a traditional bricks and mortar shop. I'll show you what's involved in opening a shop in another chapter.

Choosing the right venue to sell your goods is crucial to your success. Wherever you decide to sell your goods it has to satisfy the following criteria:

☐ be exposed to your target market;
☐ be affordable;
☐ allow a degree of flexibility;
☐ be secure and safe.

Be exposed to your target market

The reason many businesses fail is not because there isn't a demand for what they're selling, but because their products and services are not marketed at those who want and need them.

Experience

A few years ago a new business selling restored collectable and antique furniture opened in our town. The business owners put an enormous amount of time and effort into creating a very inviting shop which generated immediate interest. However, the shop was located in an area of the town where the neighbouring shops were late-night take-aways surrounded by housing estates.

Despite the initial interest, visitors to the shop were slow as few of the local residents were interested in what the shop was selling. Those who would have been interested didn't tend to go into the part of town where the shop was located.

Unfortunately late-night drunks became a problem and frequently the shop windows were broken by fighting and yobbish behaviour. The only way the shop owners could protect their business from these attacks was to install steel security grids over the window, which in turn meant that any hope of attracting passing window-shoppers was killed.

Sadly the business failed. The mistake here was that they set up a business in an area where they were not exposed to their target market. Why did they choose this area? Most likely because the rents here were far less than in the more affluent areas of our town, and not only were the rents lower but the retail area was far larger.

Be affordable

Wherever you rent it must be affordable. We'll look in a moment at what's involved in taking on a shop lease, but wherever you decide to locate your business you must be sure that the products and services you're going to offer have a fair chance of generating not only enough to cover rent, rates, insurance etc, but also pay you and give a profitable return.

Allow a degree of flexibility

One of the keys to running a successful business is to be flexible. You'll need to be able to adapt to market changes either as they happen, or preferably to anticipate them. If your business is located somewhere where you have no scope to change in any way – for example rearrange the sales areas, introduce or remove a workshop area – you will not be able to adapt to change and this will impact on your success.

Be secure and safe

In the case of the antiques shop, not only was the business located in the wrong area but it was also exposed to frequent attacks. The advantages of having a shop window for your business is that passers-by can look at what you're offering and be tempted to return to your business when you are open. If you have shutters and security doors where no one can see your window displays, you are losing out on potentially valuable sales.

Choosing where to sell your goods

There are lots of places you can market your goods. Your business could include a combination of these or just one:

- □ website;
- □ space in another shop;
- □ concession in a retail area;
- □ direct marketing;
- □ exhibition or trade fair;
- □ hotel foyer;

- ☐ train station platform;
- ☐ shops, cafés and kiosk;
- ☐ boot sales or market stall;
- ☐ shop;
- ☐ local authority concession;
- ☐ an existing business.

WEBSITE

In Chapter 8 we'll cover what's involved in setting up an online business. Whatever type of business you are planning to start a website can be a great and inexpensive way of either selling your products or promoting your business.

SPACE IN ANOTHER SHOP

Probably the most inexpensive way of getting your own shop is to hire a space in someone else's. While this can be an ideal solution for some businesses it won't suit everyone.

The type of products most suited to this type of arrangement are:

- ☐ antiques
- ☐ collectables
- ☐ jewellery
- ☐ paintings
- ☐ restored or unusual furniture
- ☐ toys
- ☐ memorabilia
- ☐ non-perishable food items
- ☐ other 'craft' items
- ☐ books
- ☐ art supplies.

Generally speaking the way these businesses are run is that you hire either a cabinet or a space somewhere in the main shop where you display your goods, for which you pay either a weekly or monthly rent. These type of shops have what's often referred to as 'easy-in easy-out' terms, which means there are no tiresome leases to deal with. You can rent your space for anything from a month to a year or beyond.

You may be required to work in the shop one day a week where you will be responsible for selling other retailers' goods as well as your own. Weekends are usually the busiest times in these types of businesses and you would do well do run your own stand/stall during these periods even though it may not be your turn.

The retailers that I know who rent spaces usually rent a number of them in businesses across the country, so achieving lots of exposure for their goods.

Advantages to renting a small space

☐ Rents are usually fairly low.
☐ It is easy to get in and out.
☐ They can be profitable with the right goods.
☐ You can use your space as a marketing tool for your business. For example, you can have a display area where people can take your brochure or card and order your products online.

Disadvantages of renting a small space

☐ It can be time consuming.
☐ You often get more curious browsers than real buyers.
☐ You can suffer from theft.
☐ It is unsuitable for many businesses.

Nevertheless it's still an option worth considering.

CONCESSION IN A RETAIL AREA

An excellent way of selling your products is to take a concession either in a shopping centre with a mobile kiosk or in another retail business.

For example many garden centres sublet some of their sales areas to businesses which complement theirs while not competing with them. These businesses include bespoke garden furniture companies, pet shops, camping and accessories shops, fish shops, fencing businesses, cycle shops and so on.

The advantages of basing your business at an already an established retail outlet is that you benefit from immediate trade as the garden centre will already have an established and loyal customer base that you can sell to.

Another considerable benefit to your business is car parking. Garden centres tend to be based outside town and city centres and usually have acres of parking available and not a traffic warden to be seen.

 If your goods are heavy or bulky your customers will appreciate not having the headache of stopping outside a high street shop where there is no parking and every likelihood of getting a ticket.

Some shopping centres will allow you to rent a space in their malls where you can set up a temporary display or cart to sell from. Again the main advantage here is you'll have an instant customer base and won't have to shell out on advertisements telling everyone where you are.

One drawback of taking on a concession is that it can be relatively expensive. However I think that instant savings on things like business rates, insurance, water rates, advertising etc, combined with the fact that you will have access to a large and ready-made customer base, can make this a very worthwhile option.

DIRECT MARKETING

Another thing to consider is whether or not your products could be sold by direct marketing techniques. By this I mean purchasing specialist mail order lists and then writing direct to your target market. Most people will describe this as 'junk mail' but if used correctly, targeted mail shots can bring about immediate, impressive results. If you don't believe me then over the next few weeks start taking a closer look at your junk mail. You'll see that it comes from some very credible businesses such as banks, insurance companies, shops, clothes companies etc.

If it wasn't worth doing do you think these highly successful businesses would bother?

How to run your own direct marketing campaign

You will need to obtain an up-to-date mailing list that you can work from. Several marketing companies specialise in selling mailing lists and their advertisements can usually be found by searching on the Internet.

Most companies will offer a service where you can buy a printed mailing list or pre-printed mailing list labels with the names and addresses already on. Although you can save yourself a considerable amount of time by purchasing pre-printed labels there is a big disadvantage to doing this. Remember that your business will not be the only business to have purchased this mailing list, which may mean that your target market becomes familiar, and understandably fatigued, with seeing the same label. So my advice is to purchase the list and then either make up your own labels or if your handwriting is up to it (handwritten envelopes get more attention that printed ones) handwrite all the envelopes.

Before purchasing a mailing list make sure:

- ☐ **You are buying from a reputable source.** If you can't see any client testimonials either on the marketing company's brochure or website they're probably best avoided.

☐ **The list is up to date.** The cheaper the list the more out of date it is likely to be. Ask the company representative to explain not only how they compile their lists but also how up to date they are.

☐ **Quantities.** You will need to buy in sufficiently large quantities to make your campaign work. Depending on what you're selling you can expect a positive reply of approximately 1 per cent. Thus if you're sending out 1,000 letters you can expect 10 positive replies.

Lots of books have been written about direct marketing and if you are thinking of using this marketing technique for your business I would recommend you do further research before buying any lists.

 TIP Although it can be expensive to run a direct marketing campaign it can be well worth it.

EXHIBITION OR TRADE FAIR

Exhibitions and trade fairs can be great places to promote your business.

Exhibitions and shows

Exhibitions are usually open to the public and vary in size. For example, both the London and Southampton annual boat shows attract thousands of potential customers while a local plant or stamp fair may attract far less. However, the potential suitability of a show should not be judged solely on how many visitors it attracts. The most important thing to get right is to make sure that the show is attracting your target market.

Trade fairs

Trade fairs differ to shows in that they are only open to the trade. For example there are gardening trade fairs where everything from plants to the latest garden machinery are exhibited. If you're looking for agents to sell your products then a trade fair is the place to find them. Even if your products are unsuitable to exhibit, trade fairs are an important way of keeping up to date with what's going on in the market where you'll be operating.

Where can you find them?

There are literally hundreds of exhibitions and trade fairs going on throughout the year. The Internet is a great place to find out what's happening, as is your favourite hobby magazine. If you're really stuck to find an exhibition then phone up one of the distributors or manufacturers of a product you buy and ask them they know of any trade fairs or exhibitions.

Getting your own stand

One of the disadvantages of exhibiting at one of the major shows is that because they are so successful it's usually difficult to get a stand and once you get it, it can be very expensive. Smaller shows usually don't fill up as quickly and it's not too costly to rent a stand.

Depending on what you're selling, exhibitions and trade fairs can offer excellent potential. I know of a number of small, independent boat builders who exhibit at two annual boat shows and fill their order books for the following year, which justifies the relatively high price of having a stand there. I also know of other businesses who simply sell their relatively inexpensive cleaning products at these shows and also make sufficient sales to cover their rent, staffing costs and return a healthy profit.

HOTEL FOYER

Depending on your products, hotel foyers can offer excellent potential for a variety of hobby businesses where you can sell souvenirs, crystals, pictures, paintings, craft items, local walking excursions, cycle hire, tours etc.

 The advantage of having your business based in a hotel foyer is that you have an instant shop without all the usual additional business costs such as business rates.

How to set it up

☐ Draw up a list of potentially suitable hotels in your area. You're looking for busy, quality hotels which enjoy all-year-round trade and have enough space in their foyer to site your display cabinet and desk.

☐ Go through your list and identify the hotel that you would most like to trade from and then the next one and so on until you have a numbered list.

☐ Find out the name of the manager and whether or not the hotel is part of a chain of hotels, and if it is the details of their head office. Do not mention at this time what you are looking to do. You're only concerned with getting contact details.

☐ Draft a suitable query letter, which must highlight the benefits to the hotel of agreeing to allow you have a concession in their foyer. Remember you must offer them some powerful benefits, for example, 'Your guests will appreciate being able to view our superior locally-crafted gifts, many of which are not available in the local shops.'

☐ Suggest either paying them a rent or commission on your turnover.

☐ Initially write to the top three hotels on your list. If these are part of a hotel group then you will need to write to the group's chief executive in the first instance. Say that you will phone in the next few days just to make sure they have received your letter and answer any initial questions they may have.

☐ Make your follow-up phone calls and try to gauge whether or not the initial hotels are interested.

TRAIN STATION PLATFORM

Station platforms are also worth considering as a potential location for your business. Much will depend on what you're selling as to how suitable a railway station would be as a location.

 One of the advantages of being based at a busy railway station is the sheer volume of pedestrian traffic that passes through each day.

There are a number of ways you could approach setting up your business. You could either rent an existing kiosk from the railway company, provided of course they have one free, or alternatively you could buy one or have it built.

How to go about getting a site

First find a railway station that would be suitable. If there is already a trader running the type of business you're proposing it's unlikely that your offer would be entertained. For example, most train companies are awash with offers from entrepreneurs to set up food and café businesses. When I spoke to a representative from one of the large train companies she told me that there would be little point in anyone trying to get a catering concession on their busiest platforms as there were already too many. She did go on to say that they would always be pleased to hear from anyone with ideas other than food and drinks.

Once you've identified a potential station then all you have to do is find out which company has the franchise for operating the platform and get in contact with their head office.

CAFÉ, SHOP OR KIOSK

If your business involves creating your own paintings, pictures, crafts, guide books etc, then as well as marketing them online you could also offer them on a sale-or-return basis to local cafés, shops and kiosks.

Getting others to market your goods in return for a commission is the oldest, and probably most reliable way, of building up your sales. Greetings card manufacturers are masters of this form of marketing.

How it works

- ☐ Put together a selection of your products and work how much commission you could comfortably afford to pay someone for selling them on your behalf.

- ☐ Draw up a list of prospective retailers. The reason for working to a pre-prepared list is that in the event you get a hostile reaction from one retailer you won't be put off. Instead you can simply cross their name off your list and continue with the next. Working with a list gives a more targeted approach.

- ☐ Prepare a price list for your products. Try to make it as easy to read and attractive as possible, and either print or photocopy enough lists to cover all your prospective retailers plus some spare ones.

- ☐ Set aside some time to visit all your prospects. The most productive way is to set specific goals. Instead of simply saying that you'll visit all these shops in the next few weeks, set aside a few days and devote this time entirely to visiting your prospects. Not only is it much easier as you will get into a regular sales routine, but also more effective because you're less likely to leave it on the to do list.

Making your presentation

If you haven't already done this sort of selling it can be somewhat daunting. However it is also very easy because you're not actually selling anything – you're giving your customers a way of earning additional sources of income, a powerful benefit!

Generally speaking you will have to make your presentation by cold calling your prospects. I'd advise you don't try to phone and make an appointment as it's unlikely they'll agree to one. Retailers are used to representatives cold calling and most will tell you fairly quickly whether or not they're interested. If they're not, fine. Don't dwell on the rejection, just get on with working through your list.

When you walk into a card shop, café or kiosk, ask to speak to the manager. (The manager may of course be the business owner who may actually be the one you're already talking to.) As soon as you meet the manager/owner introduce yourself. Say that as a local artist/photographer/craftsperson you'd like to offer them the opportunity to sell your products to their customers on a sale-or-return basis.

It's important you use the SOR (sale or return) method – this is standard practice for selling such things as cards, photos, paintings, guide books etc. Obviously if you can get your retailer to purchase a quantity of your goods then great, but a more likely starting point is for you to get your goods on display.

The benefit to the retailer is that there is absolutely no outlay on additional stock. The benefit to your business is you now have a retail outlet from which to sell your goods without having to pay large overheads. All you pay is commission.

How much commission should you offer?

This will depend on your product but most retailers will expect somewhere around the 30 per cent margin. Some will settle for less and others might want more so be prepared to negotiate.

Be careful of offering different commission deals to retailers, as if one finds out that you've offered a better deal to another you'll lose that account. Although many retailers compete with each other much of this is done on a friendly basis with many traders knowing each other. When something new comes on the market it's likely to get discussed and the first topic will be how much they can earn from it. If you find when making your presentation that one retailer will only accept your products on the basis of getting an unreasonable commission, then politely walk away.

When leaving your products you will also need to leave a copy of your stock sheet recording:

- □ an individual description of each product;
- □ retail price of each product;
- □ quantity of products left;
- □ date you'll be calling to restock and take your money.

Collecting your money and restocking

You'll need to work out a cycle of when to go and restock your product and collect what's owing to you. All you have to do is check what stock is left against your original list.

As you work through your round you will find that some retailers will already have done a stocktake and have either a cheque or cash ready for you, while others will be in state of complete chaos and might even say they can't pay you today as they haven't enough money in the till or some other excuse, which is why it's so important to have the agreed date entered on your original stock sheet.

What to do if they don't pay

It's important to have a pre-agreed date so that if you have problems you can remind them that you did check with them to make sure it was a convenient date to return. Don't get angry or demanding as there may actually be a genuine reason why the retailer can't pay you. Prior to your arrival he might have had to pay an unexpected bill or has simply had a poor week's sales takings.

My advice would be to check your stock and replenish where necessary and then agree another date to return. If after this date you're still having problems then you'd be wise to pull out and cut your losses. If the amount that you are owed is large then you should seek to recover your money via the small claims court or by employing a specialist debt recovery firm.

A word on merchandising

One of the biggest problems about using this method is that you will not be the only business competing for space in other people's retail outlets. There will be lots of other companies vying for floor and shelf space who will employ all sorts of techniques to make sure their goods are the most prominently displayed. Don't be surprised if you return after your first month to find you cannot locate your products at all. It won't be the retailer's fault, it will be because other companies employ merchandisers whose job it is to make sure their products stay at the front and others as much out of sight as possible.

If this is happening to you and your sales are suffering then it's time to start your own proactive merchandising. Hopefully the locations you've chosen aren't too far from where you live and you can pay regular visits to your retail outlets. If other merchandisers push your products to the back, you do likewise to theirs bringing your products to the front. As you live locally you will be able visit more regularly and thus win the battle. It'll soon become apparent to the competition that if they touch your display you will return to put it right.

Consider providing your own display stands

It might be worth your while investing in display stands for your products. Certainly this will open up the potential of even more retail outlets who otherwise wouldn't be able to display your products owning to lack of shelf space. Check the Internet for suitable suppliers and make up some advertising logos to go with them.

BOOT FAIRS AND MARKET STALLS

Although I'm not a great fan of boot fairs, they are nevertheless an excellent outlet worth considering to sell your products from.

Just like any other outlet or venue you will have to do your research prior to committing to setting up your stall or stand. The best way to tackle this is to visit as many boot fairs in your area as you possibly can. Remember that most of them will be on at the same time, usually Saturday/Sunday mornings. So allow yourself plenty time for your research. Assess each one and make sure you look closely at the people who are walking around. Ask yourself if these people are going to be interested in what you're selling. If they are, great. You've got yourself a relatively inexpensive part-time outlet for your business. If you think your products or produce aren't suitable then don't despair. Check out all the other boot fairs in your area and don't overlook the indoor markets.

LOCAL AUTHORITY CONCESSIONS

Your local council may provide the solution of where to base your business.

What's involved in taking on a local authority concession

Depending where you live, your local authority may provide concessions for:

- ☐ fast food outlets
- ☐ crazy golf
- ☐ cycle hire
- ☐ boat hire
- ☐ beach goods
- ☐ cafés.

There are a number of way of obtaining a concession:

- ☐ Bid on an existing tender when it comes up for renewal.
- ☐ Purchase an existing concession.
- ☐ Suggest a concession by putting together a proposal.

Bid on an existing concession

The law requires your local authority to offer all concessions for tender once the original concession period has come to an end.

Usually these concessions are advertised in your local newspaper under the public notices section. You can also contact your local council and ask to speak to the concession officer who may be able to give you some indication of what will be coming up for public tender.

Most concessions work on the following basis:

1. The concession is advertised under the public notice section of one or a number of local papers inviting interested parties to make a written request for an information pack.

2. Information packs and tender documents are then sent out. The pack contains information on the concession that is being offered, including any special requirements.

   For example, if it is a boating hire concession there may be stipulations that you must supply your own boats, undertake all maintenance of the lake etc.

   You will also be informed of the date by which the council must receive your written tender bid. If your bid is received after this date it will not be considered.

3. Tender requirements will vary on the concession being offered but most will require you to confirm what rent figure you would pay were you awarded the concession together with other relevant information such as what experience you have in running this type of business etc.

4. Tenders are sent in using a pre-addressed envelope clearly marked for the attention of the officers who will be deciding on who to award them.

5. The envelopes are all opened by at least two council officers and a decision made. This decision is then placed before the relevant council committee for final approval and the successful party is notified.

It's worth knowing that the council are under no obligation to award the concession to the party who bids the highest rent figure. The final decision will be made on number of factors including:

☐ **Performance of the previous tenant** and whether or not they are bidding. If the previous concession holder has managed the business professionally and given a good service to the public it is likely that the council will look favourably on their application as they have proved their capability.

☐ **Experience of running the type of business** that is on offer. Again if someone can demonstrate a particular expertise the council will naturally be more inclined to take their offer more seriously than someone with no experience.

☐ **The rent being offered.** Councils have a duty to the public to ensure that they are getting the best possible return on their concessions, which means that although they don't have to accept the highest bidder, they will have to explain their decision to the committee (made up of elected councillors) if they don't go with the highest bid.

Unless you're already running the concession you won't really know how much to offer in rent. But this shouldn't deter you as everyone else (apart from the existing concession holder) is in the same boat.

Purchase an existing concession

Every so often concessions come for sale. The advantages to purchasing an already up and running concession is that you will be able to see the trading figures, talk to the business owners and investigate locally how well the concession is doing before investing you money.

A disadvantage is that even though you have purchased the business you will still have to submit a tender in the same way as everyone else when your concession term runs out.

Probably the most important question you want answered when considering whether or not to buy an existing concession is to find out why the business is up for sale. It's a good idea to do your own research in addition to the reasons given in any sales particulars. It may be up for sale because the local authority is unhappy with the way it has been run. If this the case do you really want to buy something that already has a poor relationship with the landlords?

As with purchasing any business, you should always employ professional help including a solicitor and an accountant. You will also need to have 'due diligence' undertaken which can be organised by your accountant. Due diligence is a legal term which means having the books and trading claims made by the current owner checked. You also need to check with the local authority that they have granted their permission for the business to be sold.

Suggest a concession

Another way to get a council concession, as we did with our cycle hire business, is to suggest your idea to the council. Provided they have suitable premises or a space available then you're halfway there. All you need to do is convince the council that the business you are proposing would be of benefit to the public and hopefully improve the area.

To suggest a concession:

☐ If possible identify a suitable vacant council-owned property or piece of land where you would like to base your business.

☐ Have a clear idea of the type of business you are proposing to run. In our case this was cycle hire and even if we didn't get a council concession we still planned to go ahead with our venture. So when we came to meet the officers from the council we knew exactly the type of business we were going to set up and were confident with our business plan.

☐ The council won't be particularly interested in what's in it for you – they'll want to know how the wider community will benefit from your proposed business. Therefore make sure you have at least two powerful 'what's in it for them' benefits before you make your initial approach.

Be patient

The key to working on any project that involves the council is to be prepared for sometimes unexplained and lengthy delays. So you must be patient. Getting irate and impatient will not do your cause any good. In my experience the people you will be dealing with – the council's concession officers – will be just as eager as you to see your business up and running and benefitting the local community. However councils are political to the point of tediousness, which means that in all probability everyone from the person who replenishes the loo rolls to the chief executive will probably have to be consulted on your proposal before any go-ahead can be given.

Be flexible

In the event that your proposal is turned down don't be afraid to ask why. It may be that you can revise your proposal and resubmit it so that it fits in more with the council's ethos and requirements.

Don't give up

This is true with everything you do. Sometimes it's easier to give up than put in that revised submission or tweak your idea so it fits into the council's greater scheme of things. Whenever you're tempted to give up, take a small break and clear your head of negative thoughts, get on your bike and go for it again. The things that are really worth getting in this life are often those which we have to fight hardest to achieve.

WHY DO BUSINESSES COME UP FOR SALE?

It's a common misconception that the only reason businesses come up for sale is because they are doing badly. Certainly some businesses will be selling for this reason, but by no means all. Retirement and ill-health force many otherwise profitable businesses to be sold. I've read recently that many successful family businesses are being sold because no one in the family wants to take them over. So there can be a whole range of reasons for businesses coming on the market.

Remember: if you are considering buying a business you should take professional and impartial advice before making any decisions.

Summary

1. When deciding where to sell your goods and services from remember there are lots of options available to you.

2. Hiring space in another business's retail unit is an excellent way of keeping your costs down and making your venture more financially viable.

3. There are times when it will be more cost effective to buy an existing business than start your own. Don't be afraid to investigate these possibilities.

4. Many local authorities offer retail concessions, which can offer attractive prospects in terms of low rents and prominent positions.

5. Beware of shark landlords. Most property leases that you will be offered require you to upkeep and maintain someone else's business. Never underestimate how much this could cost you. Could your business support maintaining a property as well as returning a profit?

6. A high street shop isn't the only option available to you. Look for other low-cost opportunities.

8
YOUR BUSINESS ON THE WORLD WIDE WEB

The Internet offers unlimited potential for home-based entrepreneurs.

Undoubtedly, the greatest single improvement to the fortunes of the home based entrepreneur has been the arrival of the Internet.

Where else can you launch a worldwide business for less than the price of a month's advertising in your favourite magazine?

But despite the opportunities, the Internet is awash with global business failures.

There are any number of reasons for this, but lurking somewhere will either be one or a combination of these factors:

☐ Complete lack of understanding on the part of the business owner as to how the Internet works.

☐ Poorly-designed websites that make the business look amateurish and give the impression of being run from the entrepreneur's spare bedroom.

☐ Websites that are not designed to attract visitors to the site.

So what can you do to ensure that your website does what you want it to?

To answer this question you need to ask yourself *What's your objective in having a website?*

☐ Do you want a site that solely promotes your business and gives information about the services you offer?

☐ Or do you want a website that sells your products online?

☐ Or a combination of sales and promotion?

Before you go any further with your business website you need to be clear about your objectives.

Don't work under the misapprehension that simply because you have a website, visitors will come flocking to your site. The reality is that bringing customers to your website can be a full-time task. Once you get them there your website has to be absolutely right or they'll click their way out to your competitors.

Make no mistake about it – the Internet is cut-throat and there is no place for half-measures, poorly-designed web pages or sites that don't take credit cards.

There are three areas that you need to look at:

- ☐ Creating a website for your business.
- ☐ Marketing your website.
- ☐ Staying ahead of the competition.

Creating a website for your business

As I said earlier, before you go any further and even attempt to build your own site or commission someone to do it for you make sure that you have clearly identified your objective in having your own website. This is absolutely crucial to your future success.

For example, my businesses include a gardening business, cycle shop and boat hire. The objectives for each of my sites differs considerably.

My primary objective in having a site for the **gardening business** is to promote my main gardening business, which is maintenance and landscaping work.

So my site includes:

- ☐ details of the services we offer;
- ☐ reasons why someone should choose my business over my competition;
- ☐ testimonials from delighted customers who have used our service;
- ☐ gardener's diary;
- ☐ contact information;
- ☐ details of any special offers we're running;
- ☐ pictures of work that we have completed.

The site's primary objective is to get people to contact us as opposed to selling them anything. Therefore the success of the site can be gauged in how many enquiries we get through it. The process of turning those inquiries into actual orders is done offline when I go and visit prospective clients.

The main objective for the **cycle business** website is:

- ☐ to sell cycles and accessories in our shop.

The objective differs entirely from that of our gardening business, because not only do we want our website to be a marketing tool for our business, we also want to sell our products online.

The success of this site can be measured in how many new customers it brings to our cycle shop, and how many bikes and accessories we actually sell.

 TIP Write down now what is your site's main objective. Do this and you're halfway towards winning the battle!

BUILD YOUR OWN WEBSITE OR EMPLOY SOMEONE?

When it comes to creating your own website you'll have to decide whether or not you want to create your own site or have someone build it for you.

Personally I prefer to build my own websites for the simple reason that I can update them whenever I like without having to pay fees to a web designer.

The main advantages to creating your own site are:

- ☐ that it is cheaper than employing a designer;

- ☐ that you retain control over your site and can move it to another server if necessary;

- ☐ that you have more control over bringing visitors to your site by adding guest books, free give-aways etc;

- ☐ that you can play around with your site until you get it right without having to pay a designer to do it.

The disadvantages are:

- ☐ unless you do it properly it can look amateurish and destroy your business's credibility;

- ☐ it can be time consuming;

- ☐ you need to know what you're doing and be computer literate.

THE EASIEST WAY TO BUILD YOUR OWN WEBSITE

Sign up to a hosting company which offers template building

You can create a professional-looking site without having to have specialist knowledge. For example, most template websites are simply a matter of pointing at a menu and clicking the feature you want, then adding the text in the boxes.

There is an ever-growing number of companies offering these ready-made templates for your business, but you need to be careful as the quality of the templates can range from absolutely garbage to excellent. Most sites offer a free trial where you can sign up for 24 hours and try out the templates before committing yourself. It's well worth doing this.

Most of these sites also offer to register your chosen domain name for a small fee, which is often included in the price of the hosting. While undoubtedly this is a good idea, make sure that you do not get them to register your domain name until you are absolutely certain that you want to use their templates. Otherwise you may find they will charge you a fortune to transfer your domain name to another competitor.

Build your own site using software

If you have a basic knowledge of HTML or you already have web-building software, for example Dreamweaver or Microsoft FrontPage, you can either build your own site or purchase a ready-made template and then adjust this to suit your needs.

The disadvantage is that you will still need to pay a hosting company to host your site and you will also need to register your name.

My personal preference is to have it all with one company and then if either you need help or there is a problem you only have one company to contact.

Free website hosting and free template

There a number of companies that will allow you use their templates free of charge including hosting your site on one of their servers, but in return your site will either have to display their ads, or visitors will be bombarded with annoying pop-up ads.

My advice is that you should avoid these at all costs. Regardless of how hard you try you simply will not be able to encourage visitors to take your site seriously if their viewing is constantly interrupted by pop-up ads. Neither will you inspire confidence and credibility.

Have a page on an online directory

This is where you buy a page on another website's directory. I can see absolutely no advantage in doing this. The success of your site will depend on factors outside your direct control. You will have no control over the marketing of the parent directory site or have any influence over the direction it goes.

If you're just starting out I would suggest you join a hosting company where you pay a monthly fee for your site, which includes web page templates to get you started and allows you to add outside features like guest boards, newsletter sign-up scripts and so on.

Whatever you choose make sure:

☐ you can update your site content whenever you want and you are not charged for this;

☐ you can add features like guest books, e-zine subscription scripts, credit card processing and so on;

☐ the host site is reputable and you can see examples of other customers' sites. Most sites do this as a matter of course; if you don't see any email them with your request before you decide to sign up;

☐ there is no requirement for you to run others' advertising on your site;

☐ that you can include search engines 'meta tags' in your pages.

DESIGNING YOUR WEBSITE

Always try to make your site interesting and unique, but remember your design should be appealing to visitors and search engines.

With an ever-increasing and bewildering amount of websites available in any particular area your site will have to be good enough to encourage visitors to come in and spend some time. We'll look at the various ways to make your site both interesting and interactive in just a moment, but first I want to introduce you to the two most important principles of good web design:

1. Your site must be search engine friendly.
2. It must be visitor friendly.

Search engine friendly

Make it your number one priority to make your site as search engine friendly as you can. To do this you will not only need to include key words in the main text of your site, but you'll also need to include key-word meta tags in your HTML coding.

There's nothing difficult about doing either of these things. If you've created your own site you can go to http://www.free-webmaster-tools.com/Meta-Tag-Generator.htm where their online software will generate free meta-tags for your website.

Try also to make your domain name relevant to what you're selling online as search engines also search under domain names. However, depending on the area that you're going to operate in, this isn't that easy as the obvious domain names will probably already be taken.

A good domain name will enhance your search engine ratings enormously.

Before adding key words to your site be careful that your site actually contains content relating to these key words. When search engine spiders, or worse still editors, visit your site they will be unlikely to list it if it doesn't bear any relation to your key words.

If, for example, you have a site selling camping gear and you include in your key words 'maps', 'guides', 'camping directories', 'camp sites', but your site doesn't actually contain any of these things you're in trouble. Not only are you running the risk of not being included anywhere by search engines, but equally importantly even if you are listed and visitors come to your site having searched under 'camping directories' they will rightly expect that this is, amongst other things, what you are offering. The chances of them staying in, let alone buying from a site that clearly isn't what it says it is, is highly unlikely.

When it comes to key words and meta-tags, honesty pays.

Visitor friendly

It's amazing how website owners think that visitors to their site want to be bombarded by music or other silly gimmicks like annoying things flying around the screen and getting in the way of seeing what the site has to offer.

If you're ever tempted to include music, remember this. Most work places in the country now have Internet access and I know from previous experience working in a large office that employees often spend time surfing the net when they should be doing other things. But what happens if your music blares out of their speakers?

Music and over-reliance on pop-up ads, gaudy colour schemes and poorly structured pages, will drive visitors away from your site in seconds. Once they're gone, that's it.

When coming up with a suitable design for your website try to keep it simple so that it's:

☐ easy to navigate, which includes providing a navigation bar on all your pages;

☐ easy to read – the colour of the text doesn't clash with the background colour of the page;

☐ free from large graphics that take time to download.

Spend time looking at as many websites as you can. Save the ones you like in your favourites folder. When you feel you have exhausted your search go back through them and start pruning your list. Strike off those that don't immediately grab you and then keep on going until you are left with about three or four websites that you really like, and build or model your own around their design.

I'm not suggesting you copy or mimic other people's sites but get your ideas for colour schemes and navigation structures from these. Surf any of the top search engines and you'll immediately notice that they all bear similarities to each other. This isn't because they are trying to clone their competitors' sites, but because certain colour schemes work better than others.

For example, how many times have you visited a website where the colour of the text clashes so much against the page's background colour that you can't read the writing? Or you visit a site, find what you want to buy but give up after many unsuccessful attempts trying to find how you buy it?

EMPLOYING A WEB DESIGNER

As I've said earlier, I personally prefer to build my own sites either using templates or website software such as Microsoft FrontPage. However there are certain businesses where the investment in hiring a company to design your website is well worth it.

If part or all of your business is going to involve taking online bookings, then you'd certainly benefit from a website where visitors can check availability and make and pay for their bookings online.

 The key to running any successful online business is to make it as easy as possible for your customers to spend their money on your site.

From the moment your visitor arrives at your site you want them to know that you're not only open for business, but here to help.

Imagine walking into to a high street travel agent and making an enquiry only to be told they'll get back to you sometime in the future. Whilst some people might go home and wait, most won't and will go into the next travel agent and book their holiday there.

It's the same online. One of the Internet's primary advantages is that everything is immediate. You can download brochures, prices lists, buy goods, book holidays and flights all at the click of a button. So if your business is going to be operating in these areas I recommend you consider employing a specialist.

Where do you find a designer?

I regularly get emails and telephone calls from companies trying to sell me web design. Occasionally I've been tempted to ask them to give me a quote and without exception I've been disappointed. Rather than offer bespoke web design packages they've offered to create up to six websites for me to choose from, which appear to be nothing other than cheap-looking, uninspiring website templates. When I've told them that I want to be able to update the content of my site regularly, they've given me a ridiculous price to do this.

By far the best way of finding a website designer for your business is to find a number of sites that you like the look of. Usually somewhere at the end of the home page will be a little logo or message saying who built the site. If there isn't one, send an email to the company saying how much you like their website and would they please let you have the details of the company who designed it.

But make sure that:

- ☐ you like the person who is going to be working on your site;

- ☐ you get a written estimate for your website package;

- ☐ you read a copy of the company's terms and conditions and you understand and are happy with them;

- ☐ you know how much the whole package will cost including hosting fees etc, and what will happen after your first year. Some companies may offer what appears to be a great deal in year one but will then charge you a fortune thereafter.

Marketing your website

Creating your website is really the easiest part of setting up your online business. The hardest part, as with all businesses, is to get visitors through your doors, and once in, to buy from you.

Working on the assumption that you are going to be using your website both as a marketing tool for your business and a place where customers can buy your goods, you're going to have to work to a strategy if you are to succeed:

1. Bring visitors to your website.
2. Once they've arrived, get visitors to buy whatever it is you're selling.
3. Get them to come back again.

GETTING VISITORS TO YOUR WEBSITE

Obviously you're not going to be able to market or sell your products and services to anyone unless you actually get them to your site. There are a number of ways you can do this:

- □ upload your site to search engines
- □ list your site on specialist directories
- □ links
- □ webrings
- □ adwords at Google
- □ affiliate programmes
- □ contribute to other sites' newsletters and e-zines
- □ offline marketing techniques.

Search engines

One of the most frustrating things about search engines is that it can take a relatively long time before your site gets listed. My own experience has been that this can be anywhere between three to six months. Of course it may take you longer depending on your site and the market you are going to be operating in. However, I believe the wait is worth it and I also believe that given the time it might take to get your pages listed you should do this as soon as you can.

 Regardless of any other technique you use to bring visitors to your site you must never ignore search engines. At the time of writing, search engines are still responsible for bringing the largest volumes of surfers to websites.

Search engines work on the principle that surfers type key words into their search fields and then the search engine suggests a list of potentially suitable sites.

While every search engine may have different criteria for listing sites, most will use ROBOTS, or spiders, to search the Internet for pages to list. Most will also have a facility on their home page where you can suggest a site for them to look at.

You can suggest your site by submitting your URL (Internet address). The advantage of doing it this way is that rather than waiting around for their BOTS or spiders to find your site, you're suggesting they come and visit. Even though most will visit your site it still takes time for your pages to get listed, if at all.

I mentioned earlier the importance of making sure that your site is as search engine friendly as possible and that your key words accurately reflect what your site is about. This is important as when the search engine's agents visit they will go through all the pages of your website and check to see whether or not your website actually is what it says it is before they'll consider listing you.

 Remember that search engines are businesses. The quality of their service relies on the accuracy of the sites they suggest when people put key words into their search fields, so it's essential the information they recommend is as accurate as possible.

Before submitting your site to search engines you should:

1. Make sure that your site is finished. This means no 'under construction' signs or 'coming soon' messages.

2. Draw up a list of all the search engines that you would like to have your site listed on. Obviously there are the main ones – Yahoo! and Google, but don't overlook the smaller engines and particularly any ones that relate to your hobby or interest.

3. Set aside some time and sit down and submit your URL to all the engines on your list. I've found doing this in one session to be far easier than on an ad-hoc basis.

4. Keep your list and check back at regular intervals to see whether your site's been listed. Remember it can take a long time before you get listed, sometimes as long as a year. Don't under any circumstances be tempted to keep re-submitting your URL until your site gets listed. Be patient and keep monitoring.

You'll often hear about companies claiming that they can ensure your site is uploaded to as many as 800 search engines. Of course they charge for this service and the costs can be high, plus there's no guarantee of what service engines you will be listed on.

Both your time and money would be better invested promoting your own site because your primary objective is to promote your site, whilst these companies' objective is to make profit from you.

The Internet is continuously changing so it's worth spending some time investigating further how search engines work and what you need to do to ensure your page is listed.

Specialist directories

Every hobby will have its own specialist directory website, many of which will be run by amateur enthusiasts as opposed to businesses. It's well worth getting a link on these sites and you'll find that most will include your site within a few weeks of you submitting your information.

The way to find the best directories is to use search engines. In the search field type in the sort of key words that you would expect that visitors coming to your site would use. The search engine will then suggest a number of sites and you should go through these and pick out any directory sites. Obviously if they're easy to find via search engine they're worth having your site listed on their directory.

Many will insist that you post a link from your site to theirs before they will consider listing you. If this is the requirement then make sure you do add their details in your links section before registering.

Links

Getting a link on the right website can result in visitors flocking to your site. I have had thousands of pounds worth of business from one website's links page.

Again what's needed here is a proactive approach, which means visiting as many sites as you can, compiling a list of these sites, and then contacting them asking them to place a link on their site. Your email request should include the fact that you'd be pleased to put a reciprocal link on your site.

The easiest way to find the best sites for links is to learn from your competitors. So if you haven't already, get a list of your competitors' URLs (website addresses). Then go to the search engine AltaVista, which is located at: http://www.altavista.com.

Once there you can find where your competitors are linking by entering link:competitorsdomainname.co.uk.

For example, let's say you're going to be selling kites and one of your main competitors is John's Classic Kites and their website address is www.johnsclassickites.co.uk. All you'd have to enter is links: www.johnsclassickites.co.uk. In a single search you will bring up all the sites your business should be linked to if at all possible.

The golden rule when it comes to asking another site to include your link is to read their links policy. Here they will tell you their submission policy, which could include that you must have a link on your site linking back to them before they will consider you. Or that you have to display one of their banners, or any one of a number of other things.

If you don't hear from them after a few weeks send them another polite email chasing them up.

Webrings

Webrings are ideal for hobby businesses because, unlike traditional search engines, webrings are usually run by enthusiasts for enthusiasts of a particular hobby or interest.

The advantages to promoting your site by joining a webring are:

☐ they cost nothing to join;

☐ provided your site fits in with the webrings genre, there's no reason why you won't be listed;

☐ some webrings will include you immediately or shortly after you join.

The first thing you need to do is identify which webrings would be suitable for your products or services. You may already know of a webring that might be suitable and if this is the case then all you have to do is send a request to the owner to join their ring. The webring owner will then visit your site to see whether or not it's suitable in terms of content, ethos etc. If it is you'll be accepted and sent some HTML code and graphics or banners that will you have to include on your site. As soon as this is done visitors to the ring will be able to visit your site.

The two main webring directories can be found at http://www.ringsurf.com and http://www.webring.com/rw. You can also search under key word 'webring' using search engines.

If you can't find a suitable webring for your site then you could start your own. To do this you can apply to Webring or Ringsurf or use any of the major search engines. As soon as you get another four websites to join your ring you will be listed in the main directories.

With the growth and popularity of the Internet I think you will find a number of rings suitable for you to join. If you don't, ask yourself why.

 While not finding a suitable webring shouldn't stop you from going ahead with your business, it does suggest that maybe your business idea needs some more research.

Adwords at Google

At the time of writing the search engines Google and Yahoo! both offer businesses an opportunity to promote their website through an 'adword' scheme.

You bid on a certain amount of key words or phrases, that visitors might use to search for whatever it is you're selling. Which page your site gets listed on will depend on how much you bid.

For example in our Dutch bike business we could go to Google or Yahoo! and bid on the words 'Dutch bike'. Lets say we offer them 5p a word. This means that as soon as someone searches Google and enters the key words 'Dutch bike' they will at some point be presented with our site. And as soon as they enter our site through the search engine our account at Google will get debited by the amount we have bid on the word.

You open an account and then pre-pay an amount into it, which is then debited until either there is nothing left in your account or you pay more money in. How high your listing gets in the search engine will depend on whether you have been outbid on that particular key word.

Because if someone else is also selling Dutch bikes and they bid 10p on the same words their website details will be listed before ours.

The system has its advantages but the biggest drawback is that you are being charged for every visitor who comes to your site via this search engine, which mightn't be that cost effective. Nevertheless it's worth checking this scheme out to see if it is suitable for your business.

Affiliate programmes

Affiliate programmes operate on the basis that either you sell other businesses' goods and services from your website for which you earn a commission, or other websites sell your products and you pay them a commission.

Probably the most popular affiliate programme on the Internet is run by the giant online book retailer Amazon which has successfully run their affiliate scheme since 1996. You sell their goods from your website and earn a commission. This is how you do it:

1. Fill out an online application form to become an affiliate.

2. Amazon then visit your website and assess it for suitability and compatibility with their own goals and ethos.

3. If you are accepted you will be given special log on details and when you visit Amazon's website you can choose whatever goods you want to sell on your website.

4. You then cut and paste simple HTML code into your website, which displays whatever products you have chosen.

5. When visitors 'buy' from your website they will be automatically taken to Amazon's site where the sale, including processing of credit cards etc, takes place.

6. Each sale earns you a commission, which you can either take as an Amazon gift voucher or have paid into your account.

Most affiliate programmes work on this basis. There are all sorts of programmes that you can join from selling books to flights. Even the main DIY companies are now offering affiliate programmes.

 You will only earn commissions if your site already has customers coming to it. Joining a programme won't actually drive customers to your site, which is why it's well worth considering offering your own affiliate programmes.

There are two ways you can organise your own affiliate programme. Either offer your own programme by advertising it on your website and contacting other websites that you think might be interested in selling your goods and services. Or join one of the marketing companies which specialise in running affiliate programmes and for a fee they will recruit affiliates on your behalf and work out which one has sold what and to whom.

The advantages of working with a specialist marketing company are that your programme will gain immediate credibility which is something that can be difficult to achieve on your own. They also take away the headache of trying to work out which of your associates has sold what. Obviously the more products you offer through your site the harder this will be and the only reliable way of working out your affiliate sales is to purchase specialist software. This software could cost you anywhere from £200 to £20,000 depending on what you require.

At the time of writing http://www.affiliatewindow.com is probably the UK's largest affiliate management company. It's free to sign up to their website and browse all the affiliate programmes that you can apply to join. They also offer merchant schemes where they will, for a fee, manage your affiliate programme for you.

If you want to go it alone and purchase your own software or find out more about running your own schemes, the following websites should be useful:

☐ http://www.affiliatezone.com
☐ http://www.affiliateshop.com
☐ http://www.myaffiliateprogram.com.

Specialist companies come and go and it's always worth doing your own checks to find out the most up-to-date affiliate programmes and software tools. All you have to do is search the major search engines using key words 'affiliate programmes', 'affiliate software' or 'run your own affiliate programme'.

The power of newsletters and e-zines shouldn't be underestimated when promoting a new site. There are literally thousands of newsletters and e-zines published every second and the reason for their growing popularity is that subscribers benefit from reading the latest news and hot tips about whatever interests them and advertisers get to promote their website.

Many of the larger newsletters and e-zines now sell advertising space along the lines of a magazine or newspaper. Rates can be expensive and unless you've got something either unique or with worldwide appeal, I'd recommend you invest your time and energy in promoting your website in other ways.

Offline marketing techniques

As well as promoting your site online you should also consider some offline marketing, especially if your site has some sort of local appeal.

For example, our gardening business site has been set up primarily to promote our services in our immediate locality. Obviously there is a limit to how far we will travel and even though our site is up for the whole world to see, we're really only interested in promoting it locally.

Our offline marketing techniques include:

☐ **putting our website address on all our promotional literature** including business cards, brochures, posters, flyers and even on our T-shirts and fleeces;

☐ putting our **website address** on our company vehicles;

☐ having our **website address** as part of our letterhead;

☐ **a paragraph in every letter we write**, saying that if you want to see examples of our work and read what our customers say about us visit us online at www.paulpower.co.uk;

☐ **press releases and letters to the editor.** Writing to your hobby magazine and letting them know that you've just opened a new, specialist website is a great way of getting free publicity. If this doesn't work you can also write to the editors of newspapers and magazines asking if their readers would help you with your site by sending you their favourite tips or helping with someone other problem.

Part of our sales policy for our gardening business is that we don't pay for advertising. We run our own direct marketing using techniques we've perfected over the years we've been trading. But if we were to advertise, I'd include our website in every ad we run.

It's amazing how many companies don't include their website in their advertisements or even on their business cards. I'm always intrigued why they don't and whenever I ask it usually comes down to the same old problem – the website address is too long for the small advertisement.

This is one of the problems if you choose to host your website with a free hosting service. Rather than have a short, crisp, domain name you'll end up with something that no one will ever be able to remember and you won't be able to include in any of your publicity material.

 Think carefully before deciding on a domain name. Choose one that people will remember, and that looks good on all your publicity.

Staying ahead of the competition

As we've seen, getting visitors to your site is only one half of the battle. Now you've got them coming you want to ensure they're going to pay regular return visits.

If you advertise your business in your hobby magazine your potential customers receive a regular copy of their favourite magazine, either monthly or quarterly, and as soon as they see your advertisement are reminded of what you're offering.

This sort of continued exposure to your sales message is vital to stimulate sales. Experts believe that potential customers often need to see your sales message as many as five times before making a purchase. If this is true it means that unless you encourage visitors to make regular repeat visits to your site you are losing out on an enormous amount of potential sales.

ENCOURAGING VISITORS TO RETURN TO YOUR SITE

1. Ensure visitors bookmark your site.
2. Run regular competitions.

3. Provide tips of the day.
4. Offer free samples of your products.
5. Run your own newsletter or e-zine.
6. Create your own mailing lists.
7. Include an advice column.
8. Have a visitors' forum where issues can be debated and discussed.
9. Include a recommended links section.
10. Include job opportunities pages.
11. Have book reviews and product tests.

Ensure visitors bookmark your site

While some visitors will find your site through links on other websites, search engines and your ongoing marketing, many others will simply land there, not too sure how they got there. This sort of thing happens to me regularly where I'm looking for something, then follow links and more links and eventually find a really useful and interesting site. Then once I've left the site I've been unable to find it again. The solution is to bookmark it.

The way to get visitors to bookmark your site is to ask them! Of course to do this you need to offer them a benefit. For example let's imagine you're running a site for sailing enthusiasts. Visitors will need to see some immediate benefit to bookmarking your site. So if you say,

This site is regularly updated with
the industry's top sailing jobs.

Bookmark this site now to make sure you
don't miss out on the best opportunities.

You have a textbook marketing strategy, which is to offer a benefit followed by a call to action.

 Don't only include an invitation to bookmark on your home page. Many visitors may reach your site in different ways. Include invitations and reminders to bookmark your site on a number of different pages.

Run regular competitions

Offering visitors the opportunity to win something from your site is not only a great way of getting them to return but it's also brilliant for getting them to sign up to your regular newsletter or e-zine. This way you can keep them stimulated with all the latest news from their favourite hobby as well as regularly exposing them to your sales message. (We'll look at what's involved in writing your own newsletter later.)

☐ **Prizes**: Make sure that the prize you're offering doesn't stop people from buying your products. For example if your top-selling item is a unique guide book and you offer this as a prize, you may find that a proportion of people who would otherwise have purchased your guide book will postpone this in the hope they'll win one. The best prizes to offer are those that don't compete with your own products and services but have some relevance to your visitors.

☐ **Benefit:** There must be some benefit to you to offering visitors the chance to win something. The most important benefit is to have people sign up to your regular newsletter so that you can keep in touch with them. Therefore make sure that in order to enter your competition they have to sign up to your newsletter.

☐ **Regular prizes:** Keep your site fresh by offering regular prizes so when visitors do return they can see the content has changed and the site will appear more alive and fresh.

Provide tips of the day

Hobby businesses are ideal platforms for providing tips of the day. I know of one model boat builder who subscribes to as many sites as he can just to get the tips. He's adamant that finding out about shortcuts is well worth it. And he also buys regularly from the sites which offer tips.

You can write your own tips, which can be one simple sentence or include more elaborate tips with drawings and pictures.

Don't forget also to encourage site visitors to submit their tips, which will not only reduce your workload but also make the site more sticky as visitors will get a buzz from seeing their tip online.

 Create an archive where visitors can browse through previously published tips.

Offer free samples of your product

This won't suit every business, but if you can allow your visitors to sample or experience a free trial of your product or service it is an excellent way of both keeping people coming back to your site and getting new business.

Magazine publishers use this marketing technique all the time to sell subscriptions. They offer an initial free trial period of their magazine, after which you can either cancel your subscription or keep it going. It's a great way of generating instant customers. Who can refuse a free trial period?

Could this sort of marketing be used to promote your products or services online? Products which can be offered as free samples include:

☐ samples from guidebooks, recipe books, how-to style books etc;
☐ trial subscriptions to hobby magazines, newsletters etc;
☐ allowing visitors to advertise their own goods for sale free of charge on your website message board;
☐ free delivery on orders over a certain value.

The most important thing when running any sort of free giveaway or special offer is that it must have a sense of urgency. The best way to do this is to give your offer a cut-off date.

Take advantage of our free give away:
Book and pay for the walking holiday of your choice
before 31 March and we will give you two extra days completely free.

If you advertise that you regularly run free offers visitors will be encouraged to return to your site. A great way of making sure they do is offering them the opportunity to sign up for your regular newsletter where they'll be the first to hear about your free offers.

By getting visitors to sign up to your newsletter you'll be able to remind them that not only are you still around and offering terrific products and services, but also giving away some great offers.

Run your own newsletter or e-zine

The most important thing to remember when creating your e-zine or newsletter is that there must be a powerful benefit to get your visitors to subscribe to your listings. There's little point in saying 'Sign up for our free newsletter', as visitors won't bother. Most of us suffer from email overload and the last thing we want is yet more of it.

So make sure you offer a powerful benefit: 'Be the first to hear about our regular give-aways and special offers by signing up for our free newsletter.' Or just include the benefit in the title of the newsletter. For example, our gardening newsletter is called *Top Tips For Gardeners*, which in itself is a benefit.

I searched around for ages trying to think of a suitable title for our newsletter and eventually sat down and wrote down all the things I was going to include in my publication. When my list went on to several pages I began to realise that what I was planning to put together wasn't a newsletter, but a book! So I went back through my notes and scaled down what I was planning and found the only way I could really put together something useful and beneficial was to offer readers the benefit of my practical gardening experience in the form of tips. I've now built up a loyal readership who not only read my e-zine but also contribute to it by emailing me their tips.

Create your own mailing lists

Make it a habit to collect email addresses. Collect them when customers order your products, enquire about your products, pay for your products. Building your email contact list should be one of your primary and ongoing objectives.

 TIP   Time your emails to fit in with the seasonal swings of your business.

If your business is selling walking holidays then send your e-zines to coincide with annual holidays, bank holidays and so on.

Another way to collect email addresses is to have a guest book on your site. Visitors have to sign up to your guest board before they can post messages. As part of their membership you can send them your regular e-zine, which of course they can opt out of at any time.

There are some people who should be on your list. To get the following people on your email list you will need to be proactive. If you wait until they join of their own accord it might never happen, so contact them and ask them if they would like to join. I've yet to have anyone say no.

1. Editor of your local paper.
2. Editor of your favourite hobby magazine/newsletter.
3. Your financiers, if you have any.
4. Your bank manager.
5. Your suppliers (suppliers will be better able to serve your needs if they know more about your business).
6. Managers of any professional/trade organisations that you belong to.

It's important to get these people on your e-zine circulation. Many, if not all, will be impressed that you've bothered to ask them. As well as increasing your businesses credibility, you are also building on existing relationships.

Setting up an automated newsletter

The greatest advantage of having an online business is that it never closes. Long after you've gone to bed for the night people can be browsing your products and services, and hopefully either requesting more information or buying online. Even though there's no one actually running your site, your site needs to be able to run on autopilot, which is why you need to use what is known as autoresponders.

Here's how they work.

Sign up to a site that offers an autoresponder service (see below). As soon as you become a member you can then cut and paste some codes into your site, which will create a visitor sign-up box on your web page.

The code can be customised so you can include your powerful benefit message to hook subscribers into signing up. As soon as visitors sign up you will be sent an email notifying you of this and the visitor will get an automatic email back from the autoresponder, but it will appear as if it's come from you. Again, you can customise your message to say whatever you want.

If you are offering a newsletter then say something like, 'Thanks very much for signing up for our newsletter; the next issue will be delivered to you shortly.'

Your visitor's email address is then automatically added to your subscription list and next time you write your newsletter you can send it using your autoresponder, which will email it to all those on your subscription lists.

 An autoresponder is not just useful for sending out newsletters. You can use it for a whole range of marketing and sales devices.

Here are some other ways to use it.

☐ Instead of displaying your prices on your website you can invite your visitors to submit their email address using your text box link (autoresponder) promising them you'll email them a current up-to-date price list by return. You can send them a quick follow-up email a few days later asking them to contact you if they have any questions or would like to book. You can continue to send them emails (without overkill) at regular intervals announcing price increases etc.

☐ Use the autoresponder to send out free information. For example if you're running walking holidays you could invite readers to sign up to receive a free walking guide, which would then be automatically emailed to them. You could then set your autoresponder to send them a follow-up email in a few days time inviting them back to your site as you've now either updated the content, reduced prices, added new products etc.

☐ If your hobby business involves cooking, invite your visitors to sign up for some free recipes. Again your autoresponder could send these one at a time over how ever long a period you wish. This is a great way of building up client trust and allowing potential customers to get a taste of just how great your business is.

Used correctly autoresponders can send your sales rocketing, be careful you don't use them to the point of overkill or your customers will get so fed up they unsubscribe.

The most popular free autoresponders can be accessed when you sign up to http://www.freeautobot.com. The advantage to using this site is that you can pre-write a whole number of emails which will then be automatically sent at the times you pre-program. For example, your first email could be a complete price listing for your products followed up a few days later with a special offer if you buy today. This can be followed up a few weeks later, with another free offer.

I also like Constant Contact (http://constantcontact.com), which I believe is excellent for anyone wanting to publish their own e-zines or newsletters. This site has lots of brilliant features and your newsletters are made to look striking and professional. This site will offer to send your newsletters free to your first 50 subscribers after which you pay a nominal monthly fee. If you're really serious about setting up your own newsletter this site is definitely worth checking out. What I like most about this and Freeautobot is that your emails will not come with third party advertisements – something I believe you should avoid at all costs.

Lots of companies offer free web hosting and free autoresponders and it's tempting to sign up to them. All too late you realise that your emails or website are surrounded with all sorts of advertisements, which will do nothing for your credibility and will undoubtedly kill any off any chance you have of encouraging new business.

Include an advice column

The reason hobbies offer such great business potential is that at any given time there will always be newcomers to your particular interest and their quest for knowledge will be insatiable. By including a free advice column on your website you will encourage repeat visits, build up a loyal readership and get instant credibility as an expert in your field.

The following tips should help you run your own advice column.

☐ **It must free!** Don't be tempted to charge a membership to access the advice section. Rarely does this work and even if visitors do pay you to access this area of your site their expectations may well exceed what you're capable of offering and thus damage your main objectives – either to sell them a product or service or promote your business.

☐ **Make it interactive.** Even if you are an expert in your chosen field you should make your advice column more interactive by getting your visitors to post their questions and then inviting other visitors to answer them. The advantage of doing this is that you will attract more regular visitors who will want to give advice as well as simply reading your answers. You'll also find some engaging debates will take place as visitors disagree with one another's advice, making your site even more popular. Just make sure you include a disclaimer somewhere to the effect that you take no responsibility for the advice given and that this advice may not necessarily reflect your own views.

☐ **Keep an archive.** As your site grows in popularity and you get more and more material in your column break it down into sections and keep it in archives. This will allow visitors new to your site to search under different categories and make it easier to find the information they're looking for. It will also reduce the number of people posting repeated requests for advice that has already been discussed.

☐ **Monitor your column.** It's important to make sure that posters aren't being rude or aggressive to each other. Your aim is to provide a friendly, supportive advice column where visitors don't feel intimidated.

Have a visitors' forum

This is similar to the above. You can either just run an advice column or extend it to something a little more like allowing your visitors to post items for sale, items wanted, personal messages etc.

 The more interactive and interesting you make your forum the more people will come back to it.

Again there are lots of companies that will provide you with a free visitors' forum board, which you can customise to knit into your own site. To find a suitable one search 'free forum board for your website' and go through the lists of sites offering this. Again make sure that visitors won't be beaten to death with free advertisements and annoying pop-ups every time they read or post a message.

Include a recommended links section

As well as actively encouraging your visitors to suggest suitable links for your site you should also search for your own sites to include. Draw up a list and contact them all asking whether or not they would like a free link on your site and in turn asking them if they would they put a reciprocal link to your site.

Whatever you do don't be tempted to charge people to put links on your site as this doesn't work.

Don't forget to make a list of your competitors' website addresses and find out where they are linked to, then approach these sites and ask them to add your site to their links.

Remember to check through your links regularly to make sure that they are all working and the sites they relate to are still relevant to what your site is offering.

Include job vacancies

Adding links to job vacancies on your site is always worth considering as so many people now use the Internet to search for a new job or career.

There are as number of ways you can do this:

☐ Include a situations vacant section on your visitors' forum.
☐ Search for interesting vacancies and post links to your site.
☐ Include a situations vacant column in your newsletter.

My favourite way is to include a round-up of interesting job vacancies in your newsletter. Do this and you're adding another powerful benefit for people to sign up to your newsletter.

All you have to do is spend a little time every month looking through your magazines and other websites and then include this information on your site and in your newsletter.

Have book reviews and product tests

If you're stuck for things to get your forum off the ground, you could create a number of sections including book reviews, product tests, price comparisons etc, and encourage your visitors to post their views.

What makes this worthwhile is that if someone posts a review of a well-known book or product the search engine robots and spiders may well index that page using the book or product title as a keyword, which could bring lots of visitors to your site that you wouldn't normally get.

How much time do you spend on your website?

You may have come across Internet business opportunities where they conjure up the image that running one of these businesses only involves a few minutes of your time answering emails while your website does all the work.

Don't be fooled. Starting and running an online business takes just as much time as running any other business. Of course the main advantage of having an online business is that it's open when you're doing other things and reaches a greater and more diverse market place than any traditional shop.

You should spend as much time as you possibly can actively promoting your website and making sure that the content is interesting, fresh and appealing and that all working parts, guest books etc actually do work. We'll look in a moment at how you can run diagnostic checks on your website, but get into the habit of checking everything regularly. Particularly features like 'buy me now' buttons, shopping carts, online forms etc.

Get more out of your time:

☐ Set yourself daily, weekly and monthly goals and tasks.

☐ Every day, whether on or offline, do something to promote your site.

☐ Do what you say you will. If you promise visitors a weekly/monthly newsletter, then deliver on this promise.

☐ Monitor the volume of traffic to your site and try out different ways of increasing your traffic.

☐ Make sure the content pages are up to date and relevant. How many sites have you visited in the summer where the home page still has an autumn or winter theme?

Obviously you can save lots of time by making your website as automated as possible, but you will still need to promote your site making sure that you expose your business to the widest possible audience.

 The more time you invest in developing and promoting your online business the greater the rewards.

I can't imagine you would want to spend anything less than a couple of hours a day, five days a week on your site until it really gets off the ground. Whenever you hear those Internet business gurus flannel on about days spent lazing on the beach or the golf course or sailing your yacht around the world, be very sceptical. Successful online businesses don't just happen – they are created and re-created until they achieve their goals to sell or promote your products and services online.

IS YOUR SITE WORKING AS WELL AS IT COULD BE?

If you have built your own site and are going it alone you must be absolutely sure that your website is running correctly. Some of things you need to consider are:

☐ **Browsers.** Although your website might look fine through your Internet browser this doesn't mean it will look ok on them all. Check how your site looks both through Internet Explorer and Netscape browsers.

☐ **Screen size.** Lots of people now use laptops and small screen monitors. How does your site look through a laptop screen or a small monitor? A common and easily made mistake is to create a site that fits wonderfully into your own cinema screen size monitor without making sure it'll fit into a comparatively tiny laptop screen.

☐ **Pictures.** A pet hate of mine is arriving at a website I'm interested in browsing only to find the pictures are so huge it seems to take forever for them to download. Make sure that your pictures, graphics, banners etc aren't slowing down your site. Where possible try to run your images through a software program where you can resize everything so it all downloads really quickly.

☐ **Music.** Beware of the consequences of adding music to your pages. The quality of the reproduction will depend on the speed of your visitor's Internet connection. Remember also that unless your site is actually music related most visitors will neither be impressed or encouraged to return if they're greeted with music on their arrival. If, and this is a big if, you must have music on your site make sure you allow your visitors to turn off the music and display your 'click here to turn the music off button' where everyone can see it.

As well as making your own checks you can also run some online tools, which will check that your HTML code, links etc are all in good working order. Some sites that offer this service include Site Inspector: http://www.siteinspector.com, and Net Mechanic: http://www.netmechanic.com/toolbox/html-code.htm.

Check to see if you're listed in the search engines

One of the most frustrating things about search engine submissions is that they won't tell you when and if your pages have been listed. The last thing you want to do is to keep re-submitting your site – do this and you run the risk of being accused of spamming and you'll never get listed.

An easy way to see if your site is listed is to go the search engine AltaVista (http://www.altavista.com). Once there check by entering the following in the search field: url:*yourdomainname*.co.uk/directory/page.html.

You will then be able to see where you are listed. As well as the above you can also go to any search engine and enter your domain name to see if any of your pages are listed.

Don't forget also to go the main search engines and use the key words that you would expect those looking for your site to use. For example, if you're running painting holidays in Wales, then go to Google or Yahoo! or one of the other main search engines and check to see what comes up.

As soon as you see a competitor's site write down their domain name and use the technique I showed you earlier to see who they are linked to, which is where you want to be also.

As I said earlier, there are a number of commercial sites who, for a relatively hefty fee, promise to submit your site to lots of search engines. They'll only *submit* your site to these search engines; there's no guarantee that your pages will get listed.

A number of sites that offer a submission service are listed below. You may find that the cost of purchasing their submission package is justified depending your site's objectives.

- □ Site Announce: http://www.siteannounce.com.
- □ Submit it: http://www.submit-it.com.
- □ Get Submitted (web hosting, marketing, site submission). http://www.get submitted.com.

Software and sites are changing all the time so play around with search fields using key words such as 'submit your site to search engines' etc.

Do you know who is visiting your site?

I like to know who is visiting our websites as not only does this help with determining how successful our promotional strategies are, but it also means we can then tailor our products and services to our visitors.

There are a number of ways you can find out more about your visitors. For example, your website host may provide you with a log report recording your site's activity, or you could add a tracking service to your site.

Extreme Tracking (http://www.extreme-dm.com) offer a free tracking service. All you have to do is register with the site and then follow the online instructions. They will give you some HTML code to paste into your pages and this will record your site's activity.

If your provider already supplies you with log files then you'll need to be able to interpret the data by subscribing to a web traffic analysis service, for example Analog: http://www.analog.cx.

eBay

eBay needs neither introduction or explanation. At the time of writing it is the world's largest online market place and a virtual Mecca for hobby enthusiasts.

OPPORTUNITIES FOR HOBBY BUSINESSES

eBay offers enormous opportunity for any collector both to sell and source their goods. Some collectors I know have shut their shops and now trade exclusively online while others have kept their shops, but vastly increased their sales by selling on eBay.

My own view is that not every business will suit eBay retailing. In fact in some cases selling your goods via their auction process may actually devalue your products as everyone bidding will expect to get them at a reduced price. For example I've noticed that the specialist Dutch bikes that we sell in our business seldom manage to achieve their reserve price.

However this hasn't stopped me from using eBay. We've purchase all sorts of bits and pieces at hugely reduced prices for our business. Because eBay works as an auction the effects of supply, or should I say over-supply, has both a dramatic and near instant effect on prices.

We have found eBay an excellent place to purchase:

- □ quality used and often near-new office equipment
- □ tools for our bike and gardening business
- □ low-cost packaging materials for our mail order business
- □ stationery packs
- □ accessories for our hire business
- □ memorabilia for use in our marketing campaigns.

Before we purchase anything for our business we now check on eBay. Doing this has not only saved us thousands of pounds but also made us far more conscious of how much we spend. Prior to eBay we wasted hours searching through catalogues checking for prices only to choose a supplier, contact them and then find out they were either out of stock or there had been a price increase.

 TIP Setting up and starting your business is probably going to cost you far more than you originally anticipated. Try to source all you can using ebay or similar auction sites.

I know of one mobile caterer who spent an absolute fortune on new catering equipment only to find that he didn't like the business he'd got into. When he went to sell his expensive equipment he found he could only get a fraction of what he'd originally paid for them. Why? Because the company that had sold him all this equipment sold 'business packages'. In other words they sold him a business idea. Buy one of our super-duper catering trailers and become the next McDonald's. Of course he wasn't alone and judging by the pages and pages of this sort of equipment that come up on eBbay every week it's clear how many 'business opportunity seekers' didn't find this sort of business worked.

So if your goods and services aren't marketable on eBay, don't despair. It still an excellent place to save money.

Summary

1. Every business should have an Internet presence.

2. Create the best website you possibly can. Remember your website is your virtual shop window. You should put as much thought and effort into creating your online image as you would if you were to open a high street shop.

3. Your site must be 'sticky' if it is to succeed. Not only will you need to encourage visitors to come to your site, but also to return regularly.

4. eBay offers enormous potential for hobby businesses both in sourcing products for your business and opening and selling online.

9

TRADITIONAL RETAILING

Home-based forever, or will you take to the high street?

With the ease and appeal of the Internet, it's all too easy to dismiss the idea of opening a traditional retail business. After all, who would want to spend all hours sitting behind the shop counter when you could be working at home at your own pace, wearing your dressing gown if so wish, and running your own online shop?

However, this rather flexible romantic view of running an Internet business is the sort of stuff that sells dubious get-rich-quick online schemes, while the reality of running an online business is somewhat different. In Chapter 8, I showed you what's involved in running your business on the worldwide web, however let's take a closer look here at the opportunities offered by traditional retailing.

IS A SHOP GOOD FOR YOUR BUSINESS?

Whilst the main ethos behind this book is starting a home-based business, eventually this same business may well outgrow your kitchen table, house, garden shed, garage, or wherever you initially locate it. There are other, and in my view, often overlooked benefits to opening a traditional bricks and mortar shop.

The benefits of having a bricks and mortar shop

☐ With the right location, you can dramatically increase your 'walk-in' sales and improve profitability.

☐ It improves your business's credibility.

☐ It improves your chances of more easily obtaining funding for your business, as banks and credit companies like to lend on bricks and mortar as opposed to kitchen tables.

☐ It creates a better working environment. Working from home can often be lonely and present a number of problems, including where to store things, conflicts with other family members, distractions, and so on.

☐ It improves the potential saleability of your business. Would-be purchasers are far more likely to buy a profitable shop rather than simply a garage full of your unsold stock and a list of customers.

◻ As your business grows, your need for larger premises will become acute. My own experience from starting and running the Littlehampton Dutch Bike Shop was that it was actually more cost effective to open a shop than to simply increase our rented storage. Nothing is worse than having to commute to a cold, facility-less container to access your stock while having your 'sales office' based online and at home.

◻ It makes it easier to employ staff. As your business grows you'll need additional staff and nothing is worse than having to accommodate them at your home, both for you and for them.

 Remember, moving out of home into a retail shop can be an enormous turning point in starting and running your own business.

Of all the businesses I've started from home, the most enjoyable moment is when you take this leap from kitchen table/garage to your first shop. It's a great feeling to throw open those doors and create a buzz of excitement, pop the kettle on, and welcome your first customers.

When our Dutch bicycle business outgrew the garage and rented containers stage, the most logical step forward was to open a shop. And so the Littlehampton Dutch Bike Shop was born. Initially the costs were prohibitive and our business struggled to meet the additional costs of renting a shop, business rates, and so on. But working from a shop gave our business instant credibility as would-be purchasers could now test-ride our bikes and visit our shop, and so overnight we went from being just another online faceless retailer to a high profile business.

IS YOUR BUSINESS SUITABLE FOR TRADITIONAL RETAILING?

Not every business will be suited to high street traditional retailing.

For example, since writing the first edition of this book the owner of our local record shop advertised his business as up for sale. At the time I was interested in the property, not because I wanted to open a record shop but because the location of his shop was in my view ideally suited for our business. When I approached the owner about taking over the property and not the business, he told me he had already sold it. At the time I wondered who would want to buy a high street record shop given that even the biggest multi-retailers were having a very difficult time competing against online companies, many of whom were operating outside of the UK. A few weeks later, a local radio DJ announced he was the shop's new owner and of course he was ideally suited to take the business to the next level. Sadly, the business has now closed its doors. At the time of shutting up shop the owner pinned a note on the door giving the main reason for closing the business as unfair online competition.

This competition wasn't just from UK online shops, but those based abroad who are able to post CDs to the UK VAT-free. Thus the benefit to the retail customer is that they're buying a product at substantially less than they would have to pay for the same product in the UK. So who could blame them for sourcing CDs online?

There's little point in debating the legalities of this or the moral issues and so on. What's important to you at this time is to ask yourself whether or not whatever you're selling, or proposing to sell, is suitable for the traditional retail model.

Traditional retail products

Products ideally suited to traditional retail sales models will include all those items that you wouldn't ever dream about buying online.

For example, would you order your bread online? Okay, perhaps you order your shopping via a supermarket online delivery service, but how many of us can resist being pulled into a shop by the gorgeous, mouth-watering aroma of fresh bread?

Consider also the pulling power of fresh fish in a traditional fishmonger's open window. More especially if the fishmongers is based on a seafront or beach. In Worthing (our neighbouring town) the fishermen regularly sell their fish from relatively primitive seafront stalls with none of the glitz and marketing of the supermarket chains. But they don't need expensive gismos to market their fresh fish. Potential customers don't need to be convinced that the fish they are about to buy is fresh as most of the stock can be seen wriggling around on the counters.

Could these fisherman sell their fish via mail order? This is doubtful, as the costs of their freezing or keeping fish cold enough to do so would be, I'd imagine, cost prohibitive. They would also lose the benefits of running a simple, traditional, cottage business.

However, could these fishermen benefit from having a website to market their business? The answer here is undoubtedly. Having an online presence would, in my view, greatly increase their sales potential as more would-be customers would be able to find them.

But on the whole they don't view the Internet as something that is suitable for them. In the past when I've asked them if they'd consider a website, they have looked at me as if I was telling them to shut their business down.

Don't also forget that there are a number of products that will do well both in a traditional retail environment and via the Internet.

For example, most quality florists now sell online – which wasn't always the case. When the Internet first opened its doors to online consumers, I recall a radio interview with a florist who argued that no one would ever buy flowers online as potential customers wouldn't be able to 'see their true beauty, and breathe in their fragrances'.

In many ways, he was indeed correct. However, what he'd failed to consider was all the potential customers who would want to order flowers to be delivered to homes, hospitals and funeral parlours located all over the country and around the world. Thus the benefit of being able to order online in the comfort of one's own home arguably far outweighs the relative inconvenience of having to visit a town centre florist with all the hassles of parking and so on. Not to mention that so many of us these days are so time poor.

 Always think beyond the market outside your own doorstep!

Those forward-thinking florists (who were at the time few in number) who pioneered the online concept reaped enormous rewards. Some American florists expanded their single shop into a prosperous global market and saw their profits soar.

But interestingly enough, those florists who opened up but only offered an Internet service don't appear to have done as well as those offering both an online ordering facility and also a traditional high street florist's.

We could speculate forever on the reasons why these anomalies occur forever, but the good news is that you don't have to speculate whether or not your business is suited for traditional retailing. All you have to do is look at other similar business models and see where they trade.

WHAT PRODUCTS ARE SUITABLE FOR HIGH STREET RETAILING?

Ultimately all products are suitable for traditional retailing. However, as in the case of the independent record shop discussed earlier, even if your product is suited to traditional retailing you must be careful. If the product you intend retailing is already widely available in what has become a fiercely competitive high street retail environment, you stand no chance of success.

Don't even contemplate taking on the multi-retailers. I continually despair when I see new businesses open in our area which are retailing products or produce that are already locally available. Most household budgets will already be overspent. Unless you live in millionaires' row, few people will buy from you if what you're offering is available elsewhere at a much cheaper price.

Just take a look at petrol stations. How many small, independent petrol stations do you know of in your neighbourhood? Personally, I can't think of a single one. Where I live even the larger car retailers have now given up on retailing fuel, as the major supermarkets have made profit making in this area next to impossible.

 The key to surviving and succeeding as a retailer is to be able to offer something different to what your competitors are doing. If all you can offer are cheaper prices, trust me, there will always be someone willing to sell cheaper than you can.

FACTORS TO CONSIDER WHEN OPENING YOUR SHOP

Okay. So you've decided to open a shop. Good for you. I love retailing and believe that provided you're operating in a niche market, tucked away in the shade out of the dazzling lights of the multi-retailers, then you really can build a successful business.

To have any chance of success, you're going to have to give careful consideration to what I call the three 'Ps', which include:

- ☐ Position.
- ☐ Promotion.
- ☐ Price.

I'd like to take you through each one of the above. So grab your notebook and a cup of coffee and let's get down to some work.

POSITION

Where you position your shop will ultimately decide whether or not your business succeeds or fails. When it comes to buying and selling residential property, estate agents will all tell you the same thing – price is largely dependent on location, location, location, and the market local to where you are buying.

Or in other words, position.

Choose an inappropriate position for your business, and it will fail. For example, let's say your cottage business involves making fresh, homemade produce. A key sales feature is that you're providing fresh, tasty, aromatic, must-have produce. However, on the downside, because of the labour involved and the quality of the ingredients, you're going to have to charge a lot more than what people would pay for off-the-shelf, factory-manufactured produce.

You can see immediately here that if you position your shop in an area where there isn't a relatively affluent population, you're going to struggle to sell your products. Unfortunately, and as you'll soon discover if you haven't already, the rental charges for shops in these affluent areas are hugely prohibitive to say the least. Even if you are based in such an area, you may still find that the only positions available to rent, if indeed there are any at all, might be what's known as 'secondary positions'.

Secondary positions

A secondary position is essentially one that is off the main high street or beaten track. In my experience, secondary positions aren't necessarily a bad place to be, provided your business fits in with what's already there.

For example, if this secondary position is in a relatively back street area surrounded by empty boarded-up shops, or nightclubs that only come alive at midnight, then you're going to struggle to find your passing trade.

On the other hand, many secondary positions can offer lots of benefits such as proximity to or availability of car parking, free or otherwise. You could also find yourself next to or near to an already successful established business whose customer profile is similar to yours. Therefore, when you open your doors you'll immediately benefit from quality passing traffic.

You should also be aware of the term 'footfall'.

In retailing, this term is taken to mean the number of people passing your shop's door over a given period. So, for example, a busy London street would have an enormous footfall running into thousands, while a quite rural area will have a substantially smaller footfall which will in turn mean cheaper rents.

Where to get figures on footfall

Many councils and traders' associations, Chambers of Commerce, and so on will keep records of a town centre's footfall. Prior to committing yourself you should always check out potential footfalls. And in my experience take your advice from traders' associations, councils and the like, as opposed to any commercial letting agents or landlords.

PROMOTION

There are two chapters on sales and marketing in this book which will give you lots of ideas and tips on how you as a business person can improve your selling and market your business. However, when it comes to opening a traditional bricks and mortar shop you need to have a very clear, predefined strategy of how you are going to promote your business.

For example, I was recently browsing through an online site that specialises in selling businesses. My attention was taken by an advertisement for a specialist independent bookshop that was for sale close to where I live and that I'd never known existed. Although the subject matter the shop specialised in wasn't really of interest to me, I was surprised that I had never come across this place. But what really did interest me was the amount of money the business had been spending on marketing itself. Compared to the turnover (the amount of money a business takes annually from sales), the costs of this marketing were huge. Then I began to notice that the shop was advertised in every one of our local newspapers, business directories, free papers, and so on. However, until now I had never noticed their advertisements. While this may have been because I wasn't interested in the subject matter the shop specialised in, I suspect it was more that the advertisements were poorly placed and failed to achieve their objectives.

When you're thinking of taking your business to a traditional retail environment, don't forget you'll need to promote it, which is an extra cost that will always add up.

PRICE

To survive as a traditional retailer, your prices must be competitive. However, if there are already businesses out there offering the same products as you specialise in then be careful. Usually, established retailers will have a regular and loyal customer base, and if the only way you can attract them to your shop is by cheaper prices then you would really be better off not taking on the additional costs and risks that go with a shop.

On the other hand, if you are a specialist operating in a niche area of the market then you'll obviously be able to charge more for your products as you've brought them to the high street. But here again you need to be cautious. If your products are also available online via your competitors be careful that your shop isn't going to be used as a showroom for someone else's online business. This is exactly what I experienced in our shops when I took on a product that had previously only been available online. Much to my disappointment and frustration, I discovered that we had plenty of prospective customers coming to our shop to see and try out this particular product, but they didn't buy. After some investigation I discovered that the company who were supplying us with the product had slashed their price to encourage more online sales. Needless to say we stopped stocking any of their products. Some years on these same distributors are now finding sales difficult as their products are now no longer available in most shops because they have become too unattractive for retailers to sell.

HOW TO INCREASE YOUR CHANCES OF HIGH STREET SUCCESS

Despite the enormous impact of multi-retailers and the Internet on traditional niche retailers, I still believe that the high street offers great potential for the shrewd entrepreneur with a keen eye for niche products. However, you need to be prepared for what will inevitably be a relatively long slog. If our experience with the Dutch Bike Shop brand is anything to go by (and I've no reason to believe we were any different to any other successful high street retailer) you will be looking at at least three years of effort before you see any worthwhile return on your investment.

So how do you survive these three years?

Let's look at some of the ways you can improve your chances of surviving your first shop and going on to build a solid, successful retail business.

To begin with, your objectives, written or otherwise, must include all of the following key tasks below:

1. Whatever it is you are selling it must be attractive enough for potential customers to want to buy it from your business.

2. You must allow yourself sufficient time to establish your niche retail business.

3. You must have either sufficient working capital or access to further funds or credit should the need arise.

4. You have to be prepared for the tough slog ahead and to make whatever sacrifices are necessary to ensure that your shop establishes itself in the fastest possible time.

Let's take a closer look at each one of these key objectives.

Is whatever you're proposing to sell attractive enough to pull customers through your door?

I'm going to be brutally honest here – no one is going to buy anything from you (with the exception of sympathetic friends and family) unless what you're offering is actually attractive enough to buy.

Your shop must be selling something that not only potential customers want to buy, but also that they're motivated enough to buy from you either now, or as a worst case scenario, in the not too distant future.

For example, I believe one of the most difficult retail businesses to run is a gift shop, and here's why. Our seaside town is surrounded by beautiful, historic towns that each summer welcome coach- and carloads of visitors. During these busy times every one of the small, colourful, interesting gift shops is packed full of people of all ages browsing their wares. But that's the problem – they're browsers, not buyers. Sure they all admire the fine glassware, the innovative kitchen gadgets, the beautiful paintings, the lovely bespoke furniture. But do they buy? Not on your life. A few do of course, but not enough to make any worthwhile contribution to the poor shop owner's profits.

So each year at the end of the season lots of the shops close down, stock is cleared away, floors are scrubbed, and up go the 'To Let' signs. And then a few months later the estate agents' 'Let Agreed' boards go up and the whole process starts again, only this time with another hopeful soul ready to sink all they possess into a venture that has already proved itself a complete failure for countless entrepreneurs before. All very sad, but in my view, entirely avoidable.

If you are to have any chance whatsoever of succeeding as a retailer, whatever you're offering must at the very least satisfy the following criteria:

1. Whatever it is you're proposing to sell it must have immediate, or as near immediate, purchasing appeal as is possible. To put it simply, if what you're offering isn't more or less instantly saleable, the chances of ever seeing your browsers return again to buy are slim to say the least. Yes, you'll get lots of very interested people wearing out your carpets, goodwill and patience telling you how great whatever it is you're selling is, but unless they're buying it there and then you're not going to earn any money.

2. Your products must be of a high enough value to make selling them worthwhile. For example, if you're planning to sell goods that retail for pence or a couple of pounds then you're going to have sell thousands of them every day before you can even think about paying your rent (let alone making a profit).

3. Whatever you're selling, provided it meets the above two most important criteria it must be easy for customers to buy. For example, if you're retailing a product that sells for anything over ten or twenty pounds you're going to have to make it easy for customers to buy whatever it is you're selling. For example, when I first opened the Dutch Bike Shop, I didn't have any facility to take credit cards. For six long months I slogged away selling bikes to excited would-be customers only to find that once it came to them having to say yes, they didn't actually say yes. Instead they said something like 'I suppose you take credit cards?' When I told

them I didn't, they would tell me they would have to think about it, after which I never saw them again. This was entirely my own fault as I should have realised that not everyone has four or five hundred pounds sitting in their wallet or current account ready to buy a luxury bicycle. And even if they did, the cash machine would only give them a maximum of three hundred. Remember, you must make it as easy for your customers to buy from you as is possible.

Grab your notebook and in great big bold letters write down the following:

Whatever I'm proposing to sell in my shop must be attractive enough for someone to want to buy from me, must be of a high enough value to make it worthwhile, and must be easy enough for the customer to buy it from me today, now, this minute.

I promise you, if you get the above right you will be well on the way to success. But if you don't, your failure will be guaranteed. So now is the time to dismiss any glorious notions you have of opening up the next niche 'gift shop', because high streets all over the world are proven graveyards for this kind of retail establishment. Remember you don't want 'browsers' you want buyers, and you also want them in such sufficient and regular quantities that they buy something of a sufficiently high value to make it all worthwhile.

I hope I haven't laboured this point too much, and if I have done I apologise. But I really do wish that I had been told the above when I opened our first shop. It certainly would have speeded up the process of going from hard struggle to profitability – and I would have made an even greater profit.

Enough said. Let's move on!

Allow yourself sufficient time to establish your business

As I said earlier, in my case it took us three whole years before we really saw our Dutch bike shop take off. Although we enjoyed a relatively high level of sales during this time, our start-up costs (including rent, rates, and so on) ate into any potential profit.

Rather than rely on taking any money out of our business during this initial period, we had to continue with our other businesses, which at the time included, amongst other enterprises, a landscape gardening business and running a boating lake. Thus we ('we' being my business partner and I) lived on the earnings from both these businesses, which in reality meant working day and night, seven days a week, for three years.

What kept us going through those initial difficult and very tiring years was that we hadn't expected anything less. In fact, looking back I think we probably enjoyed an easier ride than we thought we would. So the first, and I believe most important thing to get right in your mind about taking your venture to the high street is to remember that very few businesses enjoy overnight success, and those that do rarely if ever survive.

So make sure you allow yourself sufficient time to grow your business to a profitable stage. I met someone recently who told me that they were about to open up their own shop selling something that I believe is already available, indeed is over-supplied on the high street. They told me that they expected to take a personal salary of six hundred pounds a week pretty much immediately. When I questioned their figures and their idea they got quite annoyed and at this point I wished I had simply nodded and smiled. I'm not a betting man, but I would wager my home that this business will fail within its first three months. So how can I be so sure of this? Well I managed to glean from this person that the product they were intending to sell would retail at £1.75. Even assuming a rather generous profit margin of 50% (which is rare, indeed very rare, in any retail market), they would earn a gross profit of 87p on every product they sell. So to earn six hundred pounds a week from their business they would need to sell 1,044 of these things every week to give them this return, plus a further how ever many of these to cover shop rent, rates, light, heat, machinery costs (as the product involves their being made in the shop), raw materials, stock, and so on.

When I asked them how many of these things they believed they could make in a day, they hadn't really worked it out. By my own calculations, I estimated that even if the whole universe conspired to help them on their way, together with Lady Luck shining on them, the most they could possibly manage to make in a week would be 200. Which by their calculations would give them gross earnings (assuming they sold them all) of three hundred and fifty pounds ($£1.75 \times 200$).

It doesn't take a genius to work out that this venture will be doomed from day one, but meanwhile they're blissfully working away in a fool's paradise unwilling or unable to take advice from anyone.

There are two things I always carry around with me – a filofax for writing down my ideas and planning my diary, and most importantly, a calculator. I love nothing more than working out the figures for all my ideas. Since I am investing time and effort in carrying around this paper and a calculator, many of my potentially daft ideas have been instantly dismissed when I've worked out some provisional figures.

So if you're sitting reading this book and planning your business, get used to having a calculator around. Working through figures is part of the fun of starting and running your own business. It also guarantees that you will focus on those all-important numbers.

Have sufficient working capital in place

To survive and succeed as a retailer, you'll have to stock your shop. So your start-up costs will be relative high. And assuming that you've hit the right note, and you've created a business that has high street appeal and sells your products, you'll have to continually replace this stock. This means you will perpetually have money tied up in your business. And the more product lines you add to your business, the more money you'll have to shell out every week or month and so on.

One of the commonest reasons why many new, and otherwise promising, business start-ups fail is because the entrepreneurs involved haven't got either the cash or credit lines available to make their business successful. This isn't just my view, but one of the top reasons given by most leading banks as to why new businesses fail to succeed.

Let me give you an example from my own experiences of how lack of working capital can hinder your progress and profitability. When we first began importing Dutch bikes from Holland, the manufacturers refused to give us any credit terms. So we had to pay for all our stock up-front, days and even in some cases weeks before the bicycles arrived in our shop. Inevitably, we never had enough cash available to buy the quantities of bikes we needed to stock in order to be successful. All we were really doing was playing on the margins, so to speak. Eventually we reached the point where the only way we could ever hope to expand our business was either to try to get increased credit at the bank, or beg or borrow money from our friends and relatives. I decided to do both. Initially I approached some family members who knew how hard we were working and could also see the potential in our business. They readily agreed to lend us some working capital. Next stop was our business bank manager, who after looking (or should I say poring through) our cash flow forecasts agreed in principle to lend us the money, with the proviso that we offer our house as security for the borrowing.

I'm going to ask you a question now, assuming of course you have a home with some equity in it: would you offer the roof over your head as security to your bank to support your business venture? Difficult isn't it? Dare you risk everything, or stay on the margins playing at whatever it is you're planning to do?

I decided to believe in our business and went all the way with the bank. So far, thankfully, it has all paid off and our business has enjoyed phenomenal growth. Expansion that would not have been possible without us substantially increasing our working capital. So I really want you to understand here that working capital, that is the amount of money or credit you will have available for your business on a day-to-day basis, will be crucial to your success.

Be prepared to borrow, beg, and go cap-in-hand to relatives, friends, bank managers and just about anybody else who can help you grow your business. Do as I did if you need to by offering shares in your company to those who help you out that are directly in relation to the amount of money they have invested in your business. That way it's all above board, and provided you're successful they will see a worthwhile return on their investment that will far out-perform anything on offer from the high street banks or savings plans.

I cannot stress this enough. If you're opening a shop you will need sufficient cash or credit available to keep it stocked at such a level that it is attractive for customers to buy from you. We're in a society that thrives on 'instant'. Unless whatever you're selling is truly unique to you, few customers will wait around for you to get something in for them that is already available elsewhere. As is often the case in retailing, sales are won not on the basis of a cheaper price, but by product availability.

Never underestimate the power of the Internet and also the potential damage it can do to your sales. For example, let's say you are hugely successful in creating a demand for your niche products. Yet because of cash flow problems, and a lack of working capital, you're unable to stock your shop sufficiently to be able to offer immediate product availability. You can be assured here that rather than wait for your stock to become available, potential customers will be looking online for that availability. The sad thing is that when this happens you're actually selling for the competition.

So, please, please – get, borrow, or beg sufficient working capital to give yourself the best possible chance of success. And if you're unprepared to risk everything for your business, then perhaps this entrepreneurial life is not for you!

Be prepared for the slog ahead and making sacrifices

Opening a shop isn't everyone's idea of fun. If you're taking on the high street then be prepared to deal with an often difficult public, many of whom will have absolutely no interest in buying whatever it is you're selling. You'll have all sorts of people through your door including those who wish to steal from you, compete with you, insult you, or find out all about your business with a view to starting their own similar business. Of course, you will also see lots of genuine customers.

So every day you must be prepared to meet the challenges head on and to grow your business without being put off by those who will do their utmost to demotivate you. When we first opened the doors of the Dutch Bike Shop we had an endless stream of moaners coming in to tell us that we'd be lucky to sell one bike. Some years on and we're still growing, still expanding, and we've all had a great time. However, I can confess to having those days when I'd come home and ask myself whether it was all really worth it.

Today I don't need to ask myself this any more. I'm part of a hugely successful business, which not only gives us all great pride and enjoyment but our customers also. Yes, it's been a hard slog, which would have been made easier had I been forewarned.

I'm forewarning you now. Prepare yourself for the hard slog ahead, but also try to remember the fun and enjoyment that come with it.

A FINAL WORD ON RETAILING

My advice to you if you are going to open a traditional shopfront for your business is that you really do need to read and research as much as you can about retailing and retail techniques. As this book is primarily aimed at those wanting to start a home-based business, I can only really touch on what's involved in opening a shop. But I do believe that many successful home-based businesses will grow to such a size that opening a shop is the next logical step to take. So don't say never, never. And if you are going to open a shop, undertake lots of research and speak to as many retailers as you can in the area where you are proposing to do so. Never rely on the promises or claims made by letting agents or landlords. It's up to you, and you alone, to undertake your research.

Shop

Before deciding on a shop you need to consider carefully the costs involved, which go beyond rent. You'll have to consider business rates, insurance, maintenance, heating and lighting as well as other additional costs.

Leasehold or freehold

Just like buying a house or a flat, there are both leasehold and freehold retail properties available. With freehold property you own the building as well as the land it sits on and have full rights over the property and can sell it (subject to any mortgage conditions) whenever you wish. You're also free, subject to planning regulations to make any alterations to the building. The disadvantages to buying a freehold property is that it is relatively expensive and can be very difficult to sell in the future.

With a leasehold property you purchase the right to use the property for an agreed period of time and are bound by the conditions of the lease. Most leases will require you to maintain the property at your expense; pay either a monthly, quarterly or annual rent payment; insure the building against damage, fire etc.

Whether your property is leasehold or freehold you will also be required to pay business rates. You will also have to pay to have the property surveyed and the solicitor's fees for the new lease. It's also common in the case of a leasehold property (not that you have to agree to it) for the landlord to put it as part of the contract that you pay all their 'reasonable legal costs' in negotiating the new lease.

Questions you need to ask yourself before deciding on a property

- **Location.** Is the shop located in an area where my target market is?

- **History.** What's the shop's history? What was the previous tenant's business? Have they relocated close by or gone out of business?

- **Crime.** Is the area prone to vandalism, burglary and does it become a virtual no-go area at night? How close is it to pubs, clubs and late night takeaways?

- **Size.** Look at size from the long term. What's the possibility of expanding your business? Be realistic here; some shops are about the size of your average ensuite. Can you really fit everything in? Forget about the great rent for a minute and look at it objectively.

- **Area.** You should always pay particular attention to what's happening in the area local to your business. Is it on the up with new businesses coming in? What are the plans for new housing? Is there already a business similar to the one you're planning to start?

- **Above and beside.** What sort of accommodation exists above and alongside your proposed shop? Most high street shops have some sort of accommodation above them which often is rented out, which isn't a problem if the tenants are OK. But what if they're not? How would that impact on your business?

Don't forget to check out your landlord

As well as researching the market local to where you're planning to open your shop, you should also find out as much as you can about your future landlord. Don't be shy about this. Remember that when you make an offer to lease a shop you will be asked for references and there will be background checks, credit checks and deposits to pay, while you will be provided with no information whatsoever about who your landlord is.

Purchasing a freehold property

The obvious advantage to purchasing a freehold property is that you won't have to pay rent. However, unless you're sitting on a pile of cash it's likely that you will need some sort of finance to fund your purchase. Commercial mortgages are available in exactly the same way as you'd get a mortgage to buy a private house. You could of course find a property which has a shop with accommodation over it so you can live above your business or rent the accommodation out as additional income.

Purchasing a freehold property is a drastic move for someone setting up their first business. If you have the sort of money needed to purchase a freehold shop then you're better off buying an established profitable business. This way at least you substantially reduce the risk and your money starts working for you from day one.

How do you find shops that are available to let?

There are number of ways including:

- ☐ walking through suitable areas looking for agents' 'to let' boards;

- ☐ contacting commercial property agents and asking them to put you on their mailing lists;

- ☐ checking on websites such as *Business for Sale* and *Daltons Business* for which a relatively small fee may have to be paid. (http://www.businessfor sale.com, and http://www.daltonsbusiness.co.uk.)

My final advice on taking on a shop lease, as opposed to buying a successful business that's already established and profitable, is to think very carefully before going ahead.

 A lease agreement is legally binding and even if you cease trading after your first few months you will still be liable to pay all outstanding rents for the duration of the lease period you entered into.

10
THE MECHANICS OF STARTING YOUR BUSINESS

Every business will be unique and have its own peculiarities. To provide all the information needed to start every business would be an impossible task and so I suggest you read what follows by way of an introductory guide to what's involved. It may be that you will have to research further to make sure that the business you're planning to start complies with all the rules and regulations of the day.

The first thing you will need to decide is which 'trading identity' is suitable for your business.

Deciding on a trading identity

There are a number of trading identities that you can choose from including:

- □ sole trader

- □ limited company

- □ partnership

- □ cooperative.

It's important to choose the most suitable trading identity for your business.

If you're in doubt what identity to start with you could start your business as a sole trader and then change to a partnership or company at a later date. Changing from a sole trader to a company is relatively easy. However changing from a company to a sole trader, although achievable, is much more difficult and can be expensive.

Only you can decided which one suits the type of business you are planning to start.

SOLE TRADER

Sole trader is basically you trading as your business. For example Fiona's Flowers, or Greg's Hairdressers, or Paul Power Landscapes. It is the most popular choice of trading identity for those offering either a service or a small retail concession.

Some important advantages to trading as a sole trader

☐ **Easy to set up without any costs.** You simply trade as you are, eg Paul Power trading as Paul Power Landscapes.

☐ **Complete control over your business.** You are your business, which means you can retain complete control over all your business-making decisions without having to consult other directors, partners etc.

☐ **Easy to change to another trading identity.** It's far easier to change your trading identity from that of sole trader to a limited company. Going the other way, ie, limited company to sole trader, can be very expensive and bureaucratic.

☐ **Accounting.** Your trading accounts do not have to include a balance sheet such as you would have to provide for a company.

Some disadvantages

☐ **You are personally liable for all your businesses debts.** This liability is unlimited and should your business fail you could end up losing your personal assets such as your home, car, furniture etc.

☐ **Credibility.** While some businesses are suited to that of sole trader and customers like the idea of doing business with a person as opposed to a company, others do not. The travel business is one business where people need to be convinced that when they are paying their deposit and final holiday payments their money is being paid to a company and not an individual.

A sole trader is an ideal starting point for your business if you're simply selling something at craft fairs, exhibitions, through your own website, etc. It is also suitable for offering services, for example wedding planner, personal organiser, florist etc.

Remember that the main advantage to being a sole trader is that you can easily change to another trading identity as your business grows. My first business was Paul Power trading as Paul Power Landscapes – a sole trader – but this business is now run as a partnership.

Another advantage to you as either a sole trader or partnership is that in the event you make a loss you can deduct your losses from future profits, provided these profits are made from the same business. You can also deduct losses from other income you have gained either in the year you sustained the loss, or the previous year, including any personal income you might have.

HOW TO SET YOURSELF UP AS A SOLE TRADER

Setting yourself up as sole trader is relatively straightforward.

1. Contact the Inland Revenue

Request the form that you need to complete to register as self-employed. You should do this as soon as you start. If you fail to do this within the first three months of becoming self-employed you risk a fine of £100.

The Inland Revenue also publishes a free *Starting Up In Business* guide, which is full of useful information regarding taxation and national insurance, employing people etc.

Contact the Inland Revenue either by phone (08459 15 45 15. Open Monday to Friday 8am to 8pm and 8am to 4pm on Saturday and Sunday) or online at www.inlandrevenue.gov.uk/startingup/. You can register and download copies of their guides.

2. Your business name

We looked at what's involved in choosing a name for your business in Chapter 3, but you need to be aware that if you are going to trade using a different name than your own, you must also include your own name on your headed note paper.

Therefore if you're a sole trader and name your business Discover Cornwall on Foot, somewhere on your headed notepaper you will have to include your name, trading as Discover Cornwall on Foot.

For example, if it was my business it would read: 'Paul Power trading as Discover Cornwall on Foot'.

3. National Insurance

You will also be required to pay flat-rate Class 2 National Insurance Contributions currently at £2.05 a week, which can be paid by direct debit.

If your profits exceed a certain limit, you will have to pay Class 4 National Insurance Contributions. The present limit is £4,745.

If the earnings from your business are low then you may not have to pay national insurance, but you must apply for exemption.

4. Staff

Sole traders are often incorrectly referred to as 'one-man bands'. However as a sole trader you can employ as many people as you need while still trading as a sole trader.

The term sole trader refers to the business owner, and not those working in the business.

If you're planning to employ staff you will need to collect income tax and national insurance contributions and pay these to the Inland Revenue. Your employees will be paying tax on a PAYE basis, while you will remain paying tax on a self-employed basis.

4. Decide whether or not to register for VAT

If you decide to register for VAT you should inform Customs and Excise and register your business with them. We'll look at the factors that you'll need to consider when making your decision in just a moment.

5. Record keeping

You are required to keep an accurate and truthful record of all your business income and expenditure.

How you record these transactions is entirely a matter for you. If you wish to record them on a roll of toilet paper using a crayon, then you may. Of course it makes sense to record them in a format where you as the business owner can readily see at any given time whether your business is making a profit or loss.

Regardless of the business identity you choose, you will have to some form of bookkeeping procedures in your business. I'd recommend everyone read Peter Marshall's excellent book *Mastering Book-keeping, A step by step guide to the Principles and Practice of Business Accounting.* published by How To Books ISBN 1857038975.

6. Comply with any other regulations that may be applicable

Depending on the type of business you're going to start, you may have to register with other government agencies. For example if you're going to be preparing or selling food then you'll need to contact your local environmental health department and comply with any statutory regulations.

You're now ready to trade as a sole trader.

PARTNERSHIP

This is a similar identity to that of a sole trader but there are two people instead of one.

The advantages are much the same as being a sole trader, however when it comes to making decisions you will obviously need to reach agreement with your partner.

Having a formal partnership agreement

Partnerships work well when things are going well but if things go wrong you will need something to fall back on. For example:

☐ one partner wants to sell the business and recoup their investment;

☐ one partner no longer wishes to work in the partnership but doesn't want to sell the business;

☐ additional cash is needed to expand the business but only one partner is able to the raise the cash.

With a partnership there are lots of 'what if's to consider. Even if your partner is your husband, wife, relative or best friend you should have a formal partnership agreement drawn up by a solicitor. Remember also that over time your partner's personal circumstances may change. You might start off as two carefree friends with lots of time to devote to your business and everything go well. Then either you or your partner marries, has children, and is no longer able to devote the same amount of time that they previously did to your business.

What happens when you one of you works fewer hours than the other and still wants the same return?

Or your partner's wife decides that she too would like to be a part of the business?

Or your partner gets divorced and their husband decides that they are entitled to a share of the business because they have been married to one of the partners?

Lots of questions need to be answered before entering a partnership, which is why you will need to have a deed of partnership drawn up.

Deed of partnership

A deed of partnership is a legally binding agreement between the partners of a business. This agreement describes how the partnership is to be run as well as detailing individual duties and obligations.

A deed of partnership will usually cover:

☐ the amount of money each partner is putting into the business
☐ profit-sharing agreements
☐ hours of work for each partner
☐ salaries
☐ future changes in the partnership – what happens if one partner dies, marries or wants to leave?

Business debts are joint

Just as a sole trader has unlimited liability for their business debts, partners have unlimited liability for their business debts, too. So if your partner accumulates business debts without your knowledge, you are also liable for them.

Can more than two people form a partnership?

Yes. A partnership can be for two or more people, however only those partners over the age of 18 are legally bound by the terms of any partnership agreement.

Partners are referred to as members of a partnership.

Can there be different types of partners?

Yes. There can be general partners, sleeping/dormant partners and even companies can be partners.

- **General partners**. A general partner is one who invests in the business, takes part in its running and shares in any losses or profits the business makes. Every partnership must have at least one general partner.

- **Sleeping partners**. Sleeping partners invest in the business and share in any profits or losses, but do not take any part in running the business.
  Sleeping partners are often friends or relatives who invest in new business ventures, for example putting up some capital to purchase a business, stock, premises etc.

  The important thing to note about sleeping partners is that although they do not take any part in running the business, they are still legally jointly responsible for any business debts and losses.

- **Companies**. Companies can be partners in another business. They share the same rights and responsibilities as other partners, however will be responsible for additional tax matters and reporting obligations.

Limited liability partnership

You can also form a limited liability partnership. To do this you will need to submit an Incorporation Document (Form LLP2) at Companies House.

The following information is required:

- Name of the limited liability partnership.
- Location and address of the limited liability partnership's registered office.

☐ Names and addresses and date of births of each member.

☐ Indication as to which of these members are the 'designated members'.

Designated members have certain duties, which include appointing an auditor, signing the accounts, delivering the accounts and annual return to Companies House and notifying them of changes to the members, registered office or name of the business.

With a limited liability partnership you are also required to display your business name, which must be the name of the limited liability partnership outside all your places of business and on all your notices.

Your company letterhead and order forms etc must show the place of registration, registration number, the fact that it is a limited liability partnership and the address of your registered office.

Taxation

You must contact the Inland Revenue and inform them that your new partnership exists. You'll then be sent a partnership return, which you must complete. This will include a partnership statement, which shows how profits and losses have been divided amongst the partners.

Although usually only one member of the partnership is nominated to complete the partnership return, every partner is liable in the event of any penalty if the form is submitted late, or there is a false declaration etc.

Similar to a sole trader, most partners will pay tax as a self-employed person, which means they will be responsible for paying their own national insurance contributions.

The procedure for a partner registering with the Inland Revenue is the same as for that as a sole trader.

Likewise if your partnership employs staff, you as employers are responsible for collecting your employee's tax and national insurance contributions on behalf of the Inland Revenue.

SETTING UP YOUR BUSINESS UP AS A COMPANY

The words 'business' and 'company' are often misunderstood. Basically if you're trading as either a sole trader or a partnership, you are a business, and if you have a company you will either have a public company or a limited company.

A public company

A public company will have PLC after its name.

To form a PLC you must have an authorised share capital of at least £50,000 of which at least one quarter must be paid on each share plus any premium. This means you would need a minimum of £12,500 (a quarter of £50,000) to form one.

Every public company must have two directors and a company secretary.

A private company

When you form a private company you do not need to have an authorised share capital of £50,000 to form your company.

Neither do you need to have two directors, but you do need to have a company secretary. If you have only one director this person cannot also act as company secretary. Therefore as a minimum you will need a director and company secretary.

The director and company secretary can be related, for example husband and wife.

DIRECTOR'S DUTIES AND RESPONSIBILITIES

Becoming a company director means that you accept certain duties and responsibilities, which include:

- ☐ Acting in good faith and in the interests of your company.

- ☐ Not using the company for any fraudulent purpose, which includes defrauding creditors or deceive shareholders.

- ☐ Never allowing the company to trade while insolvent. This is referred to as 'wrongful trading' and if you do so you may have to pay for any debts incurred by the company while insolvent.

- ☐ Complying with the requirements of the Companies Act.

- ☐ Having a regard for the interests of employees in general.

HOW TO FORM A COMPANY

There are a number of options:

- ☐ Form the company yourself.
- ☐ Instruct an accountant or solicitor to do it for you.
- ☐ Purchase a ready-made company.

Forming your own company

Forming your own company can take several weeks and if at all possible you'd be well advised to employ either an accountant or solicitor to do it on your behalf, or purchase a ready-made company.

If you do decide to do it yourself you will need to get all the relevant documentation from Companies House by phoning and requesting a starter pack.

You will then need to register the company with the Registrar of Companies by sending in:

Memorandum of Association. This will include stating the name of the company, the location of the registered office and the objectives of the company.

The Registrar will need to approve the name of your company. In the event that another company is already using the name you choose for your company, you will have to come up with another name.

Articles of Association are the rules by which your company will be managed. You can either draw up your own articles, or if you don't the standard format set out in the Companies Act will be adopted.

Memorandums of Association and Articles of Association can be purchased from law stationers.

You will also need to complete the following forms:

Form 10. This is the form used to notify Companies House of the first directors and secretary and the location of your registered office.

Other details required include details of the company director's occupation, nationality and other directorships held within the last five years.

Form 12. This is a declaration of compliance.

Form 117. You must send this form in before the company starts trading.

Registration fees. There are two registration fees to choose from. You can either pay the standard fee of £20 or you can pay £80 if you want to use the same-day service.

Instructing a solicitor or accountant to do it for you. Fees charged by these professionals vary and it's worth shopping around to get the best quote. Not all solicitors will undertake company formations.

Purchasing a ready-made company. There are a number of businesses that specialise in selling off-the-shelf ready-made companies. These companies will, as the name suggests, be already formed and ready to trade complete with a company name. You can if you wish change the company name provided of course the name hasn't already been taken.

To change the company name you will need to:

☐ Convene either an annual general meeting or an extraordinary general meeting and pass a special resolution agreeing the new name.

☐ Send a signed copy of the resolution to Companies House together with a registration fee of £10, or £80 if you require same-day-service.

Businesses that sell ready-made companies can usually be found advertising in *Exchange and Mart* and on the Internet by searching under 'ready-made companies for sale'.

When buying an off-the-shelf company make sure that the price includes a certificate that the business has never traded. Otherwise you could find yourself buying a trading business and inheriting its debts.

Taxation

The important thing to remember when you choose to form a limited company is that you are going to be working for this company as opposed to being self-employed.

☐ You pay tax as an employed person on a PAYE basis.
☐ Your company also pays tax on its profits, due nine months after the end of the accounting year.

Other requirements

You are required to publicly display the Certificate of Incorporation and the registration date and you must also put the company name outside your office premises.

The following information must be shown on your company stationery:

☐ Full registered name of your company.
☐ Either the names of all company directors or none of them.
☐ Place of registration, eg Registered in England.
☐ The registered office address and the trading address of the company, indicating which is which.
☐ Company registration number.

The advantages of forming a company

There are a number of advantages of forming a company as opposed to trading as sole trader or partnership (except for a limited liability partnership).

The most obvious being that as a company director your liability for the company's debts is generally limited to your amount of shares. Your personal assets cannot be touched unless the company has been trading fraudulently or when the directors knew that it was insolvent.

A possible disadvantage is that you are no longer self-employed and are in fact an employee of your company, albeit a director. This means that even though you have invested your money into your company, you can no longer treat it as your own. Your investment forms part of your company's assets and cannot be recouped as easily as if you were operating as a sole trader.

On the other hand if you are trading as a sole trader you are actually trading as yourself, which means you do own your business. There are no company regulations and legalities to follow if you want to sell some of your business assets or release some of your initial investment.

COOPERATIVE

You could choose to run your business as a cooperative.

This form of trading identity would be best suited to a group of hobby enthusiasts wanting to set up their own business where the business assets are all owned by the workforce. Or if this is not possible immediately, then it must be the aim of the cooperative to own them eventually.

What makes a cooperative different from other businesses?

1. The management, business objectives and use of the assets must be controlled by the workforce.

2. The assets of the business must be owned by the workforce, or it this is not possible, it must be the aim of the cooperative to own them eventually.

3. The only reward for investing money for a cooperative can be interest on the loan. Any profits arising as a result of any investment should be shared amongst the workforce.

4. The cooperative should only be disbanded if all its members agree.

It's unlikely that a home-based business would choose to form a cooperative.

However it's possible that a group of home-based businesses might want to form a cooperative to produce their own goods or services etc, such as a group of candle makers, craft workers, artists etc.

Registering for VAT

At some point you will have to decide whether or not to register for VAT. I say decide because not all businesses will have to register. Before we get to look at the circumstances when you must register for VAT, let's look at VAT itself.

WHAT IS VAT?

Value Added Tax is an indirect tax on consumer expenditure collected by HM Customs and Excise. Most business transactions will involve either supplying goods or services or a combination of both.

The price charged to the consumer will have included in it an element of VAT unless the goods or services are VAT exempt. We'll look at exemptions in a moment, but basically there are three VAT rates, which are:

- □ standard rate – currently at 15 per cent (until December 2009, usual rate is 17.5 per cent)
- □ reduced rate – currently at 5 per cent
- □ a zero rate.

These rates do not apply to all goods and services because some goods are what is know as VAT exempt, which means no VAT is payable. Also supplies that are outside the scope of VAT are those that are:

- □ made outside the UK and Isle of Man
- □ not made in the course of a business.

Items which are exempt from VAT

A full list of items that are exempt from VAT can be found by contacting Customs and Excise. The following is an indication of items exempt from VAT.

Where your business activity involves:

- □ providing credit
- □ insurance
- □ health care (with some exceptions)
- □ postal services
- □ most types of betting, gambling and lottery
- □ membership benefits provided by trade unions and professional bodies.

As you can see the chances of your providing goods and services that do not have to charge VAT are limited. Broadly speaking, a Kitchen Table Entrepreneur's business will attract VAT.

How does VAT work?

Let's take the following example based on the usual rate of 17.5 per cent.

I set up a business making homemade soaps. In order to do this I have to buy in raw materials from a wholesaler and I pay VAT on these items at 17.5 per cent.

I am registered for VAT. I can claim back the VAT that I have paid on these raw materials from HM Customs and Excise. The tax that I can claim back is what is known as 'input tax'. This is done by making what is known as a return to Customs and Excise.

However, I can only do this if my business is registered for VAT. Otherwise I cannot claim back the VAT.

Then as soon as I sell these goods to my customers I must charge VAT at 17.5 per cent. The VAT I charge my customers must then be given to HM Customs and Excise and is what is known as 'output tax'.

The mechanism by which you pay Customs and Excise is by completing *a return*. So my return to Customs and Excise will comprise of two taxes – output and input tax.

My soap making example might then look like this:

I buy my raw materials for £100 plus VAT at 17.5% giving a total of £117.50.

Therefore my input tax, ie the money I can claim back from HM Customs and Excise, is £17.50.

I then re-sell these goods to my customers for £150 plus VAT at 17.5% giving a total figure of £176.25.

Therefore my total output tax, ie the money I owe HM Customs and Excise is £26.25.

My return will then be as follows:

Total output tax	£26.25
Less total input tax	£17.50
Total owing	£ 8.75

In reality I may actually be able to claim back more input tax as I can claim back VAT on anything I have to buy to produce my final goods. Therefore if I have petrol expenses I can claim back the element of VAT included in petrol and so on.

I am unregistered for VAT. Here I simply buy my raw materials for £100 plus VAT = £117.50 and then sell them to my customer without having to charge VAT.

Cost of raw materials would be £117.50 because I cannot claim back the VAT, however I do not have to charge VAT on my finished product, which means that I do not have to add 17.5% VAT to the final price I charge my customer.

When must you register for VAT

As you can see there are advantages and disadvantages to registering for VAT. Lots of smaller business decide not to register for VAT as they believe it to be uneconomical.

Examples of this are guesthouses, many of whom choose to stay deliberately small and operate below what is known as the VAT threshold.

THE VAT THRESHOLD

If the value of your taxable supplies is over a certain limit you must register for VAT. The limit at the time of writing is £65,000 per annum. The exception to this is if your supplies are wholly or mainly zero rated in which case you need to apply to HM Customs and Excise for an exemption.

Therefore if your business sells more than £65,000 per annum you must register for VAT, unless what you are selling is zero rated in which case you can apply for an exemption. This figure is usually subject to some form of change in the government's annual budget.

You can see now why certain businesses decide to run their business so they don't reach this ceiling.

Should I register for VAT if my turnover is less than the threshold?

Deciding to register your business for VAT will depend on a number factors. The important thing to know is that you don't have to apply for VAT registration immediately. You can apply at some future date. So don't feel you have to rush into this decision.

If you do decide to register for VAT you will have to be a 'business' in terms of what's required for VAT.

Broadly speaking, HM Customs and Excise define a business as being someone who is supplying goods and services in return for payment, although payment need not be in money. Your business activity must have a degree of frequency and scale over a continued period.

In other words if you're selling the occasional item here and there then you don't qualify for registration. Obviously this is to stop private individuals declaring themselves as businesses so as to take advantage of claiming back the VAT on their purchases.

When deciding whether or not to register for VAT try to look at the wider picture.

Case study: cycle hire

Let's imagine that you're planning to run a cycle hire business.

Your total hire stock is made up of 10 new bicycles which you have just purchased at £470 each including VAT at 17.5%, which equates to £70 VAT on each cycle.

Therefore the total amount of VAT that you have paid on your stock is £70 × 10 = £700. If your business is registered for VAT you can now re-claim this £700 as input tax.

But you must also charge VAT on your rentals, if you intend to rent these cycles out at £20 per day then you will have to add 17.5% VAT on top of this, which means you daily hire rate is now £23.50. You then will have to pay HM Customs and Excise £3.50 on each daily hire you make.

You decide that you will be sticking with your original bikes for a period of three years after which time you will then replace them with new bikes.

What this means is that although you have recouped £700 input tax having bought your cycles, you will now have to work out how much you will have to pay in VAT to HMCE over the three years you intend to keep the bikes.

You will also have to work out what other business costs you will incur over the next few years.

Cost could include:

- advertising
- cycle accessories
- staff uniforms
- maintenance of any business property

- ☐ stationery
- ☐ website costs.

The advantage of being registered for VAT means you can recoup the VAT element from all your business purchases where you have had to pay VAT.

Even one small advertisement in a glossy magazine can cost £200 per month plus VAT = £235. Thus over the three-year period you could claim up to £1,260 (36 months' VAT at £35 per month) on your advertising bill alone.

You may also find that you have to have your business premises painted once in the three years and provided you choose a VAT registered contractor you can claim back the VAT element.

As you can see the decision to register for VAT is something that only you can work out for your business. You need to work out your likely costs versus your sales income and see which is best.

If in doubt, my advice is not to register immediately but see how your business goes and then register later.

There are instances where you get back the VAT on certain items even though you have been trading for a period of time and not charging VAT.

Remember though if you supply only goods that are exempt from VAT you cannot claim back VAT on goods you purchase.

VAT exempt goods are different from zero rated goods.

VOLUNTARY REGISTRATION

If you decide to register for VAT when your turnover is less than the allowed limit you are doing what is known as voluntary registration.

By registering you will have to complete regular VAT returns which can be time consuming. A new flat rate system has been introduced to ease the burden of reporting for small businesses and this system is well worth taking a look at.

Where to go to get further information on VAT

It's beyond the scope of what we can include in this book to write a definitive guide to VAT. You can download all the information from the Customs and Excise website, which is located at http://www.hmce.gov.uk. Alternatively you can telephone them on 0845 010 9000.

They also run a number of business advice open days, which are free to attend and are run at various times throughout the year. These open days are run together with other agencies such as Inland Revenue, Health and Safety, Office of Fair Trading and others. Details can be found on their website http://www.businessadviceday.co.uk.

11

TEN GREAT BUSINESSES YOU CAN RUN FROM HOME

Why spend and time and money trying to come up with the next biggest business idea, when it's far easier and profitable to follow the path already laid and signposted by existing businesses?

Ultimately, there is really no such thing as a 'new business', as every new business regardless of how innovative or radical is simply a variation of an existing business model.

For example, some of the most successful and profitable large UK businesses simply retail other companies' products. You don't see large supermarket chains spending oodles of cash and time in innovating the next best washing-up liquid. Or a successful clothing retailer commissioning clothes designers to come up with a mind-blowing, wallet-opening range of clothing. Instead they simply operate on the basis that it's far easier to buy existing sought after goods and retail them at the lowest possible cost to achieve maximum profits.

I'm not suggesting you take on the supermarket or retail giants of this world, but I do think that we can all learn from their successful formula by simply adopting an existing business model and making it more profitable and more successful.

So in this chapter, I'm going to take you through what's involved in starting and running a number of home-based businesses that are worth considering if you really are serious about starting your own business.

My top ten home-based businesses include:

- ☐ Cleaning business.
- ☐ Gardening business.
- ☐ Child minding business.
- ☐ Pet sitting business.
- ☐ Greetings cards business.
- ☐ A tutoring agency.
- ☐ Bed and breakfast.
- ☐ Catering business.
- ☐ Antiques dealing.
- ☐ Internet business.

Start your own cleaning business

My favourite all-time, start your own business is the cleaning business model. This is by far the easiest business of all as you can literally start it with nothing other than your own enthusiasm and willingness to work hard.

To begin with you don't even need to invest in cleaning products or equipment as you can ask your clients to supply them. And if you think that a cleaning business is a dead-end business opportunity, think again. Some of the world's most successful franchise operations are cleaning businesses.

The advantages of starting a cleaning business include the following.

☐ It is a turn-key cash business.
☐ There is no initial capital outlay.
☐ There are a number of different business models for you to choose from.
☐ You don't have to do any cleaning yourself.
☐ You can quickly build up a profitable, saleable business.
☐ It can be run from home without ever having to rent or buy additional premises.
☐ It can operate in the private/domestic market or work in the commercial sector.

TURN-KEY CASH BUSINESS

A turn-key cash business is one where your business is cash positive. For example, you go and do the work and get paid in cash at the end of the job. So you don't have to worry about waiting for days or even months before you get paid. Of course as your business grows, you will have to organise an invoice system where you charge your clients on a weekly or monthly cycle, but initially with this business model you can generate instant cash. Depending on your circumstances this might be very necessary.

NO INITIAL CAPITAL OUTLAY

This is the great benefit of starting a cleaning business – you don't have to have any money to hand, so if you've just been made redundant, lost your life savings, or however dire your circumstances are you can start this business without requiring lots of cash.

NOT HAVING TO DO ANY CLEANING YOURSELF

The success of this particular business will very much depend on you not doing any cleaning, and instead recruiting and building up a reliable and honest team of cleaning staff to tackle all those cleaning contracts you're going to go out and win.

QUICKLY BUILDING UP A PROFITABLE, SALEABLE BUSINESS

If you offer a quality, reliable, value-for-money cleaning business, you will see your business grow from a one-person operation into something much larger in a relatively short space of time. If you don't believe me, just have a look at one of the many cleaning franchises available for you to invest in and note how they all make the same promises in terms of future growth.

Another huge benefit of this type of business is that provided you work hard enough to get it right, you will reach a stage where you have a nice healthy, saleable business.

RUNNING IT FROM HOME WITHOUT THE NEED TO RENT OR BUY ADDITIONAL PREMISES

Being able to start and build a business that you can run from your own home means that you won't have to share your hard-earned revenues with landlords who will charge you rent and local authorities who will charge you business rates. Working from home also means that you can tailor your business around your family commitments and so on.

OPERATING IT IN EITHER THE PRIVATE OR COMMERCIAL SECTOR

Some entrepreneurs might like to work with home-owners as their clients and will offer a domestic cleaning service, while others may prefer to operate in the commercial sector where they can clean in offices, factories, schools, and so on. It is possible to operate in both sectors. However, looking at those who are already running successful cleaning businesses, there seems to be a clear division between those catering exclusively for the private sector and those involved in the commercial sector.

HOW EASY IT IS TO START?

You could start tomorrow by following the quick-fire guide below.

1. Decide on what type of cleaning business you'd want to run. For example, a window-cleaning business, a general cleaning business aimed at the domestic market, or a specialist cleaning business aimed at the commercial sector.

2. Check to see what other operators in your area are charging so you have a general feel for how much you should charge.

3. Get some cards or leaflets printed and drop them through every letterbox in your neighbourhood; leave a pile in your local hairdressers, cafés, library, and so on.

4. When the phone rings, be professional when visiting your prospective client.

Dazzle them with your can-do, honest, reliable attitude. Give a fair price, which must be in line with the current prices for the work they want done. Don't be tempted to under-cut your competitors. Sell yourself and your business on the basis of your quality and reliability. Remember, your ultimate goal is to employ staff to do the cleaning for you, so you need to ensure there's enough being charged to pay them and you and to allow for some profit for your business.

5. Whenever you get a new client, soon after you've started working for them ask them if they know of anyone else who could benefit from your services.

6. Work hard and don't delay in building up a nice, large, but manageable working diary. The sooner you reach the point where you need to employ staff, the sooner you can stand back from cleaning and start enjoying running your business.

7. Make sure you understand what's involved in employing staff and also that you have all the adequate insurances in place.

TIP

Don't lose sight of your goal, which is to run your own business as opposed to being a cleaner.

The success of your business will depend on three things – quality of service, reliability, and honesty. If you cannot get these things right from day one, don't bother.

Treat your staff and customers as you would like to be treated yourself. If you only have customers and no staff, you're simply a cleaner. So remember, it's your staff that make you a business and ultimately maintain and build your reputation. And it's your customers who pay all of you.

Start your own gardening business

I started my first gardening business when I was thirteen and returned to this type of business when I found myself in a personal and financial crisis when I was in my thirties. I haven't looked back since.

With an estimated whopping 60% of UK residents seeing gardening as a chore, you can instantly see the potential market for a professional gardening company.

The gardening business model is similar to the cleaning business model, however it has one marked difference. With a gardening business you really do have to like gardening and be knowledgeable already. If you feel your existing knowledge isn't up to it, don't worry. You can study, take short courses, and so on. The most important thing is that you can easily start a gardening business right from where you're sitting now. You don't need oodles of cash, business premises, and the like. As with the cleaning business model you can even start by using your clients' tools.

The advantages of a gardening business include the following.

☐ It is easy to start with little or no capital outlay.
☐ It is a turn-key cash business.
☐ It needs no premises and can always be run from home.
☐ It can operate in the private or commercial sector or both.
☐ You don't have to garden yourself.
☐ It is easy to build up a large, profitable business with a good resale value.

As you can see, the advantages of starting a gardening business are similar to those of a cleaning business with both businesses being relatively easy to begin with either no or limited capital.

HOW EASY IS IT TO START?

Similar to the cleaning business, you can start this today with some careful research and a well-planned sales strategy. A quick-fire get started guide follows:

1. Carry out some initial research by phoning existing businesses in your area and getting a clear idea of how much the going rate is for your services.

2. Decide on what services to offer initially, taking into account your skills and experience. For example, you could simply begin with a lawn-cutting service, a leaf-sweeping service, a gutter clearing service, and so on.

3. Have some cards/leaflets printed and drop them through as many doors as you can, not forgetting to put your card up in newsagents' windows, barbers', hairdressers', doctors' surgeries, vets', cafés, and so on.

4. When the phone rings, as it will, be professional. Have a clear idea of how much you're going to charge and what you're capable of doing. To begin with don't tackle or take on jobs that are beyond your experience.

5. Successful gardening businesses are built on offering reliable, professional, value for money service.

6. As your business grows you can employ people to work for you and the ultimate point you want to get to is where you have teams of gardeners working for your business, while you take on a purely management, entrepreneurial role.

HOW MUCH MONEY DO YOU NEED TO START?

If cash is a huge problem, you could initially start by offering your services as a gardener where you supply the labour and expertise and your clients supply the tools and materials. However, fairly soon you will need to think about getting your own tools and equipment as you can then charge more for your services and specialise in whatever area you're most interested in.

 When it comes to running a successful gardening business, knowledge and professionalism are everything. Invest time and money in training both yourself and your staff.

Make sure you charge enough and don't be tempted to win new customers on the basis of being cheaper.

Only tackle the commercial market once you've got some good experience working on domestic gardens.

Start your own child minding service

With more and more women with children returning to work, the demand for quality child minding is at an all-time high.

Of course, not everyone will be suited to starting their own child minding business, but for those who are looking for a home-based business with a huge potential market, and have a real love of working with children, what better way is there to start and grow a business?

HOW EASY IS IT TO START?

Thankfully, not too easy! I say that not to put you off in any way, but of all the business models I recommend in this chapter, I believe a child minding service is the most responsible of businesses. Therefore it's only right that this kind of business will require you to be registered, have some degree of qualification, and be subject to official, outside scrutiny.

It would be beyond the scope of this chapter to give you a step-by-step-plan for how to go about getting started. In any event you will need to check what is required in terms of legislation, planning consents, and so on prior to your starting your business. This is an area which is under constant change, with new regulations being proposed and introduced in an effort to ensure that parents can safely leave their children in the hands of others while they go out to work.

That said, the essential criteria for anyone wanting to start this business would include:

☐ You must have as your over-riding goal to create a business that puts children's needs first so that those in your care are treated to a safe, warm and often stimulating environment.

☐ Not only must you be able to get on with all the children entrusted in your care, you must also be able to build meaningful and trusting relationships with their parents.

☐ You must be organised. This isn't the sort of business where you'll get away with a 'it'll be alright on the night' approach. For example, if you oversleep one morning you'll awaken to a chorus of annoyed parents banging on your door wondering why you're not up and open. This will be a one-off event, because few if any of those parents would then entrust their child to someone who cannot even manage to get up on time.

☐ You'll need to invest in toys and equipment and ensure your property is suitably set up for taking care of children.

☐ The Children Act 2004 requires you to be registered with the relevant authorities. To become registered you will have to apply and then satisfy their criteria. There's the obvious caveat that you mustn't have been convicted of an offence against a child as well as other criteria which you will have to check up on. The easiest place to find the information you'll need is on the government website which is found at www.doh.gov.uk/scg/childprotect.

☐ You'll also have to have to comply with the National Standards, which cover a range of age groups that you might be looking after. These include everything from requirements for physical environments to the your suitability as a person. At the time of writing, there are 14 National Standards for the Under Eights Day Care and Childminding, which is for England and Wales. For information on what standards apply in Scotland and Northern Ireland, you will need to contact the relevant government departments. In any event, regardless of whether you live in the UK or elsewhere, you'll need to check for all the latest requirements. As I said earlier, child care/protection legislation is subject to ongoing changes and the only real way to be up to date on these is to check all the legislation thoroughly prior to starting your business.

As you can see, this is a business where you'll need to undertake some further research and ensure that both you, and your household, are suitable to start this, but once you've decided to take those initial steps, what's going to make your business successful?

Just like every other successful business – you'll need to offer the marketplace local to you a solution to their needs. For example, it's no good offering a child care business model that is based on elsewhere in the country (or the world for that matter) if you haven't addressed what is actually wanted in your own neighbourhood. Remember that while your customers will travel some distance to you, your business will effectively depend on support from your local area. It's important to get this clear in your mind from the outset, as you really need to research what already works well in your area and what your business could bring in addition to the hopefully already good service available.

So let's look at some of the areas you'll need to cover:

☐ To begin with, compliance. As I explained earlier, you, your business, and your household must comply with some very strict legal criteria.

☐ Finding out what's already on offer in your area. It is vital you get this right – you must identify the most successful child care businesses in your area and ask yourself the question why are they so successful? You'll also need to get out there and interview mums and dads and ask them why they chose such and such a child minding service over another. And I can tell you now it will not be down to who is cheaper.

☐ Working out a business model whereby you include the essential elements of those already successful businesses while still adding on something extra to pull new customers your way. This something extra could be something as simple as you having available space in your service for new children. Very often the problem with services like these is that the really good ones will be booked up for years in advance. A bit like seats for a highly sought-after concert, or places at a school where children's names are put down the minute they're born. So don't beat yourself up looking for the perfect hook – it could be simply that you have spaces available.

☐ Costs versus earnings. This area is crucial to your business's success and future. You need to work out how much it's going to cost you to provide your service, which will include food, toys, heating, lighting, compliance costs, any remedial works needed to your home, staffing costs (assuming you might need to hire in additional help), and so on. Estimating these costs isn't easy, and I recommend you err on the side of over-spend, as opposed to seeing how cheaply you can provide your service. A good indication of how much you can charge is to phone around existing child minding services and ask them for their rates. But remember, their overheads might be higher or lower than yours. For example, their house might have a wonderfully efficient cost-saving heating system, while your home may not. Or perhaps they have family helping in running their business, while you will have to employ additional staff. So always be cautious when making like-for-like cost comparisons.

☐ Contingency planning. This is where you must think about what would happen if...and then come up with some solutions. For example, what happens if you're suddenly taken ill and cannot open – what then? I've always found the easiest ways to come up with solutions is to ask the competition. Therefore, and again when you're researching the competition, make sure you ask them what happens when they're too ill to open. They'll then tell you their contingency plan, which hopefully you can adopt as well. It may be that there's a local, suitably qualified, freelance child minder who does the rounds when someone is off sick or is otherwise away from their business.

FINDING YOUR FIRST CUSTOMERS

I say first, because this is a business that is built entirely on the child minder's reputation and quality of service. If you get it right, which I hope you do, you'll do well and quickly build a successful business. If you get it wrong, then not only will word spread about your dire service but you may also find yourself in trouble with the authorities.

With this business finding your customers is a little easier than with other businesses, as you can readily identify your target market. For example, you're only looking to market your service to those with children, and those who need someone to look after them while they are out at work, or otherwise unavailable.

There are number of ways you can market your business including the following:

1. Leaflet drops in your neighbourhood.

2. Poster/card advertising in your local supermarkets (they all have boards where for a small fee you can advertise your services).

3. A list of child minders kept by your local authority where you can ask that it be made known you're available for bookings.

4. An advertisement in your local paper. This is my favourite way because if you play it right you should get your local paper to do a news story on your new business. Something along the lines of why you've started and what you're offering and so on. It's a great way of creating instant credibility.

5. Creating and maintaining a website. This is a good idea in any event, but do remember that with this business you can only sell to those local enough to you to be able to drop their children off daily and collect them again on their way back from work.

Careful research is the key to success with this business – therefore research everything thoroughly, from what the law requires of you to what your competition are offering.

Be prepared for hard work. If you're the type of person who enjoys quiet working conditions, then this business isn't for you. You really must love working with children and have this as your primary goal.

You are offering an extremely valuable service so make sure you charge enough to make it worthwhile to you. While I'm not suggesting you embrace profiteering by looking after your neighbours' children, neither should you operate as a charity just because they happen to be your neighbours.

Interview prospective clients as carefully and with the same objectivity as you would do with your staff. You need to be sure that you can meet their expectations and that they have a realistic expectation of what you can and cannot offer.

Start your own pet sitting service

For pet lovers everywhere, there has never been a better time to start your own pet sitting service. This service works on the basis that you either pet sit your clients' pets in their homes while they're away or, alternatively, you take their pets from them and look after them in your own home while they are not around.

However, given that a gardening business is really only suitable for those who love gardening, to be a successful pet sitter you must love pets. This business demands that you're going to be looking after someone's much loved, and very often much adored, pet.

The advantages of a pet sitting service are as follows:

☐ Very low start-up costs.
☐ Extremely low overheads.
☐ Lots of spin-off potential.
☐ Quickly builds up a profitable saleable business.

WHAT DOES IT INVOLVE?

As the name implies, you will offer a service where you stay overnight in a client's home and look after their pet or pets. Your stay could be anywhere from a 24-hour period to a week or fortnight, during which you'll attend to the needs of that client's pet. This could be anything, from feeding and cleaning to taking the family dog for walks or pre-arranged visits to any appointments that pet might have (for example, a visit to the pet parlour for a pooch makeover).

What it will not include is undertaking any household chores such as gardening, cleaning, and so on. While you'll probably get asked from time to time to provide these services in addition to your pet sitting duties my advice, which is based on the experiences of others, is to make it clear from your marketing and your initial contact with your clients that pet sitting is *all* you're offering. Otherwise you will run the risk of simply being hired as offering an odd-job service. Obviously it goes without saying that you'll be expected to clean up after yourself and to hand over the house in the same condition it was in when you arrived.

Generally speaking you'll be required to stay in a client's home and to only leave the house for the occasional short trip. Your stay will usually be for a pre-agreed duration and you will need to agree in advance what this includes. For example:

☐ Duration of your stay.

☐ How the pet(s) is/are to be cared for, which would include such things as how often you are to feed them and in what quantities, and what additional services are included (for example, walks).

☐ What you are to do in an emergency – which vet you are to take the pet to and whether or not you are required to pay the initial fees (or if the owner has a pre-agreed credit limit at the surgery).

☐ What the boundaries of the house are when you are staying there. For example, which rooms you can use, whether or not you must bring your own food, and so on.

HOW EASY IS IT TO START?

Starting your own pet sitting service is a relatively easy business. Obviously, as with all the other 'looking after people or animals' businesses, you will need to have a genuine love of pets and a real willingness to create a service whereby pet owners are willing to entrust their beloved animal to your company. Once you've created a trusting reputation, building your business should be relatively straightforward. I think the most difficult thing with this business is getting started.

The most important thing to get right is to have systems in place before you go looking for your first customer. So you need to work out which animals you would be comfortable looking after. If you only like dogs, then obviously you're going to limit your potential markets. However, I'd imagine it would be quite difficult to find a suitably experienced pet sitter for a snake, so if you have expertise with reptiles then obviously you could take advantage of this by carving out a niche market within a niche market.

THINGS YOU'LL NEED TO HAVE

☐ *A responsible nature.* Pet sitting involves quite a lot of responsibility. With this business you are offering to look after someone's pet(s), which isn't unlike looking after someone's children. So you've got to be sure that you're up to the job and also capable of looking after someone's home in their absence.

☐ *Adequate insurance cover.* You'll need to be covered for third party insurance, which would encompass both you and your business activities.

☐ *Customer care contract.* You'll need to have some form of written contract which you can get your clients to sign agreeing the scope of the things your service covers. Remember, not every client will want all you're offering so you must make sure your contract is adaptable and flexible enough to cover all eventualities.

☐ *Membership of a professional body or holding pet care qualifications.* It's not essential that you have formal qualifications, or that you are a member of a recognised professional body, but there is no doubt that you should give it some thought. Certainly there is everything to be gained by working towards a professional pet care qualification and giving your business the endorsement it might need by joining a recognised trade body. For further information take a look at what the Animal Care College can offer you (www.animalcarecollege. co.uk) and COAPE (the Centre of Applied Pet Care Ethology) which offers distance learning courses (www.coape.co.uk).

Your continued success depends on your reputation. The only way to create and maintain a successful pet sitting business is to offer a reliable, quality, value-for-money service.

Knowledge is power. Learn as much as you can about animal care and behaviour.

Make sure you check any relevant legislation before you start and keep abreast of any changes when you're up and running.

This is a business where if you get it right the rewards are excellent, so make sure you pay attention to the small things like making sure you close all doors behind you and so on, ensuring that the pet in your care doesn't escape.

Start your own greetings card business

For those with a creative, artistic flair, starting a greetings card business is an excellent opportunity to work on their creative side while building a profitable business. For those who don't have the necessary artistic talent and flair this is not a problem as they too can start their own greetings card business by commissioning others to create the cards for them.

If you choose this option there are lots of different types of businesses that you could start, including:

☐ Designing and creating your own range of cards, which you can then sell yourself.

☐ Designing and creating your own range of cards, which you can then sell to retailers.

☐ Commissioning others to create cards for you which you can then wholesale to retailers.

THE MARKET OPPORTUNITY

The greetings card market offers endless opportunities for new card ideas. When it comes to cards there are all sorts of occasions to include. From birthdays, which represent almost 50% of all cards, sold to condolences cards, get well soon cards, wedding cards, mother's and father's day cards, Easter cards – the list is endless. And the good news here is that the market opportunity is always growing for those with a keen eye for an opportunity.

TYPES OF CARD

There are all sorts of card types you can design and create, ranging from simple or elaborate home-made cards to cards which unfold to sing someone a personal greeting. Some of the main types of cards include:

☐ Picture cards with a photograph on the front.
☐ Cards featuring a painting on the front.
☐ Cartoon cards.

☐ Personalised cards.

☐ Cards commissioned for specific events or occasions where the picture/cartoon/ drawings will be specific to that occasion (for example, when a member of the Royal Family marries).

☐ Home-made cards.

Within the above types of cards you'll then have a number of sub-sections, for example:

☐ Cards that come with verses or messages, or even those that play tunes when they are opened.

☐ Blank cards where the purchaser is free to add their own wording inside, writing this especially for whatever occasion they're celebrating, or remembering, or wishing for.

☐ General cards which are aimed at a particular event or occasion, such as a happy birthday, good luck with your exams, and so on. (Remember, over 50% of all cards purchased are for birthdays!)

YOU'LL NEED TO IDENTIFY A MARKET THAT YOU CAN WORK IN

Obviously the home-made card market will be aimed at a different customer than those for the mainstream market, but each business model will suit different entrepreneurs. For example, a mum with a family to raise who is looking to start a small part-time, home-based business might find working at home, making her own cards and selling them to local shops, an easier prospect to start up and run, while the person with loads of time on their hands may want to launch a full-scale business selling to the major high street retail chains.

The secret here is to start a business that suits your skills and talents and to then follow the market that is most appropriate to your work.

For example, if you're a talented artist, you could produce your own paintings which you could then use to create your own cards. Or if photography is your speciality you could use your unique photographs to create cards. Likewise, if you're a talented wordsmith or poet why not use your writing skills to create suitable verses for your cards – you can have the images created for you by commissioning artists or photographers to supply something to suit your style of work.

SELLING YOUR CARDS

You'll only be successful if you sell enough of your cards to make a profit, and once these are sold, you have to encourage these buyers to stay loyal to your brand.

Obviously the sales and marketing methods you choose will depend on the type of greetings card business you set up. For example:

☐ Home-made cards could be sold to local shops, including gift shops, craft shops, charity shops, and so on, and also by creating your own website and selling online.

☐ Professionally printed cards (where you get a printer to produce your work) could also be sold via the above sales channels, but you could also target a broader retail market that would include specialised card shops, retail chains, and so on.

☐ You could also target specific markets and sell direct to them – here, the corporate greetings card is huge. This is where businesses, charities, politicians, and so on commission cards to be designed, created, and published that are specific to their needs. Although this area is hugely competitive and probably requires a lot more legwork than any of the above, it will be ideally suited to some greetings card entrepreneurs.

☐ Book stands at trade shows and sell direct to retailers. Use Google to help you find a list of suitable trade fairs. While booking a trade stand will usually cost quite a bit, it can reduce your costs in the long run as you will get to meet and show off your wares to lots of potential trade buyers in one hit. You will also see what the competition are up to and get a feel of what's in vogue and what's outdated. This is all useful information when planning your future design and production schedule.

It's estimated that women buy 80% of all cards sold. Therefore, make sure your cards and ideas have enough girl pulling power to get you noticed and sold.

Your cards need to be aimed at a specific customer, so sit down and write a profile of the person you believe will buy these. Then try to work out if enough of these people exist to make it a worthwhile business proposition. If you're selling your cards to retailers, each retailer will want a card that's going to sell quickly and in large enough numbers to make it worth their while.

Never have your cards printed in bulk quantities until you have tried them out on your target market. For example, if you're planning to sell to retailers then take samples of your work along to their various shops and show them at card trade fairs. It is only after this, when you have worthwhile orders, that you should commit to having them printed.

Whatever market you choose to operate in, you'll need repeat business to ensure your business grows beyond just an initial sales splurge. Make sure from day one you have systems in place to capture all your customers' details so you can contact them again in the future when you launch your next batch of cards.

Create a unique, sought-after product and you cannot help but succeed. Create low-quality rubbish and no one will buy your cards – with the possible exception of a few doting relatives.

Start your own home tutoring agency

When I first researched this business, I dismissed this as not having a wide enough appeal as I had assumed, wrongly as it turned out, that you would have to be a teacher or specialist trainer to start and run this business. However, as I quickly found out, you don't. This makes this an ideal business for the home-based entrepreneur as you can use all your creative skills to get this super business up and running and earning you a profit.

HOW DOES IT WORK?

Parents today are keener than ever to ensure that their children are well educated to a standard that allows them compete for college and university places and ultimately for job places in today's highly competitive marketplace. The problem which many face is that for a variety reasons their children are not getting the one-to-one tutoring that they would like. It may be that their child is weak in a certain subject or subjects and this is where some additional tutoring would be very useful.

On the other side of the coin, you have at any given time a number of suitably qualified teachers who (for a variety of reasons) would like either some additional part-time work, perhaps retired teachers looking to boost their pension, or just those who enjoy the satisfaction that comes with teaching motivated students.

Outside of these is you – the entrepreneur looking to start a worthwhile, profitable business. You're interested in education, you enjoy working with young people and adults. You're also an organised person with an eye for opportunity and detail. Thus you've all the essential criteria to set up your own home tutoring agency.

HOW EASY IS IT TO START UP?

Starting up is relatively straightforward and won't involve you having to spend oodles of cash before you see a return on your investment. Here's a brief outline of what's involved:

1. Decide to start your own home-based tutoring agency.

2. Carry out some initial market research which should include checking out what is already available in your neighbourhood, speaking to head teachers at local schools, and checking notices in your local paper, libraries, school noticeboards, and so on.

3. Decide on a name for your business. Never underestimate the pulling power of a well thought-out name. Remember, you're selling private one-to-one education. So you really need a name that's going to create an image of a quality, trusting learning environment.

4. From your initial research you should get an idea of how much to charge per hour. Your earnings with this business will be similar to those of any other agency which supplies staff or labour. For example, a recruitment agency will charge a percentage of a staff member's salary for every hour they work in a business on a temporary contract. When deciding on a rate for your tutors, you'll need to take into account an attractive enough hourly rate for them, plus any travelling expenses, plus your commission on every hour they work. And your commission will not simply be profits in your bank account. From this commission, you'll need to cover advertising costs (which can be relatively high) as well as administration costs, for example taking and making bookings for tutors, running a tutoring schedule, sending out information packs on your service, and so on. All of these costs must be covered before you can make any profit.

5. Once you've come with an initial costing schedule, which is flexible enough so you can tweak it in the future if you need to, you're then ready to recruit your first tutors. I'll give you examples of how to achieve this in the next section on marketing.

6. When you have enough tutors to begin with, you're now ready to market your service to potential clients. I'll give some ideas on how to achieve this in a moment.

7. As soon as the phone starts ringing with prospective clients, this is where your business will really take off. You must match tutors to students, take and make bookings, work out the logistics in terms of agreeing suitable appointments for both parties – and you're away.

8. Similar to all the other business covered in this chapter, your success will depend upon the quality of the service you're offering. So you need to be sure the tutors you recruit are up to the job, presentable, experienced, and capable of delivering home tutoring. And just as important, you must ensure that the support you give to your tutors is of such a high standard that they're happy to work and stay with your agency. For example, if your organisation skills are so poor that a tutor finds themselves turning up to the wrong address (or the right address at the wrong time), then obviously you're not going to be in this business for long.

MARKETING YOUR BUSINESS

Starting a tutoring agency needs a two-part marketing strategy:

- ☐ A campaign to recruit tutors to your agency.
- ☐ A campaign to sell your services to prospective clients.

In my experience, I don't believe you could run a joint marketing campaign to cover both of these areas. For example, putting an advertisement in your local paper that advertises for tutors and also advertises vacancies for new pupils will give entirely the wrong impression. Remember, parents are ultimately looking for exam success for their children. They're going to be reading your ad and hoping to see that your tutors are well qualified, experienced, and have a track record in delivering exam results. This can only be achieved when you have assembled all your tutors and you can use their individual accolades as unique selling points.

There are a number of ways of advertising for tutors and potential clients and some of these include:

- ☐ Direct mail campaigns to local schools, asking each head teacher if they would display a poster on their staff noticeboard to advertise that you are looking for tutors.

- ☐ Subsequently, sending a letter to each head teacher asking him or her would they mind advertising your agency to the parents of the children in their school.

- ☐ Running a series of advertisements in your local paper.

- ☐ Putting up posters in local libraries, doctors' surgeries and leisure centres, as well as a direct mail leaflet drop in school catchment areas.

- ☐ Setting up a website. Again, this is a business that would really benefit from a website where parents can view your services online and see glowing references from parents and existing students.

WHERE TO TUTOR?

My own view on this is that the best place to offer tutoring is in the student's own home as you do away with all the fears that will surface when a parent has to send their child to a stranger's house. You can also use this as a unique selling point, and your tutors can also maintain the privacy of their own homes, which is equally important.

You must ensure that all your tutors are CRB checked (Criminal Records Bureau check) which you can arrange via your local council or police on payment of a set fee. There are currently two types of check you must have done – a basic and an enhanced – and I'd recommend you go for the enhanced as this way you can demonstrate that you have taken every possible precaution to weed out any undesirable people.

You must be highly organised. This is a business based on logistics – you have to juggle lots of balls in the air to make sure everyone is where they should be at the right time. If organisation isn't your forte, then this business is not for you.

As with child care, education is a priority for many parents, so you must therefore expect to have your business scrutinised by prospective parents. Be prepared to take the time to explain your services and to make sure you project a trustworthy image.

You must get your prices right, thus accordingly there isn't really a 'cheap' solution to home tutoring. For example, in 1984 when I was living at home with my parents in Ireland, I undertook additional home tutoring in mathematics. Back then my parents paid £25 an hour for one-to-one tuition. By all accounts a huge amount of money in those days, but despite these charges the teacher was completely booked up for two years in advance. So don't base your service on being cheap. No one will thank you for offering a cheap service which fails to deliver on that all important examination result.

Start your own bed and breakfast

Obviously this is a business that will not be suited to everyone as to start a bed and breakfast you'll need to have a suitable property. That said, there are many parents who, when their children have flown the nest, will find they have an abundance of time and a number of spare rooms and would enjoy the sense of companionship that comes with running a bed and breakfast.

I know a number of successful bed and breakfast owners and all of them enjoy the social interaction that their business brings. Some of them had previously run other businesses, including newsagents, cafés and restaurants, and not one of them would ever contemplate returning to their original business venture.

HOW IT WORKS

I'm sure you are probably familiar with the traditional B&B business model – where visitors stay anything from one night to a week or more and on payment of a pre-agreed rate get a bed and breakfast service. Traditionally, B&Bs tend to be cheaper than hotels and they usually enjoy a loyal following from regular customers. However, the unique selling point for most B&Bs isn't price, but comfort. A quality B&B will be seen by many as a sort of home from home, where personal service and attention to detail really count for something.

Some of the benefits of starting and running a B&B include:

☐ It is the ultimate home-based business where your home becomes your business.

☐ That even with a small number of rooms, the earning potential is excellent when compared with other businesses.

☐ You can quickly build up a regular clientele so you won't have to continually pay out for advertising.

Potential drawbacks include:

☐ You'll have strangers staying in your home and some of these people may be from a different background or culture to your existing social circle, so you need to be broadminded and generally enthusiastic about all walks of life.

☐ It can involve long hours where you're up early in the morning cooking breakfasts and your days are spent cleaning and preparing rooms, thus leaving you with little personal free time.

THE OPPORTUNITY

You may think that you could only start and run a successful B&B in a seaside or tourist area, but you can start a B&B anywhere. For example, if you're living in an industrial area you could target the commercial market by offering local businesses high quality, comfortable rooms for their visiting customers, staff and suppliers.

Colleges and universities also offer excellent potential where you can offer group discounts on rooms for visiting lecturers, students, and even family members visiting their loved ones who are at college.

When people need somewhere for an overnight stay this will also offer you a market for your rooms. So please don't limit your thinking to just holiday visitors. There's lots of other business around that you can pitch for. For example, my friend's bed and breakfast often works as a sort of overflow accommodation for our neighbours who will book rooms for their relatives when they come to stay for parties, funerals, weddings, christenings, and so on. So it's important to advertise your services in the market local to you.

If you're in the countryside, you could perhaps offer all-year-round breaks where your guests could come and experience the countryside at various times in the year. You could also perhaps team up with local farms and organise farm tours, or walking holidays, where your B&B could be used a base for these holidays.

During the summer months my friend's B&B caters for the tourist trade, while during the winter months they will fill their rooms with workers from local factories and commercial travellers who cannot find room at the local Travel Lodge. None of them struggle for business all-round and even in an economic downturn they're still busy, as those people who would normally stay in a hotel will downsize, as it were, to a B&B.

According to figures from the Bed and Breakfast Association (bandbassociation.org) this sector is 28% bigger than that of the budget hotels business market. So you can see the huge potential that turning your home into a B&B can offer.

HOW EASY IS IT TO START?

Depending on where your home is, at present and in terms of decoration, tidiness and how everything works this will determine how soon you can start your business. Although over the years I've stayed in some fairly awful B&Bs in the UK, with wallpaper peeling off the walls, cold, damp rooms, and terrible breakfasts that seem to consist of overburdening the plate with luke-warm baked beans, the general standard of B&Bs is usually very high. And I've certainly stayed in some B&Bs where the standards far exceeded those I've experienced in four-star hotels. So you really need to have your home up to scratch – tastefully decorated, clutter free, cosy, comfy and welcoming – if you're going to turn it into a B&B.

Here are some of the things you need to address before starting:

☐ Before you do anything else, pay a visit to your local council offices and check whether or not you need planning permission to turn your home into a bed and breakfast. You'll also need to register with the council's department of the environment and you'll need to take a short course on food preparation and hygiene.

☐ Your home will also need to comply with current fire regulations. Your local authority will be able to tell you what's required.

☐ You'll need to carry out your own survey of your home to work out how many rooms you can comfortably let out, what toilet facilities you can offer, where you'll have your guests sit down and have breakfast, and what provision you're going to make for families staying with children.

☐ Work out the costs of buying linen, towels, bedspreads, crockery sets, and so on.

☐ While doing all the above, check out the competition. A visit to your local tourist information shop (or if you don't have one search online for bed and breakfasts local to you) will establish the going rates. When comparing these rates, make sure you don't get carried away by assuming the rates quoted by a single bed and breakfast are indicative of all B&Bs in your area. For example, some B&Bs will charge significantly more as they will have far superior rooms with en-suites and may also have won awards and/or have been AA or RAC approved. All this adds up to boosting their earning potential, but remember that as a start-up business with no reputation or awards to trade on you may have to tailor your prices accordingly.

☐ There are a number of great how-to books around that have been written by B&B proprietors and these will often contain many tips of the trade. For a relatively small investment you could save yourself lots of bother and learn from the experts. Don't forget as well to discuss your plans with your local tourist information office (assuming you have one) as they can be really invaluable in giving information on visitor profiles, local B&B rates, and when the high or low seasons fall.

MARKETING FOR YOUR BED AND BREAKFAST

There are a number of ways to market your B&B. My favourites include:

☐ Registering your business with the local tourist information office, assuming you have one. If there is a scheme local to you where you can get your business rated by the tourist board then you should do this as soon as you can. Independent reviews of your new B&B are essential if you are to attract the right clientele.

☐ Get a professional to design a website for you. This is relatively inexpensive and it really does pay to have a professional build your website. In my experience, you'll get far more business with a great website than you will with any other advertising medium. You'll need to become familiar with how a website works and how you can achieve high rankings on the search engines, which you can either do yourself or get your web designer to show you. If possible, create an online booking system for your bed and breakfast so you can take bookings 24 hours a day, seven days a week.

☐ When paying for print advertising, be careful that the publication you choose will be able to reach your target audience. For example, if you're in an area where you get lots of walkers visiting, then advertise in those magazines that walkers will buy. If your market isn't very specific, and you're casting your net as wide as possible, then my advice would be to spend your money on a website and the overall appearance of your home as opposed to blowing a fortune on expensive directory advertising. I've yet to find a B&B (or hotel for that matter) anywhere other than by using Google on the Internet. I've no wish to go out and buy an expensive B&B directory that only lists those B&Bs which fork out for an advertisement.

☐ Network with existing B&Bs in your area. For example, when my friends opened up their bed and breakfast, they approached a number of the existing B&Bs in their area and asked them if they would recommend their B&B when they were full. Without exception all of them agreed, and almost immediately a steady flow of guests came their way as a result. And of course when my friends' B&B is full, they return the favour with reciprocal referrals.

Running a B&B isn't for everyone. However, as I said in the introduction to this section, if you like people and want a relatively easy to run, high-margin, low-risk business, then the B&B business model takes some beating. Those I know who run B&Bs are far happier, and I'd hazard a guess more profitable, than those people I know who run restaurants and cafés. The latter group always seem to be up against different problems. Whether these are staffing problems or a lack of business due to bad weather or faulty fridges, the hassle factor of running a restaurant seems to me to outweigh the benefits. On the other hand, those who run successful B&Bs seem to enjoy doing this far more and to have fewer problems.

Don't start by ripping out rooms and building extensions to your existing home. If all you have at the moment is one or maybe two rooms, then start with these and see how you go. Lots of successful boutique B&Bs started out with just one or two rooms and many have stayed this size, still managing to be more profitable than their larger competitors.

When decorating and presenting your rooms try to take a step back from your own personal tastes. Take a look at successful hotel chain rooms where the emphasis is on clean, neat, bright and fresh colours as opposed to anything too dramatic. Remember, the key to a successful B&B is to appeal to as wide an audience as possible.

Wherever possible aim your business at the local market first. Remember that at any one given time there will be countless local celebrations and get-togethers going on in your neighbourhood and many of those attending will need somewhere to stay. You could even consider offering a discount to bookings that come from your immediate neighbourhood and town.

Don't blow thousands on expensive magazine or directory advertising. Far better to invest any surplus money you have in the appearance and presentation of your property as this really will be the key to your success. The 'vacancy' sign hanging outside your door can often generate far more business than any amount of expensive advertising.

A well designed website will pay you dividends. Include pictures of your rooms, the breakfast area, gardens, and any guest testimonials. And if you can do it, try to get an online booking mechanism built in.

Start your own catering business

Very often when those entrepreneurs who have a flair for cooking think of starting their own catering business, they turn their attention to more traditional catering business models such as restaurants, cafés, pizza parlours, and tea-shops. Nothing wrong with this, however, you will need lots of cash either to buy an existing restaurant premises as a going business or to build your own.

There is an alternative, which is to start your own catering business that you will initially run from home, subject of course to how suitable your home is to this type of business and provided you get permission from your local authority's environment department.

However, if your home isn't suitable don't despair, you can still find a suitable property to operate from and subject to planning consents and the necessary registrations you can still work from relatively cheap premises. I say 'relatively cheap premises', as your business could be located anywhere, from a suitable building down the end of a remote lane to rented space in a local restaurant or hotel.

HOW IT WORKS

Your business will work on the basis of you bringing catering to wherever a client is.

For example, one day you could be providing a light buffet in the offices of your local town hall and the next a full sit-down lunch for a business meeting at company offices. The possibilities with this type of business are endless, as you and your business are no longer tied to one location.

Outdoor catering opportunities include providing the catering for:

☐ Local businesses in their offices when they're having meetings or customers visiting their premises.

☐ Events such as village fairs, shop openings, council meetings, and so on.

☐ Funerals, weddings, christening ceremonies, birthday parties, and any home-based celebration or gathering.

☐ Farmers' markets and town fêtes.

☐ Garden parties.

☐ Mobile, all-in barbeque services where not only do you supply and cook the food, but you also bring your own equipment.

You can also create your own range of home-made food products (for example, soups, cakes and cookies) which you then sell at various shows, fairs, and farmers' markets.

HOW EASY IS IT TO START?

Starting a mobile catering business is relatively straightforward and to begin with can be easily achieved on a very small scale. For example, you could start with a simple home-made soup-making business where you make the soups at home (subject to local authority permissions), which you can then market at various farmers' markets, town centre fêtes, and so on.

A more ambitious business will require greater preparation and research to get started, but don't let the work involved put you off. Your initial groundwork should include undertaking the following as a minimum:

☐ Check with your local authority as to what the current legislation is for running an outside catering business. You'll also need to speak to your council's environment department which will cover all aspects of food hygiene and safety. My advice would be to book an appointment to discuss your plans with them. They should also be able to advise you of what elementary food hygiene courses you will need to take before opening your business. Discuss your premises with them also. If you are planning to use your own kitchen at home then it will have to meet the minimum legal requirements. Ask the council officer to tell you what this entails.

☐ As you're not planning to open a restaurant or café, the location of your kitchen isn't crucial to your success. However, you will still need to be sure that the premises you choose are suitable for your business and have suitable planning consents for the preparation of food. Again, you'll need to check with your local council for advice and guidance on the current legislation. Whatever you do, don't sign a lease or rent or buy anywhere until you are completely assured you can get the relevant permissions and that any work needed to bring the property up to the required standard will not prove cost prohibitive. For example, if the premises you are considering renting consist of a derelict rat-infested warehouse with no proper sanitation it's likely that the costs will be too prohibitive for you to convert it into something that meets your requirements.

☐ Learn the trade before you start. Unlike some of the other business models (for example, a cleaning business), a catering business does require you to have cooking skills. Of late, I do wonder at the number of 'cafés' I've had the misfortune to eat in where it's blatantly obvious that those folk running the business have about as much cooking ability as my dog. So if you are considering this option, you must be a competent cook in the kind of food you're going to offer. If all you're planning to do is run a tea and coffee and sandwiches buffet at your local council offices once a month, then fine. But if you're going to undertake the larger and obviously more lucrative jobs, then you need to be skilled and capable in what you do.

ESSENTIAL MARKETING

As with any business, timing is all-important. So when's the best time of the year to start an outside catering business?

The answer to this question will very much depend on the type of outdoor catering business you're intending to run. For example, if you're planning to sell your food at farmers' markets, village fêtes, shows, and so on you'll probably find that early January isn't the best time to start. However, if you're pitching at the domestic market you could find that you do well catering at funerals, birthdays, New Year parties and the like. So much will depend on who your target market is and/or how broad the customer base is that you're going to try to sell to.

YOUR MARKETING STRATEGY

Don't be tempted to start your business on the basis of a solitary advertisement in your local paper or telephone directory. While this is one thing you could or perhaps even should do (depending on your budget and the type of business you're planning to run), it shouldn't be your only sales strategy.

This is the sort of business that needs a really clever, proactive sales approach. For example, if you're going to target the corporate market and win contracts for business lunches, then why not turn up somewhere with *free* samples of your cooking? Just show up unannounced with food, flyers, business cards and business-winning smiles and offer some tasty bites, and then move on to the next big office you can find. Just do it – get out there and sell your business. The great thing about selling food is that you can offer free samples, and how many people do you know who would turn down the offer of free food?

Some marketing ideas to get you started would include:

☐ A website, which is ideally suited for this type of business. As your business doesn't have a shopfront to speak of, you'll need somewhere where prospective customers can see what you're offering, can browse menus and products, and get a feel for you and your business. In my experience, there's nothing better than a welcoming, personal website where you have an almost personal interaction with your prospective clients. Once you're up and running you can also publish positive customer experiences on your site and if you sell at farmers' markets and fêtes, you can also upload pictures of your previous attendances at these events, hopefully showing lots of happy people munching their way through your sought-after produce.

☐ Proactive campaigns work with this business – passive advertising isn't really an option. Think leaflets, flyers, A boards, posters, free food samples, direct mailing to businesses, and networking with local councillors, local business people, and so on.

☐ Advertise your services to as many local businesses as you can who could then add your service to their existing service. For example, you should approach all the funeral directors in your area asking them if they would consider recommending you to clients who may be looking for home catering after a funeral service. Or florists, who again could help you sell your services locally to those who are buying flowers from them for a wedding, anniversary, funeral, and so on.

☐ Be proactive with the local press. Get your press releases out. Give your business a local news angle to capture the imagination of the editor of your local paper. This could be anything, from why you've started your business (for example, you recently needed a similar service to what you're now offering but were unable to find a cost-effective solution) to you winning a cookery award when you were at school, or you having been a chef at a certain hotel. Whatever angle you take, make it in some way newsworthy. You'll find the results far better than using any sort of expensive but passive advertisement.

☐ Pick up the phone and cold call as many local businesses as you possibly can to advertise your new business. Don't be shy, just dial the number and tell them how your new business could help them out. Be bubbly – or gracious, sexy, or charming – but above all, be proactive.

TIP *books small business start-ups • how to*

Outdoor catering is hard work. Not only have you to source, prepare and cook food, but you also have to set up your stall possibly at a different location every time you open for business and all this adds to your workload. You also need to add to your running costs the costs of booking stalls and transporting yourself as well as your products and staff to outdoor locations. All of this adds to the overall expense, so make sure you don't overlook these costs when quoting to prospective clients.

Your cooking must be up to a sufficiently high enough standard to make people want to refer you to their friends or families. The idea of you catering for an outside event with bought-in supermarket sausage rolls (I've seen one outdoor caterer do this recently and it was absolutely shameful what they dished up) isn't what this business is about. Your success depends on your ability to create a range of foods that people really do enjoy eating.

Beware of the costs. Catering is one of those businesses that can make me shudder whenever I think of them. For example, in our businesses our products don't have a shelf life anywhere near that of a pint of milk or a loaf of bread. If we don't sell our products today, there's always tomorrow or next week. However, this is not true of catering where your jams, soups, cookies and so on will all have to be sold within a certain period. So you need to get your quantities right. Over-production in this business will quickly devastate any potential profits.

Start your own Internet business

In 1999, I was commissioned by my local newspaper to write a piece on shopping on the Internet. As part of the research for my feature, I interviewed a number of shopkeepers, the manager of Brighton's largest indoor shopping centre, and a number of estate agents. Without exception, all of them were fairly dismissive of the Internet. The manager of the shopping centre told me that she couldn't see why anyone would want to shop this way as they'd miss the 'touchy feel' of the traditional shopping experience. One local estate agent told me that house buyers would always want to see the property first hand, and accordingly the Internet had little to offer.

Fast forward to today and were I to interview the same group of business people, I think it's fair to say that they all would agree that the Internet has significantly changed the way we all do business. Indeed in many cases, the Internet has been blamed for putting more traditional retailers out of business than anything else. I tend to disagree with this view, and believe that the smart, forward-thinking, traditional retailers who could see the Internet's potential grabbed the opportunity with both hands and used it as a tool to build stronger, more profitable businesses.

For example, around the time my feature on shopping on the Internet was published, a relatively small, independent cycle shop owner with one business in Portsmouth could see immediately the potential the Internet offered his business. And while his competitors were moaning about unfair competition from online retailers, this Portsmouth cycle shop entrepreneur started an online business selling cycle parts and accessories. Today, this business – Wiggle – is one of the UK's largest and most profitable online cycle stores. Had this cycle shop owner ignored the potential of the Internet, he would have lost out on the fun, excitement, and profitability of creating an online retail giant, and subsequently taking a very early retirement to enjoy the fruits of his labour.

SO WHAT CAN THE INTERNET OFFER YOU?

In my view, nothing comes close to what the Internet can offer the home-based entrepreneur. For example, I have successfully grown a profitable niche cycle business from my kitchen table into a business where we now turn over in excess of a million pounds, and this figure is continually growing. The only way this growth was achieved was by taking our cycle business online and marketing to a broader audience.

So what type of online business could you set up?

The list of potential businesses is simply endless. For example, if you're a keen walker you could set up a website where you sell everything from walking guides to walking holidays and everything in between. If you're a talented chef who would like to set up your own restaurant but cannot afford the money needed to buy or rent a property, you could set up your own online cookery school.

Whatever your interests or hobbies or speciality, the Internet offers a relatively cost-effective way to launch a business without all the hassle and expense of setting up a traditional shop.

Here are just some ideas to get you thinking:

☐ If you're retired you could set up an online group where you arrange days out, holidays, or excursions for like-minded people who want to make more of their retirement but perhaps are living alone and lacking in confidence or companionship.

☐ Whatever your area of expertise – whether it is cooking, carpentry, gardening, pet care, and so on – you could set up an online business where others can visit your site to find answers to their questions and also to buy products and services specifically catering for their interest.

☐ Start an online magazine covering your chosen field. In 2007, the BikeRadar website (www.bikeradar.co.uk) was set up as an online forum and point of information for cyclists. This site quickly became popular with all sorts of cyclists and earns its profit from selling advertisements online.

☐ You could start your own dating agency, or a website where people can find like-minded travelling companions or someone to join them on day trips or cinema or theatre visits.

The potential here is enormous and the great thing about the Internet is you can test-drive your business idea on a very small scale before committing huge amounts of money. For example, a friend of mine makes bespoke miniature figures for dolls' house collectors, model railway enthusiasts, and so on. For years she had to invest in expensive magazine advertising to reach her target market. At one time she even opened up her own shop, but the overheads were too great and she was quickly forced to close. However, along came the Internet and immediately she could see its potential. She has since opened up her own website and is selling her pieces all over the world.

HOW EASY IS IT TO START?

Of all the business models I've discussed here, starting an Internet business is the easiest one to get up and running and is also the one most suited to being a home-based business as you can get. Contrary to what you might think, you don't need lots of technical know-how or to be able to write your own codes or HTML scripts. All you need to do is come up with an idea for an Internet business, and as with all business ideas you'll need to research it thoroughly until you get to the point where you have a business opportunity as opposed to simply a 'good idea'.

Once you've got your business worked out – whether this is arranging walking holidays in Ireland or selling pet rocks online – you'll then need to create an online presence, which could include:

☐ A blog.
☐ A page on a social network site.
☐ A traditional website.

Blogs

A blog is a bit like an online journal where you 'blog' about all the things that interest you. For example, if your main interest is in hill walking, you could start a blog detailing all your experiences, both good and bad, and reviews of outdoor gear you've tried as well as you experiences of walking in various places. If your blog is good enough you'll quickly build up a loyal readership and you will then be ready to open up your blog to carrying paid advertisements, or indeed bolting on a online shop. I like blogs and I have a few favourites which I read regularly and have made purchases from on the basis of those products and services endorsed and recommended by the blogger.

Social networking sites

The popularity of social networking sites beggars belief. Not only do celebrities now use social networking sites as a way of promoting their latest album, track, film, or book, but new talent has also managed to get their music played and listened to where all other conventional routes have failed them. For example, the singer Colbie Caillat was discovered on the social networking site MySpace (www.myspace.com), while still others have found fame on other social networking sites such as Facebook and Bebo.

Setting up your own page on these sites is as easy as it gets and you don't need any specialist web-designing knowledge. Once you are up and running you can then spend your time and energy building a site that showcases what you have to offer and use that further to build your own online business.

For example, I know of one entrepreneur who wrote a downloadable ebook, (which is a paperless book which you download online, usually either free or for a very low cost) on how to wash a mountain bike. In its first outing, this ebook was downloaded an incredible 45,000 times! Given that to download this subscribers had to give their name and email address, this entrepreneur then had an audience of 45,000 people to sell his specialist bike cleaning fluid to. I cannot think of any other advertising medium that would generate such a response for so little investment.

A friend of mine who is an artist has used his web pages on a social networking site not only to sell his work, but also as a way of recruiting models, promoting his exhibitions, and building brand awareness of his work.

Website

A fully automated website where visitors can not only browse your products and services but can also buy them online using a credit card is vital to your business success. One of the main features of a successful online business is the ease by which visitors can access information on your products and services and buy them online.

Once again, you don't need to spend thousands on this. You can do it yourself using one of the many 'create your own website' companies which will offer you a template website by which you can create your own site. Our site at the Littlehampton Dutch Bike Co (www.dutchbikeshop.co.uk) has been built using Mr Site's take away website. I first heard of Mr Site in the national press when it won a number of awards for offering low-cost web start-ups. As the Littlehampton Dutch Bike Shop was a low-cost start-up, I didn't have any money to commission a website designer to do it for me. So I used Mr Site, and to date we've achieved over a £1million pounds of business by using this website, which costs us less than a hundred pounds a year.

My advice when it comes to starting an online business would also be to start with a low-cost/no-cost easy entry and to work on building up the number of people visiting your site. Once you've achieved this and some early sales success, you can then reinvest some of your profits into creating a really superb website which can take online bookings and so on.

By far the greatest advantage of starting an Internet business is that you can do it from wherever you are. Even if you don't have Internet access at home or own your own computer, you can still run your business from the local library, internet café, and so on.

I've sold bicycles while I've been mountain biking in Greece, cycling in Ireland, and sitting in bed feeling highly sorry for myself with 'man flu'. It's a great flexible business model that offers so much potential to people of all ages and abilities.

Just think, there was a time when eBay didn't exist. Yet speak to anyone today, young or old, and most of them will recognise the business name eBay. And then you have all the specialist online advice sites that can help with making purchasing decisions – for example, money supermarket (www.moneysupermarket.com) or Go compare (www.gocompare.com) for car insurance and so on.

TIP *how to books • small business start-ups*

Think big and think global. An online business can reach anywhere in the world. So don't limit your business to the market that is local to you.

Beware of how fickle the website surfer can be. Regardless of how much money you spend bringing visitors to your website, social networking area, or blog, if you're not up to date or good enough the competition are only a click away. Never take online visitors for granted. If you don't give them enough good reasons to buy from you, there are plenty of others who will take their money.

Beware of copycat businesses starting up on the back of your success. I've had this happen where another 'entrepreneur' has simply copied our products and tried to pass them off as the genuine article. One business even went so far as naming their own business after ours so it looked as if it was our subsidiary. Although this is illegal, there's little you can do to stop it as many of these copycat online businesses will be set up using post box numbers and overseas addresses. Beware of this sort of thing happening and make sure you buy up all the relevant domain names for your business. For example, if you're calling yourself 'joepublicshops. co.uk, make sure you also buy up the .com name (i.e., joepublic shops.com) and so on.

Make your website as personal as you can by including your details and where possible even your photograph. Remember, shoppers can't meet you in person so you need to convey honesty, reliability, and so on. Also take time to ensure that you publish on your site any and all positive feedback from your customers (often known as customer testimonials).

The Internet is a constantly changing environment so you must, *must* update your site regularly. Remember, the competition are only a click away. . .

Start your own antiques business

If you have a passion and enthusiasm for collecting antique items, why not turn your knowledge and experience into a worthwhile business? The great benefit of becoming an antiques dealer is that you can run your business to suit yourself. For example, you could begin this in your spare time by attending auction houses and then selling at selected fairs and exhibitions, all of which you can pre-plan. Once you're up and running and have a feel for the business you could then move on to a full-time operation where you can either rent part of an existing shop or open your own business.

HOW DOES IT ALL WORK?

The main difference between this and a traditional retail business model is that the stock you source will be unique to your business. For example, let's say you have a special interest in china and glassware. So off you go and source some interesting pieces at auctions, which you know are easily re-saleable. Once you've bought your stock you're then free to sell it. I'll introduce you the most common methods of selling antiques in a moment, but for now let's stick with the key differences in your business model. Unlike other retail models, when you price your pieces you will base your price on two very important criteria, which are:

1. Uniqueness.
2. Sought-afterness.

Provided you've purchased wisely, you should incorporate these two selling features in everything you purchase. Compare this to other retail models, where unless you manufacture your own product, there will be other retailers selling exactly the same items as you, and therefore you could end up with unsold stock as others cut their prices to the bone or there's an oversupply of whatever it is you're selling.

On the other hand the prudent, careful eye of the antiques dealer means they will buy only what they know they can sell for a profit and also relatively quickly.

You have two main options open to you as an antiques dealer as to what you can source and sell:

☐ Small items, for example glass, china ware, toys, jewellery.
☐ Larger items, which would include things like furniture.

The advantages of selling smaller items is that you can easily transport them, both from where you've bought them and to sale venues, and also they are easy to store.

An advantage with the larger items is that they'll usually have greater profit margins than smaller pieces, however this also means they'll cost more for you to buy per item.

Similar to any other retail business model, you must buy your stock for as low a price as you can possibly get and sell it for maximum profit. Your success and profitability will depend on a number of factors:

☐ Your ability to negotiate and seek out antiques.

☐ Your ability to turn around your stock quickly enough to maintain a steady flow of cash in your business.

☐ How much profit you make on all your transactions and not just the one lucky sale or the one lucky find. Don't get carried away with stories of dealers wandering through boot fairs and picking up some sought after, extremely valuable relic where the boot fair seller had no idea as to its true value. While I'm sure these sorts of tales have indeed happened and do still occasionally happen, a single, potentially lucky find isn't the way to run a profitable, sustainable business.

WHERE DO YOU GET YOUR STOCK?

There are a number of ways to source stock, including:

☐ Auctions.

☐ Antiques fairs.

☐ Scouring the ads in your local newspaper.

☐ Online auction sites (e.g. eBay) where items come up for sale without anyone really knowing their true value.

☐ Proactive buying, by you placing ads in magazines, local newspapers, and so on looking for items.

As with every other small business, the secret to successfully sourcing your stock should be for you to specialise in a small line of certain items. That way you'll quickly establish yourself as an expert and will then be able to adopt some tried and tested routes to getting the best stock. You'll get to know which auction houses you can do business with, and those that don't suit your specialist market. Likewise with antiques fairs, you'll soon get a feel for the best ones for your market.

How much stock you carry at any one given time will be largely down how much money you have available to tie up in that stock. Remember, when you sell an item from your stock this item will eventually need replacing if you are to stay in business. For example, let's say you trade in specialist china pieces and that initially you have £1,000 available to invest in start-up stock. Once you've used up your stock budget, and sales start coming in, these monies are obviously not just profit but the retail price less the trade price less any costs you have incurred sourcing and selling the stock – and it is this money that you can either take out of your business or reinvest it to increase your stock. However, if you get to the point where you are making no reinvestment in stock but are spending all the revenues from the items sold you will be left with nothing. The antiques trade isn't a business where you can simply phone the wholesalers on a Monday morning and order more stock.

HOW DO YOU SELL YOUR GOODS?

The first thing to note here is that you can sell anywhere in the UK that you wish to, but in some areas (or possibly all areas, depending on what the Home Office is currently planning to introduce) you may have to register. Somewhat bizarrely, some areas such as Kent require you to register, while other places don't. The only reliable way to find out is for you to check with the local council's trading office on where it is you're planning to sell.

There are a number of ways to sell your antiques, including:

☐ Renting space at an existing antiques shop. For example, I live near Arundel in West Sussex where there are a number of antiques shops, many of whom advertise space to rent in their shops. The rent will usually include that you must undertake to work in the shop for a pre-agreed period each week. The benefit of this to you, the trader, is that you're free to buy and sell your stock elsewhere while others are selling your goods for you. Of course, this isn't always a great idea if you have others who don't share you passion, enthusiasm and knowledge for whatever it is you're selling, but generally speaking it's a worthwhile mutual arrangement.

☐ Opening your own antiques shop. This is not to be recommended for novices to the business and you certainly need time to learn the trade and work out what find for you and what doesn't. It's always difficult to start a new antiques shop on a high street as you will need time to build up a reputation and you will also need to be in the right area.

☐ Booking a stall at an antiques fair. You'll find details of all the various fairs, dates, times, locations, and so on online by searching on Google and buying magazines relating to the antiques trade.

☐ Online. You could create your own website and sell your antiques online, however the disadvantage of this is that not every antique line will be suitable. For example, mail ordering antique china runs the risk of damage to the pieces while in transit. On the other hand, pop or theatre memorabilia are ideally suited to being posted.

☐ By reputation. This is where you build up your reputation in your chosen field and regulars buy from your latest collection, which you could market by sending them lists of what's available or they could check out your website. You'll also find new customers will come to you because they've heard you're a specialist in a particular area.

☐ Online auction sites such as eBay. These can be suitable for certain antiques, for example post cards, theatre memorabilia, and so on.

☐ Specialist websites. One example here is Abe Books (www.abebooks.com) which specialises in out-of-print, rare and first edition books.

To be successful, you must have a genuine passion for antiques. Even if you don't know anything specific about antiques now, but are still passionate about them, you can learn the trade. What you cannot do is become passionate about something that really doesn't interest you.

Start this as a hobby business and work your way up to becoming a full-time dealer. Don't rush, take your time, and build your business slowly and carefully.

Beware at auctions that you don't get sucked into a bidding war and end up paying over the odds for a piece you'll struggle to sell at a profit.

Antique dealing is a business where haggling over prices is expected. Beware of this when buying but also be aware of this when selling, as if you ticket price your items with small margins, you'll have no room for negotiation and selling will become difficult, tedious, and unprofitable.

INDEX